DOING SURVEY RESEARCH

A Guide to Quantitative Methods

PETER M. NARDI

Pitzer College

Boston ■ New York ■ San Francisco ■ Mexico City ■ Montreal
■ Toronto ■ London ■ Madrid ■ Munich ■ Paris ■
Hong Kong ■ Singapore ■ Tokyo ■ Cape Town ■ Sydney

Series Editor: *Jeff Lasser*
Series editorial assistant: *Andrea Christie*
Marketing Manager: *Krista Groshong*
Composition and Prepress Buyer: *Linda Cox*
Manufacturing Manager: *Megan Cochran*
Editorial-Production Coordinator: *Mary Beth Finch*
Editorial-Production Service: *Shepherd, Inc.*
Electronic Composition: *Shepherd, Inc.*

For related titles and support materials, visit our online catalog at
www.ablongman.com

Between the time Website information is gathered and then published, it is not
unusual for some sites to have closed. Also, the transcription of URLs can result in
unintended typographical errors. The publisher would appreciate notification
where these errors occur so that they can be correct in subsequent editions.

Credits: Materials from SPSS are used by permission of SPSS, Inc. (Chicago, IL:
SPSS 10.0 for Windows, 1999) and from the General Social Survey (GSS) by
permission of the National Opinion Research Center (NORC).

Library of Congress Cataloging in Publication Data

Nardi, Peter M.
    Doing survey research : a guide to quantitative methods / Peter M. Nardi.
        p. cm.
    Includes bibliographical references and index.
    ISBN 0-205-34348-1
    1. Social surveys. 2. Social sciences—Research—Methodology. 3. Sampling
(Statistics) I. Title.

HN29 .N25 2003
300'.723—dc21

                                                                2002034283

Printed in the United States of America

10 9 8 7 6 5 4 3 2   07 06 05 04 03

CONTENTS

110834

CHAPTER FOUR
Developing a Questionnaire 57

The strengths and weaknesses of different types of survey methods are discussed. The focus is on learning how to design a questionnaire: How to write attitude, behavior, and demographic questions and to format a survey. Ways to code responses and prepare data for computer analysis are also presented.

CHAPTER FIVE
Sampling 96

This chapter explains random probability sampling and describes different methods for obtaining samples. Longitudinal and cross-sectional research designs are discussed, as well as different types of probability and nonprobability sampling, and the idea of sampling error.

CHAPTER SIX
Presenting Data: Descriptive Statistics 115

Understanding how to describe findings using graphs, tables, and statistics is the focus of this chapter. In addition, the emphasis is on learning to make decisions about when to use the mean, median, mode, standard deviation and understanding the concept of the normal curve and z-scores. Concepts of probability and statistical significance are introduced.

CHAPTER SEVEN
Analyzing Data: Bivariate Relationships 139

This chapter discusses how to read and construct cross-tables of data and decide which statistics to use to measure association and correlation. Understanding how to reject or accept a hypothesis using the appropriate statistics to assess bivariate relationships is highlighted.

CHAPTER EIGHT
Analyzing Data: Comparing Means   164

This chapter shows how to assess differences between means using t-tests and analysis of variance. As with other bivariate data analysis, knowing when to use these statistical procedures and how to interpret them is central to testing hypotheses.

CHAPTER NINE
Analyzing Data: Multiple Variables   180

This chapter focuses on the analysis of three or more variables to answer more complex research questions. It discusses when to use and how to interpret multiple regression analyses and how to perform elaboration techniques with control variables.

CHAPTER TEN
Presenting Results, Making Conclusions, and Writing Reports   203

In this final chapter, learning to write a report of the research project is emphasized, along with the key elements that go into a presentation of your study. Understanding the different audiences reading a report guides the preparation of the findings.

PREFACE

Not too long ago, a student entered my office, visibly upset and seeking answers. She wanted to know why "everyone" in class was doing better than she was when none of them studied as much as she did. Or so she claimed. When I suggested that this may not have been true, I also hinted that it was possibly the case, and that until we had some evidence to support the connection between hours studied and grades, neither of us could claim to have the answer for what was simply an opinion or, at best, an observation based on a few selective cases.

And thus we embarked in the development of a research project to answer this question, an exciting journey that required the juggling of a variety of issues, skills, and decisions. How many times, though, have we been faced with such a daunting task and had no idea how to get started and what to do next? Throughout our education and careers, many of us are asked to gather data, interview people, analyze findings from a survey, or complete an original senior thesis or major project at work. How to initiate a study, construct interesting and relevant questions or hypotheses, develop reliable and valid measurements, gather a sample of respondents, and interpret statistical results before writing up the findings, all require practice and skills that often come only from having done such a project in the first place. People learn to do research by doing research, but they can't do research well until they learn the ideas and become familiar with the assumptions and techniques behind it.

This book is intended to guide new researchers through this process, to get them started on the research journey, and bring them to a point where they feel ready to tackle an even larger major project. It focuses on *quantitative research methods* and, in particular, those involving *questionnaire surveys*. Many agencies and organizations ask employees to carry out short projects requiring questionnaire designs to assess client services or organizational needs, measure workers' satisfaction levels, or evaluate social programs and new policy implementations.

For many undergraduates, a large, complex research project, such as expected in a Master's or Doctoral program, is not likely to be assigned; yet many social science majors require a senior thesis or some evidence of carrying out empirical research that answers specific questions as part of a methodology or statistics course. Minimally, people are expected to be critical evaluators of research, to read tables of data, know which statistics to use under different circumstances, and interpret results, even if they are not obliged to calculate the statistics mathematically by hand. Those who continue on to graduate school will be required to take more advanced statistics and research methods courses in preparation for a master's thesis or doctoral dissertation.

This book is intended for those who want to learn how to do quantitative research for a project in an undergraduate course, as a degree requirement, or as part of their work for an organization, and for critically understanding and interpreting research they read in their daily newspapers, in reports carried out in the workplace, and in scholarly journals. The goals include:

- Providing hands-on experience in developing, carrying out, and concluding a quantitative research project
- Reviewing previous research in the professional journals to clarify ideas and develop hypotheses
- Learning to construct valid and reliable measures for questionnaire surveys
- Developing sampling strategies
- Deciding on which statistics to use when analyzing data
- Reading and evaluating tables of data and statistics that appear in newspapers, reports, and academic journals
- Making interpretations about the data and writing conclusions about the initial research questions or hypotheses.

The objectives are targeted to social science students and to those in the workplace who must perform some institutional research or evaluation surveys for their job. Learning how to do research, making decisions about which statistics to use when, and how to interpret statistical analyses are goals for everyone in today's research-oriented society where questions about the reliability and validity of data from a study or pubic opinion poll come up routinely. This book helps in achieving those objectives.

Information is organized in the sequence of a research project; that is, it begins the journey with a discussion of the purpose of doing research (Chapter 1), how to do a review of relevant articles related to the topic (Chapter 2), and how to formulate and operationalize a set of questions or hypotheses that can be studied with limited financial resources and time (Chapter 3). Too often, methodology books provide techniques that can only be accomplished successfully with large sums of funding over longer periods of time than people typically have to complete a study.

The chapters then continue along the research journey and focus on developing an effective questionnaire (Chapter 4), designing a sampling strategy (Chapter 5), learning how to use elementary statistical techniques and perform basic data analysis (Chapters 6 to 9), and interpreting data and making conclusions about the original research questions when writing different kinds of reports (Chapter 10).

In some chapters, examples from actual research studies and scholarly journals, as well as information from popular media (such as polls and surveys in newspapers and on television), illustrate the ideas and statistical concepts. In addition, there are four kinds of exercises at the end of each chapter:

- *Review:* What do these Key Terms mean? The reader is asked to review the concepts and definitions presented in the chapter.
- *Interpret:* What do these real examples tell us? The reader is encouraged to make sense of information and data from research journals and popular media.
- *Consult:* What could be done? The reader is given an issue or problem that requires advice about what could be done, based on the new material presented in the chapter.
- *Decide:* What do we do next? This exercise carries over from one chapter to the next and asks the reader to design the next step in a research project focusing on the relationship between television viewing and what people feel and do about racial issues and stereotyping. Using the same topic in each chapter encourages the reader to link concepts and demonstrate cumulative knowledge. By the end, the reader might have decided on a research design, carried out the writing of a questionnaire, analyzed the survey results, and written a final report.

Doing well-designed survey research is an exciting journey that begins with curiosity and ends with a clearer sense of some possible answers. The results might not be definitive and the knowledge gained may be tentative, but we surely are one step closer at the end to knowing more about the topic than when we started out. Like all adventures, the trip can be fun, tedious, nerve-wracking, and exhilarating. Let's go!

ACKNOWLEDGMENTS

This book would not be possible if it weren't for the hundreds of students who learned the material with me in my Quantitative Research Methods classes at Pitzer College in Claremont, CA. They allowed me to make mistakes, try new ways of communicating complex ideas, and tolerated my bad jokes. These students and my wonderful colleagues in Sociology at Pitzer College are hereby acknowledged for all their inspiration.

Encouragement, support, love, and humor from Jeffrey Chernin while writing this book cannot be overstated. This is for you, especially when you have to show me the data.

CHAPTER ONE

■ ■ ■ ■ ■

WHY WE DO RESEARCH

LEARNING GOALS

In this chapter, the differences between everyday thinking and scientific thinking are discussed. An argument is made about the advantages of doing survey research and understanding various kinds of research: exploratory, descriptive, explanatory, and evaluation. The chapter concludes with a comparison of quantitative and qualitative research methods. By the conclusion, you should be able to give examples of everyday thinking, discuss the components of scientific reasoning, list the different types of research methods, and describe them.

Remember the time you asked one of your parents to buy a particular pair of expensive running shoes, or to let you go to a party, or to do something just because "all the kids" were? Well, the astute parent would question this and wonder if it were really true that *all* your friends were actually involved. "Why not collect some data first and then report back to me about what percentage of your friends own those clothes or are getting their driver's licenses?" That's what parents trained to do survey research might say!

Too often we make conclusions about entire groups of people based on observations of only those we know or see around us. Or to put it more scientifically: Too often we generalize about an entire population based on a nonsystematic method of collecting data from a biased sample. This is one of the major differences between everyday experience and scientific thinking. What follows is an argument for doing things more systematically and scientifically than usual, and a justification for doing quantitative survey research as one approach to understanding how and why humans think and act the way they do.

EVERYDAY THINKING

How we see the world around us is shaped by a variety of forces which include the books we read, the television and movies we see, the culture's

1

rules and guidelines for good behavior we repeatedly hear, and the teachings from the religious organizations and schools we attend. It is also highly influenced by our friends—the peer groups we spend a good deal of time in and from whom we learn. But so many of these social forces are linked to each other in ways that tend to reinforce our already-held values and beliefs. Conclusions based on networks of friends and family members are hardly useful, then, in trying to understand how most other people think or behave.

The trick of socialization, to paraphrase writer Carlos Castañeda, is to convince us that the way we see the world is the only reality, one supported by social consensus. By experiencing more diverse cultures and meeting a wider range of people we come to understand that to make conclusions based simply on the way our friends and family live, what they believe in, or how we were socialized, is limiting. Too often those with whom we associate are similar to ourselves in values and beliefs; we end up selectively sampling like-minded people and erroneously concluding that "everyone" experiences reality in the same way we do.

Although we seem to manage fairly well on a daily basis, our everyday experiences are often based on methods that can lead to problematic decisions with outcomes that can seriously affect our lives. Imagine if some friends told us that they were able to stop flu symptoms and prevent a recurrence of a cold simply by eating only the white filling in a chocolate cookie everyday for a month. Would we rush out to buy bags of these wonderful cookies and use them to ward off the flu instead of getting a vaccine? It certainly would be more fun (and fattening), but not likely to keep us from getting the flu. What if they told us to take Vitamin C? Would we run to the store to get some, or would we critically inquire about the research that supports this general statement?

Every day we make conclusions and act on them with similarly limited information. Recall how sometimes you answer the telephone and it confirms exactly whom you just suspected would be calling: "I knew it would be you on the other end. I could tell by the ring!" Never mind that you don't remember the number of times you did not guess accurately, or that you normally speak to that person around the same time and day of the week as this call.

Or recall the time you rushed out to buy something based on the testimony of one person who swore how terrific that CD or book was. Or how you ran to the nearest movie theater to catch a film your friends exclaimed to be the best ever and some critic called "the best film of the year" even though it was only March. Although it would be impossible and crazy to survey a large number of people every time we need to make a decision to do something, be aware of how the process of making a choice is often not much more systematic than believing the person with the secret cure for the common cold. Yet, we make such decisions because we know from experience ("empirical data") that this particular friend's recommendations have almost always been reliable.

What we do in everyday life is typically the result of some less scientific thinking than the procedures we would expect policy makers, or neurosurgeons, or airline pilots to follow when they are in control of our well-being. In other words, what we need to consider is how ordinary thinking differs from the systematic methods needed to understand complex social behavior and attitudes. By doing so, we begin our research journey on the correct foot.

The characteristics of ordinary, everyday thinking and inquiry include:

- Biased questions
- Limited sampling
- Selective attention, perception, and retention
- Inaccurate generalizations

Biased Questions

Did anyone ever ask "Do you really want to go to that Arnold Schwarzenegger movie?" and say it with an air of disdain? It would be difficult to answer "yes, I really do want to see it" since the questioner was implying that the film was so bad no one in his or her right mind could really want to go. And remember the time someone wanted to know the reasons why everyone was so dissatisfied with the workplace, thereby assuming that "everyone" was unhappy and all we needed to do now was find those reasons? Consider the research question usually worded this way: "Why is it that I study more than the other students yet they get better grades?" and the implications already formed by the phrasing.

In each of these three cases, everyday nonscientific thinking leads us to ask questions that are already *biased* or slanted in a particular direction. The first, perhaps more rhetorical, question is already providing the answer in the way it is worded. It does not allow for a full range of possible answers, so the only conclusion would be that everyone who was asked the question in this way in our survey does not want to see the latest Schwarzenegger movie. We'd be making an accurate statement of what was uncovered, but the answers are only as good as the way the question was framed and applicable just to the *limited* sample. The tendency, of course, is to *generalize* to all people, that is, to make conclusions about people not surveyed using the information obtained from those that were.

Similarly, the second question proceeds from a *selective* assumption that may not be accurate so the only answers we get from a survey of employees' experiences are negatively *biased* ones about the organization. How many times do we really ask "Why is this workplace such a happy one?" with the same enthusiasm and inquisitiveness as we asked why people are dissatisfied with work? Or more accurately, how often do we ask what they think about their workplace, without qualifying it as good or awful when we inquire?

With the third question about study habits, we are talking ourselves into believing something that may not be true, but asking it in this form just the same. Rarely do we, in everyday talk or thought, put it the following way: "I wonder if there is a relationship between the amount of time people study and their grades." We often begin with a particular viewpoint and proceed to ask questions from that selective position, sometimes not even aware that we are doing so. Thus, the answers we get tend to verify what we already believe and give us a false sense of having found some objective and honest answers. We now have the reasons why our *limited* sample of employees hate the cafeteria food and falsely *generalize* that everyone hates the food because we never found out how many liked it in the first place.

Our daily interactions with friends, family members, and the people we encounter on a routine basis rarely require anything more scientific. Ordinary discourse contains many such poorly worded questions and biased assumptions, and the world manages to keep going. However, imagine the consequences of asking questions in these ways when trying to understand more complex and important behaviors and opinions or when attempting to develop public policies that can seriously affect people's lives. No one should think that an educational institution, for example, can create rules to require a certain amount of study hours per week simply based on the findings of a survey that only asks why those who study less get better grades. Should the human resources office really modify an organization based on the results of a survey focused only on the dissatisfaction of its employees?

Everyday thinking, in other words, typically employs biased phrases and other nonscientific styles of framing questions when making sense of the world we live in. The results of these queries may help us decide which movie to watch, but they are not useful when it comes to making choices that affect social policies or arriving at conclusions fairly and consistently. How we can improve the way we ask questions and minimize the biases that derive from faulty wording is discussed in more detail in Chapter 4.

Limited Sampling

Most of the time we make sense of reality by reflecting on the experiences we've had. It is not too difficult to figure out how our friends feel about various rules, political leaders, music, and television programs. We are generally good at assessing the climate of opinion about controversial topics among our peers and those whom we encounter regularly in our living spaces. Unfortunately, there is also the tendency to take these limited experiences and then assign them to ever larger groups of people.

"Everyone I know hates the food in the cafeteria"—so it must be bad. "I talked with others in the class who have good grades and they're not reading the assignments"—so it doesn't matter how much one studies. "No one I know liked that movie"—so it must be failing at the box office. While it may sound reasonable to make such concluding statements, the problem of course is that we have simply taken the opinions or measured the behaviors of those we already know and then made the assumption that they are somehow representative of "all" people: "But, Mom, *everyone* is going to be driving this year to school." But if they are our friends, they are likely to be people who share our tastes and values.

People forget that most of the time our lives are constrained and limited by the social spaces we inhabit. Race, social class, gender, sexual orientation, and religion are just some of the many characteristics which provide different experiences and push us into living in unique subcultures and communities. Everyday life is often a series of encounters in limited areas. We rarely get to move outside of our circumscribed environment and, when we do, we do not always see what is there. It is part of human existence to *selectively* attend to, perceive, and retain information. After we have arrived at some belief about people or assumption about some events, we use these beliefs to focus our attention mostly on those aspects that already fit our

■ ■ ■ ■ ■

BOX 1.1

EVERYDAY BIASES

A great source for studying how people selectively see the world, make use of limited samples, generalize to people not studied, and ask questions in biased ways, is to read the "Letters to the Editor" in local newspapers. Soon after a major shooting occurred in a suburban high school a series of letters appeared in the local paper, each with its own explanation for what happened and each likely representing the writer's own personal values and biases. These letters included the following reasons:

1. life in white monotonous suburbia and the alienation that results;
2. Republican congressmen who refuse to pass legislation controlling guns;
3. parents who neglect their kids' depression and isolation;
4. schools that allow hate-filled speech and all sorts of taunting and teasing of kids who are different; and
5. legal abortion and the theory of evolution both of which lead to a devaluation of life.

Take a look at your local paper and see how many examples you can find of everyday, nonscientific reasoning.

assumptions. We typically see only those dimensions and we tend to remember better just the events that verify our already held beliefs. That's what the process of selective perception, attention, and retention is. It's difficult to experience reality differently from the way we are taught, and contradictory evidence usually shakes us up to the core.

Selective Perception

How many of us actually noticed what our boss or favorite professor wore yesterday? Most of us don't *attend* to or pay attention to such things unless we have a particular interest in evaluating someone else's clothing styles. And even if we did notice, what aspects of the clothing did we even see? We tend to *perceive* only some things, in this case, perhaps just the shoes or the type of shirt. And when we do make note of them, for how many days do we *retain* this information? Can we actually recall what we had for dinner or what our best friend wore a week ago?

As a result, for us to suggest that we understand how other people feel or behave based on our own limited sampling, selective perceptions, and selective retention is problematic. At best, we could say that we have a sense of the way the people in our lives approach the world. To use that everyday information, though, to enact policies or change the rules of the game for everyone else would be overgeneralizing and unethical. *Overgeneralization* occurs when we attribute patterns to an entire group and make conclusions about a wide range of people or events based on a few observations. The limitations imposed by our everyday investigation of only the people around us restrict our use of that information for scientific purposes. How best to sample and generalize, and how to go beyond the convenience of talking to those whom we already know, are the topics of Chapter 5.

SCIENTIFIC THINKING

In order to be able to make accurate and honest conclusions about human behavior, we are required to go beyond the components of everyday thinking. While those techniques and styles may help us get along in our daily lives, the job of measuring various aspects of the social world and people's beliefs and behaviors demands a more deliberate approach. Certainly intuition can play some role in arriving at conclusions and making decisions, but would we really want someone about to operate on our body to do so guided by today's horoscope or by some hunch and intuition?

We would hope surgeons base their decisions on techniques and knowledge gained from decades of scientific studies and research. Although understanding study habits and grades is hardly as important as brain surgery, if we were to enact some policies and procedures that can have positive or negative impact on students' well-being, then investigating patterns of studying also deserves some rigorous and systematic methods. Developing policy or making conclusions about social life is best accomplished with the assistance of scientific procedures rather than with a dependence on the everyday thinking described previously. Science is certainly not the only way of arriving at information, but it may be better suited for specific kinds of questions.

Scientific thinking is characterized by:

- Empirical observations or data
- Systematic and deliberate methods
- Objective, intersubjective, and replicable procedures

Research Design and Empirical Observations

Let's consider what these mean and see how they differ from everyday thinking. In order to be more confident that the findings on which our policies will be based or the conclusions we make about social relationships are accurate, we need to develop scientific methods for gathering our observations. We need a *research design*, or a plan for translating our research objectives into measurable and valid information. Simply making decisions based on what we see happening among our friends and the people we encounter is not a reliable procedure for generating ideas about larger groups or categories of people. Yet, one of the basic principles of science is involved in everyday thinking; that is, we regularly make observations and collect data.

Empiricism states that the only source of knowledge is experience, especially of the senses. We understand the world through observation (data collecting), not just through speculative thinking or theories. At some point, to be scientific, we must encounter the reality that is out there and experience through observation whether the educated hunches or ideas we proposed in our theories are substantiated.

Systematic and Deliberate Methods

Empiricism is also part of the everyday procedures we sometimes erroneously use to make conclusions, so other elements are essential. These observations must also be *systematic*, *objective*, and *replicable*. This is where issues of representative and random sampling, measurement reliability and validity, and other methods used to make observations come into play, as discussed in later chapters. By spelling out clearly the details of how we are to measure and who we are to observe—and "what" we will do to get the "who" to do the "how"—we are engaging in the methodical step-by-step procedures of research design that make scientific thinking more *systematic* and deliberate than everyday thinking. Although such procedures don't always guarantee completely accurate results, they do eliminate many of the errors that are part of ordinary, nonscientific observation procedures, and allow us to generalize and arrive at conclusions about larger numbers of people or events.

Objective, Intersubjective, and Replicable Procedures

Some might argue that the elimination of errors and biases is what makes science more *objective*, that is, less dependent on emotion or personal prejudices and values. Because the procedures have been systematically detailed, other researchers could *replicate* the study (i.e., repeat it using the same methods and similar sample) without interference of individual biases. Of course, researchers have biases and hold a wide range of values that not only may affect the topic they choose to study, but could also influence the procedures they develop to make the observations and collect the data. After all, scientists engage in everyday thinking and employ selective perception as well.

There is nothing wrong with this subjectivity; indeed, it is a key process in uncovering the multiple ways people understand reality differently. Rather than assume that certain expressions or concepts are objective, we sometimes need to recognize that there are alternative meanings attached to those concepts. For example, when a questionnaire inquires about marital status and the range includes "married," "divorced," "widowed," and "single/ never married" categories, how are these options viewed by gay and lesbian respondents who are living with someone of the same sex in a romantic relationship? What if respondents were cohabiting with and not legally married to an opposite sex partner for fifteen years and the relationship ends, are they still "never married" or "separated/divorced"? Subjectivity provides the insights and meanings others have about social behavior and attitudes, and contributes new ways of developing measurements more comprehensively. We cannot, however, use subjective perspectives as a sole research method if we plan to make scientific generalizable observations.

If the procedures are comprehensively described and others with differing values and beliefs use them in their research to achieve similar results, we can more confidently conclude that the methods and findings were less affected by any personal biases of the researcher. Perhaps a better word than "objectivity" to describe what is going on is *intersubjectivity*, or what Ira Reiss (1993: 6) suggests happens when people with differing perspectives collectively agree on a particular way of seeing reality: "So we can define objectivity in science as those views of the world that come to be agreed upon by the community at any one point in time."

Finding the "truth" about human behavior and social processes is an ongoing goal of the social sciences. Knowledge is achieved and "facts" are built incrementally over time. The information we get at any one point is an approximation of the truth and is constantly being modified, clarified, and expanded with each new study. This is why it is so important to develop scientific ways of measuring and thinking about patterns of social behavior and attitudes in order to achieve the basic goals of research.

THE PURPOSES OF SCIENTIFIC RESEARCH

Research on human social behavior and attitudes is conducted for many reasons, including to explore, describe, explain, and evaluate for the purpose of understanding an issue in depth, arriving at decisions, and making predictions.

Exploratory Research

Sometimes research is conducted for exploratory reasons, that is, to get a rough sense of what is happening on a particular topic for which we don't yet have enough information. People use *exploratory research* to assess the opportunities for undertaking a study, to try out various methods for collecting information for a proposed larger study later on, or to learn the language and concepts of the topic used by those who will be studied. Exploratory research also has been designed to ascertain the needs and goals of a particular organization (often called *needs assessment research*) in preparation for a study or evaluation. *Focus groups*—a collection of respondents organized in a group discussion format to present their ideas about a subject—are frequently designed to achieve many of these objectives.

Let's say we are interested in understanding more about what concerns students about their educational institution that may cause them to drop out or stay in school. Although we could consult the many studies that have been done on dropouts, we have reason to believe that the unique dimensions of this school are particularly important to consider. So we design a study to explore what is going on at this school by developing a series of focus group discussions with students to learn their language, topics, and ways of viewing the institution in order to construct a better questionnaire for a later research project.

Descriptive Research

A typical goal of exploratory and almost all kinds of research is to provide basic information describing the topic and respondents involved. *Descriptive research* is often the first step in most research projects and the primary objective for some, like the U.S. Census or the General Social Survey and similar large surveys designed for gathering information. If we were interested, for example, in understanding the relationship between the number of hours spent studying and grades earned, we need to get descriptive information

■ ■ ■ ■ ■

BOX 1.2

DESCRIPTIVE RESEARCH AND SCIENTIFIC THINKING

If we were interested in understanding drug use and nonuse patterns among Asian American teenagers and depended on everyday thinking, we could make conclusions merely by looking around a high school and arriving at some description of who was using what and how much. Yet, this "research" would in no way be systematic and we might erroneously make inaccurate generalizations. Consider instead this excerpt from a study by Nagasawa, Qian, and Wong (2000: 596) which uses data from the Asian Student Drug Survey funded by the National Institute of Drug Abuse. Notice how a more scientific data-based approach results in descriptions that remove some of the errors of everyday thinking and false generalizations to an entire racial/ethnic category:

> . . . it is inappropriate to lump Asian and Pacific Americans together into a single racial/ethnic category. Our data suggest that Asian and Pacific Islanders differ significantly in drug and alcohol use. For example, Pacific Islanders have the highest use of marijuana and cocaine. Among Asian Americans, Filipino youths are most likely to use marijuana and cocaine, while Chinese youths are least likely to do so.

about the characteristics of the students (gender, race, etc.), what their grades are, how many hours a week they study, how many years of education they already have, and how many hours a week they work or participate in sports or other activities. The goal of such a survey would simply be to present basic information profiling the respondents (referred to as the *demographics*) and describing the issues under study.

Explanatory Research

Once we have some descriptive information we might then want to uncover the reasons why a relationship between grades and hours spent studying differs for the students we sample. We do this kind of research in order to *explain* relationships, to uncover the reasons "why" or "how" some social phenomena occur among respondents. *Explanatory research* is designed to answer the "why" question: why there is a range of behaviors or opinions held among people surveyed. Why don't they all have the same attitudes toward capital punishment or vote in the same way? Ideally, we want to be able to explain or perhaps predict these opinions and behaviors with efficient, less complex reasons or causes.

Remember when a romantic relationship ended and we wanted *the* explanation or cause for it not working out? We'd all like to have just one simple reason (such as, "it was the other person's fault"), but we know down deep that there are many reasons, since most complex behaviors and attitudes require more than one cause. However, the "law of parsimony" suggests that we should look for the fewest number of reasons (causes, explanations) to account for most of the differences (variation) that exist among our respondents in the behaviors or attitudes we are attempting to study.

Evaluation Research

We are typically interested in understanding the causes of human social behavior and people's opinions about a variety of issues. Sometimes, however, research is conducted to evaluate specific outcomes and to provide the explanations for why and how a particular result occurred. Applied or *evaluation research*, as it is called (see Rossi and Freeman 1996), focuses on problem solving and measuring the results and specified outcomes of the implementation of various social programs and policies (the "causes"). Many educational institutions also develop evaluation tools to assess students' achievement of the intended objectives and goals of the schools.

For example, a university wants to know whether its study abroad program results in students achieving an intercultural and international understanding of people and issues. It creates a new type of program designed to produce such understanding. Evaluation research would focus on the objectives of the program and assess whether the new study abroad experience directly resulted in any change in behavior and attitudes.

Decide and Predict

With information collected systematically, those responsible for a program or policy can make informed decisions about what dimensions need to be changed, enhanced, or removed. Using research to *decide* and *predict* outcomes is a central goal of much research, especially evaluation and explanatory research. By figuring out the causes of behavior or opinion, we use this information to make informed decisions about future events. One goal of research is to estimate what might happen after the research is completed, that is, to make forecasts about a company's future earnings, or to estimate the impact certain social policies will have, or to guide us in making *decisions*. Wouldn't it be great if teachers could present information to their students demonstrating that there would be a high likelihood of success in school if they put more hours into their studying? Wouldn't it be a worthwhile goal of research to be able to understand the causes of earthquakes or tornadoes and use this knowledge to *predict* their occurrences and make decisions about building codes and other modes of disaster preparation?

Cause and Effect

However, to determine causation, it is essential to (1) establish that a relationship (or correlation) exists between the alleged cause and the observed outcome or effect; (2) determine the time line of occurring events, that is, the cause must precede the behavior or opinion in time; and (3) eliminate other plausible explanations or alternative causes. If we can show that (1) there is a connection between hours studying and grades; (2) the grades come after the amount of study hours claimed (it is possible that someone with low grades could increase the number of hours studied as a result of the grades); and (3) no other possible explanation exists for the grades, such as number of hours working at a job, bad teaching, or time spent at parties, then we can more confidently conclude that how much students study explains a good deal of why they achieve various grades. We usually are not able to explain why one particular person does well or not, instead we may have found an explanation for variation among a sample of students. Most social science research is focused on understanding differences among aggregate groups of people, not in explaining or predicting one individual's behavior or opinions.

All three of these elements must be present to declare a cause and effect relationship. Too often, in everyday thinking, people assume that correlation is the same as causation. Just because two variables are related, does not mean we can conclude that one *caused* the other.

Concluding Thoughts on Scientific Methods

For us to describe, explain, and predict with any accuracy, it is necessary that we develop a research design of scientific procedures and avoid the kinds of everyday thinking that could lead to incomplete data and erroneous conclusions. While it is often tempting to make decisions, explain causation, and predict the future based on psychic powers, intuition, and "gut feelings," these are not particularly useful skills when convincing funding agencies, public policy makers, or methods professors that what we have uncovered is accurate and unbiased.

This is not to say that scientific procedures are always ideal and problem-free. There are many behaviors and opinions that elude the methods of science. How well can we really measure and explain the process of falling in love, predict who will successfully be our best friend, or fully understand religious fervor? Many have tried, but sometimes more abstract ideas require other kinds of methods besides quantitative scientific ones, or should be left to the work of poets and artists!

The research problem or the evaluation questions must determine the methods. And for most of the issues social scientists study and the complex behaviors we want to understand, scientific thinking and procedures work well. Yet the method should not precede the problem to be studied. Before

■ ■ ■ ■ ■ ▬▬▬▬▬▬▬▬▬▬▬▬▬▬▬▬▬▬▬▬▬▬▬▬

BOX 1.3

CORRELATION OR CAUSATION?

Sociologist Barry Glassner (1999) in his book, *The Culture of Fear,* uncovers numerous examples of why people fear the wrong things, many times due to making false conclusions about causation. Consider his argument about the fear of "road rage." Many people are concerned about the increase in shootings, attacks, and other exhibitions of anger that are taken out on drivers on today's streets and highways.

Explanations for this alleged increase in road rage suggest that we are increasingly living in a society where community no longer exists, individualism reigns, and a generation of young people have not learned the proper values and courtesy due to declining importance of family, schools, and religion. Let's assume for the moment that what is contained in these supposedly causal explanations actually has occurred (we really should first explore whether there is a decline in values or if an increase in individualism does exist). Even if declining values about community are related to increases in road rage, how can we be sure they are *causes* of road rage? Perhaps individualism is the result of an increase in crime on the roads and comes after in the time sequence. Or maybe there are plausible alternative explanations, such as an increase in media coverage of these occasional road rage events. That's what Glassner (1999: 5) concludes when he argues that road rage is partly a media-created myth and that the attention by TV news shows and others creates a false impression that these roadside shootings are rampant on today's highways: "The more talk there is about road rage, the more likely are newspaper reporters, police officers, and insurance agents to classify as examples of it incidents that they would have ignored altogether or catalogued differently in the past."

we choose a questionnaire survey approach, we should consider the different kinds of methods that can be used to study human social behavior.

RESEARCH METHODS

Doing survey research is a skill, an art, and an intellectual process involving collaboration, patience, and creativity. As Lauman, et al. (1994: 57) claim, "In practice, survey research methods, like many specific scientific laboratory techniques, remain more an art than a science." Survey research is also a choice of one method among many from which to select. As such, choosing to conduct a quantitative approach to understanding the social world can only answer some questions. It is not ideal to begin by saying "I want to give a questionnaire out but I am not sure what my topic is yet." Research questions must come first, and then the choice of the relevant method to study them should follow.

There are many different ways of gathering data, depending on the questions we are asking, whom or what we are studying, the financial and time limitations of our project, and the amount of detail we desire. Each method not only comes with strengths and weaknesses that must be evaluated carefully before selecting, but it also comes with a set of assumptions about the nature of knowledge, beliefs in the efficacy of science, and other philosophical questions about how we can make sense of the world in which we live. Most methods can be combined to study a topic (often termed *triangulation* when two or more measures or methods are used), and several of them share similar procedures, sampling strategies, and ethical considerations. Larger research textbooks (such as Babbie 2001 or Neuman 2000) provide more details about the different methods and the scientific assumptions that go with them. Because the focus of this book is on quantitative survey methods, here is a brief overview of other research methods, with key points to consider when evaluating whether questionnaire survey methods are best suited for a particular study.

Experimental Designs

When interested in understanding how the manipulation of a variable can explain specific outcomes on another variable, some researchers find it useful to conduct experiments (see Campbell and Stanley 1963). A classic *experiment* research design typically involves comparing two groups, one called the experimental group, the other the control group, to both of which respondents have been randomly assigned. In the experimental group, the researcher conducts some treatment on the subjects and measures its effects in comparison to another group that does not receive the treatment or to a group receiving a different kind of treatment.

Experiments typically occur in laboratory settings where the researcher can control the environment to prevent other possible causes from affecting the outcome of the treatment or experiment, thereby insuring internal validity or accuracy and perhaps allowing for generalizability, or what is sometimes called external validity (see Chapter 3 for a discussion of validity). Experimental designs are also suited for testing specific hypotheses and for doing applied evaluation research, rather than for conducting an exploratory study.

Imagine we are interested in understanding the impact on teenagers of an educational film about prejudice and racism. In the classic experimental design, we would randomly assign the teens to two groups. Each group completes a questionnaire focused on attitudes toward minorities and other indicators of prejudice. The experimental group views the video (the treatment) while the control group does not, or perhaps sees a different one if we were interested in comparing films. A few weeks later, a questionnaire on racism is given to the two groups and comparisons are made. Ideally, those who watched the film now have lower prejudice scores than the group who did not see the film; we infer that the film was partly responsible for this change. There are many variations of this classic experimental model, many of which are used in evaluation research and by experimental psychologists and social psychologists.

Qualitative Methods

If the goal is to understand human behavior in its natural setting and from the viewpoint of those involved, then an appropriate method is often a qualitative one, as opposed to a quantitative method in which predetermined categories and a more structured scientific approach are involved. Qualitative research explores new topics by getting into the settings where people carry out their lives. Anthropologists typically use qualitative methods to understand a culture, and some of the earliest sociologists (often referred to as the Chicago School of sociology) were pioneers in using these methods to study how people lived in small towns and urban centers (Plummer 2001).

Field research, participant observations, open-ended interviews, and focus groups are some of the common types of qualitative research methods (see Denzin and Lincoln 1994). At some level, they all involve observing what people do, what they produce, and how they interact verbally and nonverbally. For example, if we wanted to understand how people make decisions about what food to eat in the employee cafeteria, we might do better observing them than to ask such questions days later on a questionnaire. Going to the cafeteria, taking extensive notes about the kinds of people who choose different foods, observing how much they eat, listening to how they interact with other diners, talking with them about their choices, and so on, are just some of the methods of a qualitative approach.

Trying to understand with more depth and sensitivity people's subjective understandings while acting in their social situations is the main goal for qualitative research. We typically do not get to study a very large number of people using qualitative techniques compared with survey research, but we usually get more details and a stronger sense of the variety of ways people engage with the world around them. It is a technique ideally suited for doing exploratory research as well.

Content Analysis and Archival Research

It is not always necessary to study people and their behaviors and opinions. Occasionally we might be interested in understanding what they produce and to see how these might change over time. *Content analysis* involves the study of artifacts, usually written (such as diaries, newspapers, biographies, and official documents), but also visual and other forms of communication. It is based on developing a way of coding and classifying the information (the content) in the documents or media being studied. Content analysis is often used in coding answers to open-ended items on questionnaires (see Chapter 6 for a discussion about this). It includes qualitative methods and sometimes the quantification of information. For example, we can study the content of radio talk shows and code the broadcast in terms of how liberal or conservative the views of the host and the callers are, as well as tabulate the percentage of men and women who air their opinions. Or we might be interested in researching the images of gays and lesbians in television shows and do both a quantitative analysis of the number of characters as well as a content analysis of how they are depicted in these shows: Are they portrayed in stereotypical ways? What are their issues? Are they shown in relationships or isolated?

Let's say we are interested in evaluating newspapers' editorials toward capital punishment. We would develop a sampling scheme, read the editorials and construct coding categories, and then evaluate the articles in terms of those codes, perhaps pro- or anti-capital punishment, in all circumstances or in certain ones, for first offense or other, and so on. Sometimes this work involves searching archives and other *historical* documents for information about capital punishment in the nineteenth century, for example. *Comparative* research could also include looking at editorials on capital punishment or laws in other countries.

Quantitative Methods

Many times researchers are interested in describing the number of people involved in certain behaviors or holding specific beliefs. Some want to make use of archival data that have been collected by others over the years, such as all the information gathered during a census. Others like to focus on explaining the way people act or in predicting how they might act in the future. Underlying all these is an assumption that social phenomena can be systematically measured and scientifically assessed. For many of these kinds of questions and assumptions, the use of quantitative methods is most appropriate, as we have been discussing in this book.

Some of the techniques involved in content analysis, experimental designs, archival analysis, and in-depth interviewing make use of quantitative approaches. Structuring questions, developing categories and variables, and counting responses and observations are just some of these techniques. An easy way to remember the differences between quantitative and qualitative research is to think about how someone reviews a movie. If a reviewer goes into details about the acting, the camera work, the screenplay and dialogue, and the grand meaning of the story, then she is providing a qualitative analysis. If a reviewer simply says, it's worth three stars or two thumbs up, he has given a quantitative response with fewer details, but a convenient summary evaluation.

Quantitative methods involve writing questions for surveys and in-depth interviews, learning to quantify or count responses, and statistically (mathematically) analyzing archival, historical, or our own data. A most common form is a self-administered questionnaire. Questionnaires are ideally suited for respondents who can read, measuring people's attitudes and opinions, and when we want to get a very large number of respondents too difficult to observe with qualitative methods.

Doing survey research well is the theme of the rest of this book. It focuses primarily on questionnaires with samples of people, but many of the techniques described apply to other situations and methods. The first stop on the research journey is learning to create good research questions and generate problems to evaluate. In the next chapter, we look at ways to find ideas that are best served using the scientific methods of quantitative inquiry.

REVIEW: WHAT DO THESE KEY TERMS MEAN?

Biased questions	Experiments	Qualitative research
Causation vs.	Focus groups	Replicable procedures
correlation	Inaccurate	Research design
Content analysis	generalizations	Selective attention,
Describe, explain,	Limited sampling	perception, and
explore, evaluate,	Needs assessment	retention
and predict	Objective and	Systematic methods
Empiricism	intersubjective	Triangulation

INTERPRET: WHAT DO THESE REAL EXAMPLES TELL US?

1. What are the errors in everyday thinking contained in the following *Letters to the Editor?*
   a. "As a parent, I am glad that private and parochial school teachers are not required to go through the training given to public school teachers. If they did, those schools would have the same problems and bad education public school kids face."
   b. "If we institute national standardized testing it will lead teachers to teach only what is necessary to pass the test. This isn't what teaching is all about."

2. Here are descriptions of articles appearing in the academic journal, *Sociological Perspectives*. For each one, based on what is stated here, say whether the main goals of the research are to describe, explain and/or predict:
   a. A study by Nagasawa, Qian, and Wong (2000) looks at the likelihood of drug use and nonuse among Asian American teenagers. Earlier, this chapter

presented some descriptive results, but the research also investigates social control and peer group theory to understand why variations in use and nonuse occur among different Asian American groups.

b. Research by LeBlanc and Wight (2000) documents the characteristics of people who serve as informal caregivers of people with AIDS in Los Angeles County and the San Francisco area. Caregivers are more likely to be male, in their late thirties to mid-forties, white, and highly educated but with low income; many are unemployed. However, of those caregivers related to the patient, they are more likely to be female, slightly older, a racial/ethnic minority, and earn less money compared to those caregivers who are nonrelatives.

c. A study by Adams and Serpe (2000) finds that people who are better integrated into their local community (that is, how happy they are with neighbors, how much they have in common with them, and how satisfied they are with their city or town), will be less likely to fear crime and perceive themselves vulnerable to assaults.

CONSULT: WHAT COULD BE DONE?

One of your friends tells you that she heard from a friend that students living in Sanborn Hall have the highest grades on campus and suggests that you should move there next semester. When you do so, your grades will go up, she says.

1. How would you respond to this statement?

2. Is this an example of everyday thinking or of scientific thinking? In what ways? What would be the purpose of doing some research on this?

3. How would you respond to the cause and effect statement your friend is making?

DECIDE: WHAT DO YOU DO NEXT?

You are asked to do a study looking at the relationship between people's television viewing habits and their opinions about racial and ethnic issues and stereotyping, and their actions toward people from diverse backgrounds. Does TV viewing have an impact on their attitudes and behaviors toward diversity?

1. Give examples from everyday thinking that you have heard about this relationship. What are the errors in making conclusions from these examples?

2. Provide examples of studies you could do whose purpose is to (a) explore the relationship, (b) describe the relationship, and (c) explain the relationship. What kinds of questions would you ask and how would they differ for each type of study?

3. What would you need to know to declare there is a cause and effect relationship between TV viewing and racial attitudes and behavior?

■ ■ ■ ■ ■

CHAPTER TWO

FINDING IDEAS TO RESEARCH

LEARNING GOALS

Discovering topics to study by searching for research ideas and finding existing studies is one of the goals of this chapter. Learning to write a good literature review is discussed, especially in the context of using theory to guide your research. The chapter also raises the ethical issues involved in doing research. By the end of the chapter you should be able to search for topics in the library and in computer databases, write a coherent and focused review of the research literature, and raise the ethical concerns various kinds of research topics might create.

You've just been handed an assignment by your boss to gather data for a work-related project about customer satisfaction using a self-administered questionnaire. Or maybe a professor is asking you to develop a research topic for your senior year honors thesis in women's studies. Now what do you do? Where do you even start? You're probably thinking: I wish I had written down all those ideas I've had over the years because now I can't think of anything to study! Figuring out what to research or how to begin an assigned project can be a daunting task for many people. For some, curiosity generates too many broad questions. Others begin with too narrow an idea that goes nowhere beyond a simple query. What follows are some strategies that can be used to develop a research agenda that is meaningful and focused and that can help in creating a successful research design.

GENERATING TOPICS

Ideas come from many sources and part of any research design is translating those ideas into reliable and valid ways of measuring them. Developing an idea that is carried out to completion in a scientific research program is a powerful and creative process. To experience taking a topic, constructing research questions, and collecting evidence to support or refute your ideas can be exhilarating. And the first step—generating researchable topics that are unique ideas—is often one of the most innovative parts.

Curiosity and Experience

Where do we get ideas and topics for research? One way is with our own *curiosity*. Look around: listen attentively to what people are asking and see what they are doing. Be conscious and questioning of your own *experiences* and focus carefully on what you read about or hear in everyday encounters. Do these lead you to wondering about something in particular? For example, you learned in a linguistics class that women's body language when listening to others speak appears to be different from men's body language. Are women nodding frequently, providing more verbal signals, and smiling more than men? Or perhaps you heard that voting patterns vary among people from different social classes and ethnicities? Maybe you overhear students complaining about certain of the school's policies. Or you might just simply wonder if studying so much really makes a difference in the grades you get.

One of the first ways, then, of generating a research topic is to use your own curiosity and experiences as a source for further inquiry. But be careful: personal experiences can result in either a topic so broad that it would be impossible to study ("are men really different from women?"), or so narrow that it would be difficult to go beyond a very limited set of questions resulting in the most specific and trivial of findings ("which is the favorite Beatle of my friends' parents?").

Assignments, Theses, and Grants

Of course, another way to find a topic is to be assigned one from a teacher, a supervisor, or some granting agency. Perhaps you get a notice (called a request for proposal or application, RFP or RFA) stating that *funding* is available for research on alcohol use among the elderly. This sparks your interest and you begin to develop some questions that you feel need answering in this area.

Similarly, you might be asked to do a *thesis* for completion of a degree in political science, for example. Reflect on the courses you have taken and see if the books you have read or the lectures you remember raise questions that need some systematic analysis. You know that the topic has to be in the area of political issues so you decide that voting behavior among young adults is something that interests you. Studying voting behavior is quite general and not focused yet, but it is a good start.

Consider a situation where you are an employee at a social service agency that specializes in working with the homeless. The agency is required to file a report at year's end about the services it provided, the kinds of people who have been assisted, and the strengths and weaknesses of the program. Your supervisor *assigns* you the task to develop a questionnaire that can be used to assess these outcomes. You may not have a choice in the topic, but you do need to make some important decisions about the research design and the kinds of issues to be covered. Again, you start out with a general idea or topic and you now need to begin focusing more specifically on its multiple dimensions.

Other Research Findings

By reading published academic research, you learn what has been done already and what needs to be accomplished. An *academic article* is a paper that has been reviewed by peers and published in a journal read primarily by researchers and scholars. Normally, these are original reports of research. Such publications as *Newsweek* magazine, the *New York Times,* or *The Economist* may be sources for original information but they often summarize and report on research published elsewhere. In such cases, they are secondary sources, not primary ones like academic journals. Your search for further information about your topic should begin with the primary literature of original research.

Sometimes your goal is to *replicate* studies. In such cases, prior research gives you the questions, methods, and information you need to redo the study with a similar or perhaps different sample. An important aspect of science is the ability to repeat results under similar conditions, or with different pools of respondents.

Another goal might be to fill the gap in the research by focusing on what hasn't been done. Most articles conclude with what the researchers couldn't do and with suggestions for additional studies. Sometimes they even suggest particular lines of research that their project has generated and that need further analysis. Not only is published research a good source for a topic, it also gives you direction once your topic has already been selected. Reviewing the published literature often continues even after you design your study; it helps immensely when analyzing data, interpreting the outcomes, and writing up the final report.

Serendipity

An idea can also derive from the research we are already doing. It is not unusual to discover a finding that was totally unexpected; this is what is often called *serendipity*. By accident, a result that wasn't anticipated jumps out, and we become intrigued to figure out why this occurred. This leads to a new line of research in an attempt to study this serendipitous finding in more depth. For example, a study is designed to assess the relationship

■ ■ ■ ■ ■ ▬▬▬▬▬▬▬▬▬▬▬▬▬▬▬▬▬▬▬▬▬▬▬▬▬▬▬▬▬▬▬▬▬▬▬▬▬

BOX 2.1

USING RESEARCH TO GENERATE IDEAS

In an article by Kramer and Lambert (2001) on gender-based discrimination in job promotion, the authors end their article—in which they found a pro-male bias in promotion not related to time on the job and education—with a section called "Directions for Further Research." They list the limitations of their study and suggest the need for better measures of social class, a consideration of the proportion of women in managerial positions, and an assessment of the positions for which women are most likely hired. In sum, they state that "further investigation of sex segregation across all job fields, socioeconomic statuses, and employment levels, and its corresponding relationship to actual promotion events, is in order." (2001: 124) After reading this, someone looking for a study to do can develop a project that assesses promotion issues and that includes various levels of jobs (managers, hourly workers, executives) in different industries (service organizations, manufacturing jobs, educational institutions), among a range of social classes, for example.

between dropping out of college and grades. Several items of information are gathered during the study, including gender, race, social class, outside work commitments, course load, and major. In the process of reviewing the data, a researcher notices that other items about whether a student was on academic probation, received low grade warnings, and had meetings with advisors, might be interesting to analyze.

Unexpectedly, after further data analysis is completed, it's discovered that some students who received low grade notices tended to drop out, rather than to get their act together and study harder. Low-income students were more likely to see these warnings as statements verifying that they were not "college material" and could not make it at the university, as they had secretly feared all along. They tended to leave college more than the middle-class students who received the notices and used them as a "kick in the butt" to work harder. Because studying low grade notices wasn't the main focus of the research, it is not possible to go beyond this anomalous finding, but it can lead to the development of another research project on how probation and low grade notices affect various racial, social class, and gender groups differently.

Whether from astute observations of the world around you, an assignment at work or school, serendipitous findings in another study, or incentives from a funding agency, a topic is generated and the process of refining it to a more manageable project starts. At this point, the primary task is to carve out something that is focused, informative, unique, and fun to do. After all, if you don't enjoy the topic, you are not going to be motivated to do a thorough job!

SEARCHING FOR RESEARCH

A good way of figuring out if an idea or research topic is still too general or too specific is to type some key words into a computer search of resources. You can always use one of the *Internet* search engines (such as Google), but this will turn up lots of information (some of dubious quality) that is not likely to serve the needs of scholarly research. Imagine, for example, how many hundreds of thousands of responses you'll get if you search for "alcohol and elderly" (I actually got 241,000). The Internet may assist you and provide the names of many relevant agencies and publications, but it is probably not the best place to begin narrowing down the topic to find relevant scholarly information.

Your goal at this point in the research journey is to search for completed academic studies on your topic. Using library *databases* and entering the relevant information generates lists of academic articles and studies focused on your subject. Still, you must narrow your focus. Be careful not to select such a specific topic that prior research cannot be found or that the outcomes would not be interesting beyond one specific answer (for example, "Did women in Florida under the age of 25 vote in the last election?"). On the other hand, too broad a topic will result in thousands of articles, such as entering "voting behavior and young adults" into a search engine for academic journals. Perhaps uncovering just a few key articles or books on the topic will assist you in narrowing your search.

You also have to begin focusing on what you really want to know; don't ask questions for which you already have the answer. For example, what is it that you actually want to learn about voting behavior and young adults? How frequently they vote, who they vote for, racial and gender differences in party registration? Once you decide on some other categories of interest, search again using several additional key words, for example, "voting behavior, youth, gender, political party" and see what happens now. Ideally, a more reasonable number of articles shows up, and you can begin the next phase of reading and analyzing the studies.

Once you have found some well-designed research and academic articles on your topic, a review can provide additional concepts and ideas for further focusing of your study. The articles also list other publications to find. Look at the bibliographies and references in these journals and see if there are some articles or books regularly cited. These might indicate a classic study in the field that is important to read, or it may simply provide a new set of articles you hadn't discovered in the database searches, which only cover a certain number of years.

Searching the academic databases can be followed up with a search of more popular newspaper and magazines, the Internet, and other media to help you understand the popular culture's take on the subject and to suggest

■ ■ ■ ■ ■

BOX 2.2

LIBRARY DATABASES

There are many resources in the library to guide us in searching for books and articles on specific topics. They are typically available through computer databases which are lists or collections of information about books and articles organized by such various fields as name of authors, title, year of publication, and key words about the topic. Most of these resources rely on a system using *Boolean* logic to search for information. Boolean logic is based on dichotomous, or two-category, questions: is it true or false? Is it an odd-numbered card and a red one? Is it a heart or a diamond? The logical operators "or," "and," "and/or," "less than or equal to," among others, form the basis for the search.

For example, in its simplest form, if we are interested in finding an article about attitudes toward capital punishment among teenagers, then we would search for "capital punishment AND teenagers." Both pieces of information need to be present in an article for it to be selected by the search engine. If we inadvertently typed "capital punishment OR teenagers" then we would get every article written about teenagers and every article written about capital punishment. Research about elderly people's attitudes toward capital punishment would appear, as well as articles about teenagers and movie attendance, for example. Check the "Advanced Search" help feature of these databases for more details.

There are numerous databases available, depending on the subscriptions the library holds. They include *PsycINFO* to search the major psychology journals; *Education Abstracts* and *Education Resources Information Clearinghouse (ERIC)* for articles about education topics; *SocioFile* for sociology; *Social Science Abstracts* and *Social Science Citation Index* for various social sciences; *Political Science and Government Abstracts* and *Public Affairs Information Service (PAIS)* for government and political science areas; *EconLit* for economics; *Anthropology Literature* and *Human Relations Area File (HRAF)* for anthropology; and *MEDLINE* for medical research. LEXIS-NEXIS is a great reference for finding newspaper, magazine, and trade publication articles.

other avenues of research. But be careful: a lot of what is in the nonacademic literature may represent inaccurate reporting of results, personal opinion, poor sampling strategies, and the other pitfalls of nonscientific reasoning discussed in Chapter 1. You need to develop a critical sensibility in order to discover the quality material when searching in this era of information overload. Journalism sometimes sounds like social science, but it rarely does more than provide information. Analysis, theoretical interpretation, and systematic evaluation are what make social scientific approaches different from popular culture writing.

LITERATURE REVIEWS

At this point, you should have narrowed your focus and found many articles and books on the subject you are studying. This doesn't mean you have arrived yet at a final topic or set of questions. *Evaluating* the previous research is an important step in developing a quality study. Not only does this provide further ideas, but it also generates a set of questions, concepts, and methods relevant to researching your topic.

When reviewing the literature, it is essential to develop a detailed *database,* either with index cards, computer programs, or simply sheets of paper in a notebook. Plan ahead and prepare a list of information you need about each publication reviewed. For example, consider the form on the next page. Make copies of this, complete one for each article or book read, and use it as a way of keeping notes. Details about the complete title of an academic article, its authors, the journal name, the publication date and volume and issue number, are just some of the items required when writing up a bibliography or list of references in a final report.

For each academic article or book, attend to the methods used: Who or what is sampled and how many, what questions are asked, what are the variables, how are they measured, what statistics or data analysis are used, are the conclusions linked clearly to the data collected, is there a discussion of the limitations of the study? What major findings result from this research? The material in the rest of this book provides information you should use to be a critical evaluator of the methods, sampling, statistics, and overall research design of the studies you read, in addition to teaching you how to do your own survey research.

Once you have assessed the studies, the next task is to decide if you want to replicate any parts of them. If so, you might consider using the same measures (such as questionnaire items with the permission of the authors) or modifying them if you are duplicating the study with a different sample. If you feel something is missing from these studies, pick up on something the authors said they wished they had done, or see if the results suggest a further line of research to take. Then consider which aspects are worth keeping and which should be changed or expanded. For example, if you believe that studying students in an introductory psychology class was a weakness in an otherwise interesting study, then choose a better sampling strategy. If you feel the questionnaire items written for a study on satisfaction in the workplace did not accurately capture what represents satisfaction in the specific workplace you are studying, then modify the questions for this particular sample. Remember, though, that comparisons with other research cannot be exact unless the same measurement tools and methods are used. But this is primarily important only if comparison or replication is your main goal.

■ ■ ■ ■ ■

BOX 2.3

CREATING A DATABASE OF REFERENCES

Title:

Author(s):

(For an article) Journal name, volume, issue, page numbers, date:

(For a book) Publisher, city, date:

Summary (sample, methods, variables, questionnaire items, findings):

Direct quotes (with page numbers)

Your opinion (strengths, weaknesses, etc.)

(continue on back as needed)

A good literature review is necessary to help design the research. There is no need to study something that has been done over and over again, unless you have a unique perspective on the subject. A good literature review is also important in assisting you in becoming more knowledgeable about the research subject. Too often, people jump into a topic and fail to understand the range of issues involved, ignore important cross-cultural or subcultural differences that might impact a study, and make the same methodological mistakes others have. Critically evaluating the historic research record contributes to an expertise that becomes relevant when presenting the findings, contextualizing the research, and responding to queries about the work.

Learning to synthesize and find links among the various studies is the next step in organizing what is read. Reflect on the readings and uncover common threads and differences that run through the work. Are there specific themes that emerge from the research that has been done? Do the findings tend to apply to some categories of people, but not to others? How generalizable are the results? Are certain measurements more effective than others when studying this topic?

Organizing your literature review into thematic subtopics is a good way to summarize what you have read, rather than writing it up in a tedious sequential review, such as "this article reported such-and-such, and this article found that, and then these authors discovered something," and so on. For example, Adams and Serpe (2000) begin their study on the relationship between fear of crime and a sense of community by first citing public opinion polls about the percentage of Americans who fear crime today. Then the literature review is divided into three subtopics: (1) "Conceptualizing Fear of Crime" in which the authors discuss studies distinguishing between fear of crime and perceptions of the risk of victimization and feelings of vulnerability; (2) "Consequences of Fear and Vulnerability," which focuses on research about stress theory and life satisfaction; and (3) "Antecedents of Fear and Vulnerability," which concludes the literature review by summarizing work focused on social integration and feelings about belonging to a community. They conceptualized and organized what they read into three meaningful categories that highlight the central themes and issues of the study. Chapter 10 presents more about writing a literature review for a final report.

THEORY AND REASONING

Theories are an important source of research ideas; they typically underlie quality research. A *theory* is a set of statements logically linked to explain some phenomena in the world around us. If a theory is used to generate research ideas about certain behaviors and attitudes, then we are using *deductive reasoning.* On the other hand, if specific observations or empirical data are used to construct a general system of linked statements, then we are engaging in *inductive reasoning.* Most research involves both processes: a review of the literature tells us what theories and explanations we can use to deduce specific research questions that are then used to get data that form the basis for inducing or modifying a theoretical perspective to explain what was observed and measured.

A major outcome of investigating a topic through a critical literature review is the discovery of theories and the development of a set of concepts and questions that can be used to test those theories or to create new ones. This set of questions or hypotheses form the framework of a research design. Learning how to write hypotheses and develop good research questions that can be translated into reliable and valid measures is the focus of Chapter 3.

■ ■ ■ ■ ■ ▬▬▬▬▬▬▬▬▬▬▬▬▬▬▬▬▬▬▬▬▬▬▬▬▬▬▬

BOX 2.4

DEDUCTIVE AND INDUCTIVE REASONING

Emile Durkheim's *Suicide* (1951 [1897]) is a classic study in which Durkheim *induced* a general theory about social cohesion and how connected people are to communities, based on data collected throughout France in the late nineteenth century. Across different sets of people, those who belonged to more cohesive groups had lower suicide rates, he theorized. Durkheim did not develop a psychological theory about why any one particular individual commits suicide, but rather a sociological one based on specific *aggregated* information (data pooled together from a collection of people). He was interested in explaining *patterns* of behavior across groups and the variables that contribute to an understanding of those patterns. By linking these observations logically into a coherent system of explanation, Durkheim induced a theory about various types of suicide, like egoistic suicide which is related to a lack of social integration.

As others have done for over a hundred years, learning about Durkheim's theory can generate new research questions. Perhaps a study on how people who have large friendship networks tend to be healthier in mind and body, or how a lack of community and shared values contributes to increases in alienation and crime, can be derived from Durkheim's ideas. Going from a more general theory of social cohesion and suicide to a specific set of topics and hypotheses for further study on community cohesion and crime illustrates how research ideas can be deduced from theory. And Durkheim's contribution to the development of sociology was this creative linking of theory and empirical data.

THE ETHICS OF RESEARCH

When you have selected some specific and manageable topics and ideas to study, the next step is to design a research plan. As you do so, it becomes important to ask whether the topic and the act of gathering information are worth the impact they may have on who or what is being studied. You may have generated a wonderful set of questions and topics, but if they put people in difficult and stressful situations, the research should not go forward. In short, before the study begins, it is crucial to reflect on the ethics of doing research about a chosen topic, with the measures you intend to use, under sponsorship (and restrictions) from the agency providing funds, and with the sample of people or institutions you plan to survey.

Every major academic and professional association engaged in research has developed a *code of ethics* to guide the collection of data. Every institution conducting research also sets up an *institutional review board* (IRB) to evaluate the proposed research using those codes before the studies get funded or can start. When human subjects are involved, the guidelines are especially required to be followed.

In brief, codes of ethics state that participants should not intentionally be *physically or mentally harmed* and their *right to privacy* must be respected. Potential for harm and threats to privacy arise in several areas and situations, including in the process of sampling, measuring and analyzing data, disseminating the findings, and using the data. As described in later chapters, it is unethical when researchers deceptively use inappropriate statistics to distort the findings, distribute portions of the study favorable to their beliefs or the sponsoring agency while concealing unfavorable parts that do not support their ideas, use the results in ways for which they were not designed, and reveal information about specific respondents who were assured confidentiality.

Confidentiality needs to be emphasized when information identifying respondents can be linked to their specific answers and is revealed only to the researchers for the main goals of the project. *Anonymity* can be assured when there is no way of connecting any identifying information with the person completing the survey. Respondents do not give any names or code numbers linked to their names. Confidentiality is not the same as anonymity: anonymous information is always confidential since it can never personally be linked to anyone, but confidential information is never anonymous since it is known who completed the survey.

Although it is not always clear-cut in advance whether a research topic and the questions asked will invade people's privacy or cause mental or physical danger, it is important to discuss the potential impact the study might have with those involved. This is essential in order to eliminate any situations where intentional harm could occur, and to inform people what is going to happen in the study so that they may determine how much loss of privacy is at stake and decide whether or not to participate. This is what is called *informed consent*. For example, it would be ethical to tell participants that a questionnaire contains items related to alcohol use and family issues, and that they are not obliged to complete items that might disturb them. In this way, should those with a painful family history of alcoholism feel uncomfortable about the project or answering certain questions, they would have the chance to opt out. Of course, this might affect the outcome of the study because it alters the nature of the sample responding, but ethical concerns take precedence.

Similarly, volunteers for research must participate of their own free will. Being part of a captive audience—whether in a classroom or a prison—can be a form of coercion unless there are opportunities to decline involvement. For example, the Code of Ethics for the American Sociological Association (ASA) states: "When undertaking research at their own institutions or organizations with research participants who are students or subordinates, sociologists take special care to protect the prospective subjects from adverse consequences of declining or withdrawing from participation" (for a complete copy of the Code go to this Internet link: *www.asanet.org/members/ecoderev.html*). However *voluntary participation* can affect the outcome of a study if the sample ends up composed only of respondents who are willing to get involved. They may be very different kinds of people from those who declined, and depending on the research topic, this can result in distorted findings.

When there is any danger of physical or mental harm, consent must be given, usually in writing, and it must not be obtained through any form of coercion or misinformation about the project. Researchers must balance the amount of information they need to give with the amount necessary for respondents to arrive at a decision. Sometimes disclosing too much about the research can affect the outcomes of the study. Knowing you are part of the group getting a fake (placebo) vitamin, for example, may affect the results. In no case, should the researchers *deceive* the participants about the project. Of course, informed consent may not be needed if the questionnaire does not have the potential for harm, or at least no greater harm than what occurs in everyday social interactions, for example, when asking people anonymously about their favorite books, movies, and other hobbies. Occasionally, *debriefing* people (informing them about the complete objectives and methods of the research) after they participate in the study is a good way of providing information that, if given at the beginning, might have led to biasing the results.

In any case, we need to determine ahead of time whether a project has any potential harm, how we will minimize it if there is any, what mechanisms are in place to guarantee the confidentiality of the data gathered, and how much we will tell the participants before and after the study. This is the kind of information typically presented to an institutional review board which determines whether the design of the study (the sample, measurements, outcomes, uses of the data, consent, and privacy concerns) meets the ethical standards of the profession and sponsoring institution. The following guiding principle of research is clearly stated in the ASA's Code of Ethics and applies to all fields of study (just substitute "psychologists" or "anthropologists" or "political scientists" or whatever profession for "sociologists"):

> Sociologists respect the rights, dignity, and worth of all people. They strive to eliminate bias in their professional activities, and they do not tolerate any forms of discrimination based on age; gender; race; ethnicity; national origin; religion; sexual orientation; disability; health conditions; or marital, domestic, or parental status. They are sensitive to cultural, individual, and role differences in serving, teaching, and studying groups of people with distinctive characteristics. In all of their work-related activities, sociologists acknowledge the rights of others to hold values, attitudes, and opinions that differ from their own.

REVIEW: WHAT DO THESE KEY TERMS MEAN?

Academic article	Debriefing	Review of the
Boolean logic	Deductive and	literature
Code of ethics	inductive reasoning	Search engines
Confidential vs.	Informed consent	Serendipity
anonymous	Institutional review	Theory
Database	board	Voluntary participation

INTERPRET: WHAT DO THESE REAL EXAMPLES TELL US?

1. An article by Daniel Mears (2001: 3) investigating supposed links between immigration and crime, includes the following in his literature review:

   > Theoretical research on the relationship between immigration and crime has been nominal. . . . [Clifford Shaw and Henry McKay's 1942] theory suggests that crime is more likely in "socially disorganized" areas marked by high levels of poverty, ethnic heterogeneity, and residential mobility. . . . In addition to [their] social disorganization theory, at least two other prominent theories have been used to examine the immigration-crime nexus. The first, strain theory, involves a focus on blocked socioeconomic opportunities as contributing to crime and delinquency; the second, cultural deviance theory, derived primarily from [Edwin Sutherland's 1934] pioneering work on acculturation, centers on the idea that certain

groups have or develop distinctive cultural traditions that either promote or are accepting of criminal behavior.

a. How is theory being used to generate ideas for a study here?
b. Is this deductive or inductive reasoning?
c. How might these theories relate to the topic of Mears' research?
d. What kinds of research questions could you generate from these very brief descriptions of various theories?
e. What are some of the ethical concerns you would raise about such a study?

2. For a study of sexual practices of Asian/Pacific Islander high school students, Schuster, et al. (1998: 223) described their procedures for administering the survey:

> Respondents completed the anonymous self-administered survey during a regular class period and sealed it in an opaque envelope. Survey administrators unaffiliated with the district proctored the classes. . . . The school district notified parents about the survey and gave them the opportunity to sign a form denying permission for their children to participate. Students could also decline participation, and names of respondents completing the survey were not recorded. Respondents were instructed to skip questions they preferred not to answer.

a. Using the Code of Ethics, how do you evaluate these statements?
b. What other ethical concerns do you feel need to be addressed?
c. What is the difference between asking parents to deny permission and asking them to give permission? What are the pros and cons of each method?

CONSULT: WHAT COULD BE DONE?

Imagine you have been asked to consult on some research projects. Discuss with the researchers the *ethical* issues involved in the following situations:

1. A questionnaire on alcohol use seeks information about growing up in an alcoholic family.

2. Prisoners in the state penitentiary can get time off if they agree to try a new kind of medication.

3. Students in an intro psychology class get extra credit for volunteering for an experimental study conducted by the professor.

4. Respondents to a survey are asked to tell about their recent sexual experiences with those of the opposite sex and same sex.

5. High school students are invited to complete a questionnaire on drug and alcohol use. Monetary incentives will be offered for completion of the surveys.

6. For a study on nutrition and performance, participants are given high fat content meals for several days before asked to solve some mathematical problems.

7. You are led to believe that you are receiving a new vitamin to help in fighting colds, but later realize you were part of the control group receiving a placebo (a non-vitamin sugar pill).

DECIDE: WHAT DO YOU DO NEXT?

You are asked to do a study looking at the relationship between people's television viewing habits and their opinions about racial and ethnic issues and stereotyping, and their actions toward people from diverse backgrounds. Does TV viewing have an impact on their attitudes and behaviors toward diversity?

1. Which databases would be most useful for a study of this kind?

2. Develop some key words that you could use in a search of databases to find academic articles on the topic.

3. What Internet sites might provide helpful information on this issue?

4. Make a list of categories and themes you would use to organize the research literature after you have reviewed relevant articles and books.

5. If you are doing a study, list the databases used, create a bibliography of at least five articles and books related to your specific topic, and write up a summary of the readings organized thematically.

CHAPTER THREE

DESIGNING RESEARCH
CONCEPTS, HYPOTHESES, AND MEASUREMENT

LEARNING GOALS

Central to doing survey research is understanding the idea of operationalization and how to go from ideas to concepts to variables. Learning the various levels of measurement is also essential for analyzing data. This chapter shows how to write hypotheses using independent and dependent variables and how to evaluate the reliability and validity of measures. By the end of the chapter you should be able to distinguish the different levels of measurement: nominal, ordinal, and interval/ratio; discuss the various kinds of reliability and validity; and write one-directional, two-directional, and null hypotheses.

Once we select a topic and review the literature, we are ready to begin constructing a research plan. A research design serves as a blueprint for the project, and must be detailed when proposing a topic for a thesis or applying for a grant. A *research design* involves several stages: (1) developing concepts that are derived from ideas, theories, or prior research; (2) taking those concepts and translating them into measurable variables (operationalizing concepts); (3) selecting the most appropriate research method to gather data (surveys, experiments, field methods, content analysis, etc.) based on the goals of the project (to describe, explain, predict, explore, or evaluate); (4) choosing a sampling strategy for deciding whom or what we want to study (the *units of analysis*), and over what period of time (longitudinal across time or a one-time cross-sectional study); (5) planning how to collect the data and who will do it; (6) deciding on the relevant statistical and analytical tools to make sense of the findings and observations; and (7) describing plans for interpreting and analyzing the results and writing a final report, article, or policy recommendation. A detailed budget should also be included as part of a research design (especially for a grant or funding agency) specifying everything from the costs of duplicating questionnaires to phone calls, supplies, salaries for researchers and those doing the data collection, computer data entry and software, travel expenses, and other related items. The remaining chapters of the book explore these steps in the research design process as they apply in particular to survey research methods.

VARIABLES AND HYPOTHESES

Creating a research design or plan is essential for carrying out a scientific study. By carefully specifying the steps necessary for researching a topic, we avoid many of the pitfalls of everyday thinking described in Chapter 1. The first important phase in this process is formulating ways to measure ideas and concepts with accuracy and consistency.

Concepts

Research is guided by a set of questions composed of concepts connected to your topic. These concepts may have been uncovered in a review of previous research and theories, or developed from your own intellectual curiosity and knowledge. A *concept* is an idea, a general mental formulation summarizing specific occurrences, such as "gender" representing such things as masculinity and femininity, or "age" summarizing specific instances of the idea of time (youth, middle age, elderly). A concept can be defined with a dictionary to produce a common usage of the word, and a search of scientific publications can result in a more suitable definition for the appropriate field of study. Otherwise, the meanings of concepts can be quite subjective and made more difficult to measure, especially for more abstract ones. Some concepts are specific and concrete, such as "height" or "academic major," while others, sometimes called *constructs*, are more complex, abstract, or difficult to define, such as "happiness." Ask many people to define the concept of "love" and you'll get everything from operas to paintings to poetry to warm puppies.

Conceptualization must occur for research to begin and what we mean by the ideas and terms used in our study should be explicitly stated. For example, if you are interested in studying gender differences in phobias, you need to be clear about your conceptualizations. Psychologists define the concept of "phobia" as a persistent illogical fear, while sociologists define "gender" as the prescribed roles that men and women are to follow in a particular culture. A good way to start a project, then, is to list the concepts you are interested in studying and then find working, nominal definitions for them.

Variables and Values

The next step is to take the concepts of the research topic and translate them into something measurable. When this is done, these concepts are called *variables* to signify the variation that might exist in the concept. Concepts that have only one fixed meaning, such as the concept of Pi (π) in mathematics, are called *constants* since they don't vary. Most concepts have multiple categories or *values* to represent the variability of the concept. "Gender" typically has two values, male and female, and "religion" can vary across dozens of categories. The subjective concept of happiness, for example, can be transformed into a variable with values ranging from very unhappy to very happy, and height could range from very short to very tall, or from two feet tall to seven feet tall, depending how it is measured. Occasionally in a study, what normally is a variable can become a constant, for example, when only women complete the survey. In this case, gender becomes a constant for this particular study and can no longer be used as a variable for further data analysis.

Once concepts have been defined and translated into variables, they require some specification about how they are to be measured, or what is called the process of *operationalization,* as described below. Measurable variables form the basis of questionnaire items which guide the collection of data. Questionnaire items are the most specific form of an operationalization, and represent what the researchers believe are good indicators of the concept. Chapter 4 focuses on writing questionnaires.

Hypotheses

Central to a research design is the construction of research questions and hypotheses to guide the project. Untested statements that specify a relationship between two or more variables are called *hypotheses.* A hypothesis is a hunch derived from an informed reading of the literature, a theory, or personal observations and experience, and must be capable of being tested. For example, a study might hypothesize that there is a relationship between employees' job satisfaction scores and the quality of the benefits provided, such as health care, vacation time, and child-care facilities. Each of these concepts is a measurable variable and a potential association is stated relating them to one another.

Independent and Dependent Variables

One goal of research is to explain why a particular variable varies; why isn't it a constant? Why don't people vote the same way, what is the outcome of a new benefit package in the workplace, why do people vary in height or hold different attitudes toward equal rights for gays and lesbians? The

■ ■ ■ ■ ■

BOX 3.1
CONCEPTS, HYPOTHESES, AND VARIABLES

Consider the following example from a published academic article. Note how concepts are introduced and defined, how they become variables in hypotheses, how they are operationalized, and which ones are independent and dependent.

A study by Jones and Luo (1999) was designed to assess whether poor people exhibit a culture of poverty mentality, and if African Americans differ from whites in their attitudes toward employment, family values, and welfare. They begin their article by discussing anthropologist Oscar Lewis' 1959 thesis of a "culture of poverty" in which poor people cope with their impoverished situations by adapting a set of psychological traits including a strong orientation to the present, early sexual initiation, and a mother-centered family. These represent a set of values and attitudes that are passed along to the next generation through a process of socialization or learning.

After discussing Lewis' ideas and other research about a "culture of poverty," the researchers use these ideas and translate the concepts into more concrete definitions and measures. They (1999: 440) write: "Contemporary culture of poverty explanations identify three distinct mind-sets that differentiate poor individuals from mainstream society: lack of a work ethic, improper family values, and an ethic of dependency."

Note how they take a more abstract concept such as "the culture of poverty" and turn it into a more manageable and specific set of ideas. For their purposes, three concepts are described to indicate a culture of poverty. But the work is just beginning. The researchers next have to define more explicitly what they mean by these concepts.

They define "work ethic" using the concepts and ideas from other research, including whether someone would continue working after he or she earned enough money to support oneself without a job, if that person sees employment as central to getting ahead, and if he or she is aware of how much motivation to work and orientation to the future people have. An "ethic of dependency" is conceptualized as attitudes toward welfare, and the concept of "family values" becomes a shorthand phrase for considering attitudes toward sexual activity outside of marriage, single parenthood, and female-headed households.

With these more specific definitions, Jones and Luo (1999: 444) construct a set of hypotheses, such as "Blacks should not differ from whites in regard to the work ethic dimension" and "Blacks should exhibit more positive attitudes toward mother-only families, out-of-wedlock births, premarital sex, and welfare." They label race as an independent variable and attitudes toward work, welfare, premarital sex, and so on, as the dependent variables. The first research question is stated as a two-directional null hypothesis (no difference between the two categories or values of the variable race) and the second is a one-directional hypothesis with blacks expected to demonstrate higher attitude scores on the dependent variables. Also notice that these hypotheses are designed for the purposes of

(continued)

BOX 3.1   CONTINUED

describing differences, not for explanation. The outcome would tell us who differs, but not why.

Now comes a key part: the researchers specify the procedures (operationalization) they use to measure these concepts which are stated as variables in the hypotheses. Jones and Luo (1999: 446) continue: "We use three items to measure work ethic. Our first item . . . assesses whether or not an individual would continue working even if she or he no longer needed the income . . . . Our second item. . . assesses whether or not an individual considers employment to be his or her most important activity. . . . The third item . . . [asks] respondents how important it is that a child learns to work hard. This item simultaneously taps the work ethic and socialization aspects of the culture of poverty."

An "ethic of dependency" is operationalized with items measuring whether respondents believe that "individuals should have to work in order to receive welfare" and "welfare benefits should be reduced in order to make employment more desirable." Approval of premarital sex, belief that childbearing should be limited to marriage, and opinion about a single woman's ability to raise children are used to assess "family values." Note that the researchers could have defined "family values" behaviorally; namely, asking respondents whether they had sexual activity before marriage, or grew up in a female-headed household, or are a single parent. However, they chose to use attitudinal measures to define the concept.

In case you are interested, they found no difference in attitudes toward welfare and family values between whites and blacks, but blacks agreed more than whites that single women can raise a child as well as married couples can. To learn their other findings, look for the article in your library.

---

outcome we are seeking to understand is called the *dependent variable* and we hypothesize that its variability in our sample *depends on* particular explanations or causes. The explanations or causes (or predictors, if you are trying to predict the variation in the dependent variable) are called the *independent variables.*

There is nothing inherent in a variable that makes it dependent or independent; it often is a function of the research question or hypothesis we develop. What is a dependent variable in one hypothesis could very well become an independent variable in another hypothesis or study. For example, you might be investigating whether the variation in the number of hours studying (independent variable) in a survey of college students affects differences in grade point averages (dependent variable), but later on you are interested in the reason that study hours differ so much (dependent variable) and whether this variation in your sample is due to involvement in work and extracurricular activities (independent variables).

Positive, Inverse, One-Directional, Two-Directional, and Null Hypotheses

Hypotheses should be clearly listed before proceeding with a study. However, it is not necessary to have hypotheses before conducting research: sometimes we create simple statements in question form to guide the research. These research questions can focus on describing information, such as "How many respondents in my study are male and how many are female?" or "What is the average score on the reading test for the local school?" Other questions attempt to explain or predict relationships or differences among concepts, such as "Are differences in levels of self-esteem related to height and weight?"

A project on grades and study habits might frame the research goals in any number of ways:

1. I wonder if the number of hours studying per week is related to grades at the end of the semester.
2. If the number of hours studying per week is low, then grades are low.
3. The higher the number of hours studying per week, the higher the grades.
4. The relationship between the number of hours studying per week and grades at the end of the semester differs between men and women.
5. There is no relationship between the number of hours studying per week and grades at the end of the semester.

The first statement is simply a research question providing a hunch about a possible relationship between the two variables. The second statement is an "if . . . then" format that specifies a particular direction to a hypothesized relationship. In this case, it is called a *positive one-directional* (or *one-tailed*) hypothesis because, as the independent variable decreases in a particular way (study hours go lower), then the dependent also decreases in the same direction (grades go lower). The statement is considered *positive* because both variables are hypothesized to change together, or co-vary, in the same direction. Conversely, the third statement is making the implication: those who study more, get higher grades. This is also a positive one-directional hypothesis.

Note that a relationship is not hypothesized about one particular person, but about grouped (or aggregated) people. Hypotheses should not be written as "If a person studies less, his or her grades are lower" since the research is not designed to get information about any one individual person. The hypothesis is proposing that across the hundreds of people researched, those who study less, tend to have lower grades. Any conclusions or predictions about one person cannot be made.

A *negative* or *inverse* one-directional hypothesis states that more hours studying is related to lower grades—a scary thought indeed! It goes in the opposite or inverse direction: as one variable increases across the sample of people in the study, the other variable decreases. If we do not want to specify ahead of time any direction (positive or inverse), then we write *two-directional* (or *two-tailed*) *hypotheses,* such as "there is a relationship between hours studying and grades." Note that the exact relationship remains unstated, and the possibility that it could be a positive one (more hours related to higher grades; fewer hours studying related to lower grades) or a negative one (more hours lead to lower grades; fewer hours related to higher grades) is left open. We have two chances to support or refute the hypothesis.

The fourth hypothesis is an example in which three variables—hours studying, grades, and gender—are involved. The expectation is that the amount of time studying and the grades obtained will not be the same for men and women. It is not stated ahead of time whether the relationship will apply only to men and not to women, or the other way around. Thus, it is a two-tailed hypothesis. Researchers introduce a third variable in a hypothesis when they are interested in multivariate analysis to see if a relationship between two variables holds up under the conditions of a third or control variable, or if they want to assess the impact of two or more independent variables together affecting the outcome variable. Further discussion of the process of elaborating relationships with additional variables is presented in Chapter 9.

The fifth example illustrates another way of writing a two-directional hypothesis: the *null hypothesis,* since it assumes that *no* relationship exists between the variables. It is a common form of stating hypotheses when using inferential statistics, since the logic of research is that you do not directly prove a hypothesis. Instead, you reject no relationship which results in the assumption that there is a relationship (a double negative is a positive!), although you haven't directly proved the statement.

Rejecting the null hypothesis is a statistically significant event and worthy of publication, announcements, and perhaps further funding. It is not necessarily a good or bad thing; no value judgment is implied when rejecting or accepting a hypothesis—you may have found a significant relationship between hours watching television per week and an increase in grades, something you were hoping would not happen—but it is something that gathers attention. The goals of your research guide you in interpreting the results, and the hypotheses assist you in scientifically designing your study.

Defining and Operationalizing Variables

With a set of questions or hypotheses, list the variables in your study and specify their conceptual and nominal definitions. Be attentive to which ones are independent variables and which are dependent. It is important that the

■ ■ ■ ■ ■

BOX 3.2

THE LOGIC OF THE NULL HYPOTHESIS

In a sense a null hypothesis exclaims "show me that I am wrong; I say there is no relationship" and you either find that you are wrong ("go ahead and reject my hypothesis, I guess there is a relationship after all") or you have withstood the challenge ("accept the hypothesis of no difference; I told you so!"). But in neither case have you proved the hypothesized relationship directly. Rather, the null hypothesis has failed to be disproved (it is accepted as is, as no relationship), or you have disproved it (it is rejected and a relationship exists. Hold a press conference!).

Here's an example in logic: you state that there are no such things as chickens with purple polka dots. You can do a census of all chickens in the world and see if this is so; if there are no purple polka dotted chickens in the entire population, then you have indeed proved your point. Realistically, you aren't going to check every chicken in the world, so you take instead a sample of chickens (more on sampling in Chapter 5), and lo and behold, none of the chickens in your sample have purple polka dots.

You have not disproved your statement: you accept it and infer that there are no purple polka dotted chickens in the world based on your sample. All you can scientifically and logically conclude is that you accepted your null statement that no purple polka dotted chickens exist. However, you did not prove this directly. Somewhere in some hidden chicken farm there might be a purple dotted chicken pecking away. If you found one, you would reject the null, and state the *alternative hypothesis* that there are some. Call in the press for a major news story and t-shirt marketing plan!

concepts that make up the variables are clearly defined before going to the next step in figuring out how to measure them. Consider a study on political attitudes and race and the following hypothesis: there is a difference among various racial/ethnic groups about their opinions of the 2000 Bush-Gore presidential election or, as stated in the null form, there is no difference in opinions about the election among various racial/ethnic groups. You assume that people's views on the outcome of that contest and the ensuing debates about "hanging chads" in Florida depend on their race or ethnicity. You list the two variables: racial/ethnic group (the independent variable) and opinions about the election (the dependent variable). This is a two-directional hypothesis since you are not predicting ahead of time which category of the race/ethnicity variable will relate to which set of attitudes about the election.

Now you must define these concepts: what does race/ethnicity represent and which attitudes do you want to assess? Do you really mean their attitudes or were you thinking to include a behavioral dimension such as for whom they voted? Once you decide on the concepts you intend to study and turn them into variables by concretely defining them in measurable ways, the next step is to specify how you are going to measure these variables. The objective is to develop appropriate *indicators* for the variables and concepts you are studying. A concept can be measured using any number of ways to show its variability. The concept of "sadness" can be indicated using one question in a survey "Are you sad?" or it can be assessed through multiple indicators such as a set of ten items that form a "sadness" scale. A *scale* is a composite measure combining responses to many questions believed to assess the same concept or variable.

This process of specifying the indicators of a concept is called *operationalization*, because we are describing the operations or procedures it will take to assign values to the variables. Think about the time someone told you that a movie was really interesting, and you asked for clarification on what "really interesting" meant. What you were doing was asking for a definition, asking how your friend measured the quality of the movie, and asking what operations he or she used to arrive at the value of "really interesting" for the attitudes toward the movie variable. The values for the variable could have

■ ■ ■ ■ ■

BOX 3.3

CONCEPTUALIZING AND OPERATIONALIZING "A VOTE"

In the 2000 Presidential election, the vote counters in Florida had to decide if someone voted for Bush or Gore. This may not seem as self-evident as both sides of the race claimed. Let's begin with the concept of voting for a candidate. The idea of voting is inherent in our political democratic system and the concept is fairly concrete. We could then look up a nominal definition in the dictionary, such as "a formal expression of preference." But we still need to spell out how this preference will be expressed. When will we know if someone voted and for whom?

If you recall, the debate in Florida centered on several different meanings for "a vote" by introducing us to hanging chads, dimpled chads, pregnant chads, and the like. The vote counters specified the operations (the rules or instructions) it took to arrive at a conclusion that the punched hole was a vote for one or the other of the candidates. For some, a vote was defined as a chad that was punched all the way through, or by others as hanging by one corner, or just pushed in resulting in a dimple. Was the intention of a bruised chad good enough, or did a card have to demonstrate a complete punch to be measured as a vote? In other words, a dictionary definition of the word "vote" had to be translated into a measurable unit with the methods of decision spelled out, or operationalized clearly and with consensus. How clear a consensus operational definition was in the Florida election remains debatable to this day.

ranged from "really bad" to "really excellent," with "really interesting" somewhere in the middle. Or "really interesting" could have been the highest accolade in your friend's measurement scale. The way a concept is operationalized needs to be spelled out in detail in order to be scientific and not lapse into the errors of everyday thinking as described in Chapter 1.

Similarly, if you define the concept of race/ethnicity as a category with which a respondent identifies, then you might operationalize the variable as a person self-disclosing as African American, Asian/Pacific Islander, Latino, White, Native American, mixed race/ethnicity, or other. Or it could be measured as the category listed on a birth certificate. The actual item we construct for a questionnaire becomes the measurement using these categories for the values of the variable race/ethnicity.

Let's say attitude toward a political election is defined as how intense respondents feel about the election results and whether or not they perceive them as fair or not fair. Attitude will be operationalized by developing a five-point measure from "strongly agree" to "strongly disagree" to assess what the respondents believe about such statements as "The outcome of the mayoral election was achieved fairly" and "The campaign used too many negative advertisements."

The conceptual definitions and operationalizations are important to describe in a study because if others wish to replicate your research, it is important that they know the steps you took to measure your variables. When they review the literature and find your study, they might agree or disagree with the way you defined and measured the concepts. So long as you are clear with what you did, you have provided readers with enough information to make a fair assessment of your work.

Clearly, the more abstract the concept, the harder it is to develop an operationalization. How would we measure "excitement" or "alienation" for example? On the other hand, there are fewer ways we can operationalize "income" in a study: Do we ask for income before or after taxes, with or without investments, per month or per year, for an individual or the entire household? But differences in the way we measure concepts can affect the outcomes and interpretation of the findings.

LEVELS OF MEASUREMENT

Operationalizing variables involves specifying levels of measurement and considers how reliable and valid the measures are. When constructing a questionnaire, it is important to understand the many ways variables can be written. Not only can differences in measurement affect the statistics used when analyzing the data (as discussed in Chapter 6), but they also determine the various kinds of information you actually get. Researchers make four general distinctions in measuring variables: nominal, ordinal, interval, and ratio measurements. In addition, variables are discrete or continuous.

Discrete and Continuous Variables

A *discrete* variable has values that do not contain additional information between those values, such as the number of children in a family. There are only exact numbers of children; there is nothing in between the counting units. Do you know someone with 1.3 children, or 3.75 kids? Type of car owned can be a Honda, a Ford, a Volkswagen, and so on, but there is no category between a Honda and a Ford. A *continuous* variable, on the other hand, has values that have information between those values. Time is measured continuously: the counting units of 1:15 pm and 1:16 pm contain seconds between them. If your watch has a seconds hand, you can measure them. In track races, you break down the units between minutes and seconds even further to hundredths of a second, and many computers calculate time in nanoseconds. We arbitrarily say "it's around 1:15" unless you're one of those smart alecks who, when asked the time, responds "it's 1:16 and 23 seconds" or "we've been dating for two months, 3 days, 14 hours, and 6 minutes!"

The distinction between discrete and continuous is useful when interpreting data since it occasionally is reported in the press that, for example, the average family size is 2.3 children. A statistic appropriate for continuous variables (a mean) was calculated for discrete data. A more important distinction, however, is the level of measurement used to operationalize the variable.

Nominal Measures

The simplest, and perhaps least useful statistically, is the nominal level of measurement. *Nominal* variables are discrete measures whose values represent named categories of classification. A measure used to list academic disciplines such as sociology, psychology, anthropology, history, and economics, is a nominal one. A number can be assigned to these categories (called *coding*) as a shortcut summary of the category, but it is not mathematical and no order to the categories is intended. On a questionnaire, for example, the variable "religion" can have the value 1 for "Catholic," 2 for "Protestant," and 3 for "Jewish," or it could be listed as 1 for "Jewish," 2 for "Buddhist," and so on. These are arbitrary numerals that do not represent any type of mathematical quantity. They're like zip codes or telephone numbers. We can't add or multiply them, or claim that our phone number is bigger and, therefore better, than someone else's. If a friend told you the type of car she drives by giving you the category number without telling you the coding scheme, it would make no sense, because it does not represent quantity. ("I drive a 3." Huh?)

In fact, we do not need to assign a number to the categories because many computer programs allow for data analysis of text, but it is a convenient way of entering data into a computer program for later analysis. There are fewer keystrokes when typing a "4" than when typing "philosophy major." When there are two categories, the variable is called a dichotomy or a *dichotomous variable.* In some statistical calculations, these two-category variables are called *dummy* variables; for example, the variable "work status" can have one category value "employed" and another value "not employed."

Ordinal Measures

When the category values for a variable are in sequence, the measurement is considered an *ordinal* variable. This is also a discrete measure but one in which the values increase or decrease in a particular order. In this case, it does make a difference which one comes before or after the other. For example, we might ask respondents to indicate their shirt size (the variable) in terms of small, medium, or large (the values). They go in order; we cannot say medium, small, large, and then assign the numbers 1, 2, and 3 to those words since they are not in sequence. If something is in category 1 it must be less than 2 which in turn must be less than 3. Or we could assign numbers the other way around: 1 can be the most, 2 in the middle, and 3 the least. Just so long as we keep going in rank order once we start the numbering.

When we are asked to line up in size places, we are using an ordinal measure to determine who is shortest and who is taller and who is tallest. We don't measure using a ruler to get the exact inches; it's just a visual estimate of degree. If we measure a variable with the idea of greater than or lesser than, we are using at least an ordinal measure. For example, you might ask respondents to disclose their yearly income using such discrete categories as "under $15,000," "between $15,000 and $20,000," "between $20,001 and $25,000," and "over $25,000." These categories are in sequence and can be coded with ordered numerals showing increasing degrees of wealth, such as a 1 for "under $15,000," a 2 for "between $15,000 and $20,000," and so on.

Yet, the ordered number still doesn't tell you the answer without first consulting a coding sheet of information. If someone responded to a question about how much he earned last year by saying "I earned 3", you couldn't tell what category of income that is just simply by the numeral. All you know is that he is earning more (or less, depending on the order) than those in the first two categories.

Interval and Ratio Measures

When the value you get tells you everything you need to know about the variable, you are operationalizing it using an *interval* variable. These are measurements whose numbers are in order with equal size intervals, but have no absolute or fixed zero as a starting point. Temperature, for example, does not begin at zero; in fact 0 degrees is not the absence of temperature, it is an actual temperature. Yet the number itself tells you what you need to know. If you ask how cold it is outside, and the response is 45, you do not need to look up what category that value represents. It is an actual number that can be treated mathematically (that is, added and subtracted). It is 10 degrees more (remember it is has the properties of ordinal measures) than 35 degrees, and 5 degrees less than 50. However, you cannot say that 40 degrees is twice as warm as 20, or half as warm as 80, since there is no absolute zero point to calculate a ratio.

When there is an absolute zero, it is called a *ratio measure*. Now a zero represents the absence of something and the start of the numbering system. There are no negative numbers below zero on this type of measure. Thus, zero weight is the absence of all weight; you cannot have a negative weight. Ratio measures allow you to use the other mathematical operations (multiplication and division) to achieve ratios and conclude that someone who is 200 pounds is twice as heavy as someone 100 pounds, or that $10 an hour pay scale is half as much as $20 an hour. Note that this is different from a measure that is used to assess the severity of an earthquake. The Richter Scale is not a ratio measure, but one in which the units are based on logarithmic calculations, so that an earthquake of 7 compared to one of 6 is an increase in amplitude by ten. So you can't always assume that a measure using actual numbers is a ratio or interval one.

Ratio measures are so similar to interval ones, except for the presence or absence of zero, that throughout the book, such variables are called *interval/ratio* measures. They are usually continuous measures, although discrete interval/ratio measures also exist such as number of books in the library, children in households, houses on a block, or any other similar counting situations. The most advanced and important statistics require interval/ratio levels of measurement.

Other Measurement Considerations

Not every measurement falls neatly into these four distinct types. Dichotomous variables technically are discrete nominal measures. However, an order exists when there are only two values: assigning an arbitrary 1 to "home owners" and a 2 to "renters" suggests for the purpose of analysis that renters are "higher" than home owners for the duration of the data analysis in this study. Therefore, dichotomies can be treated as ordinal or interval/ratio measures. Another example is an intensity measure, such as a 5-point range (often called *Likert scales*) where 1 is "strongly agree" and 5 is "strongly disagree." These are ordinal measures, but researchers treat intensity scales as interval/ratio measures when the amount of agreement or disagreement is assumed to vary in equal intervals along the points of the measure.

■ ■ ■ ■ ■ ▬▬▬▬▬▬▬▬▬▬▬▬▬▬▬▬▬▬▬▬▬▬▬▬▬▬▬▬▬▬

BOX 3.4

LEVELS OF MEASUREMENT

Consider these excerpts from published academic research and see how researchers decided to operationalize the variables with different levels of measurement :

1. "We measured marital status according to four categories: married, never married, divorced or separated, and widowed" (Jones and Luo 1999: 447).
2. ". . . we include the following characteristics of workers: *age* (measured in years)" and "*presence of work experience* . . . (1 = had previous work experience)" which is a dummy variable (Aiba and Wharton 2001: 77).
3. Each item on the Homophobia Scale (such as "Would you mind if your child's teacher was a lesbian" and "Do you think employers should be free to refuse to hire a person because of that person's sexual orientation?") was scored on a 4-point measure where 1 = no, 2 = probably not, 3 = probably, 4 = yes (Sherrod and Nardi 1998: 31).
4. Two items taken from a national survey about health and sexuality: (a) "During the past 12 months, about how regularly did you drink alcoholic beverages? Would you say that it was . . ." Daily = 1, Several times a week = 2, Several times a month = 3, Once a month or less = 4, Not at all = 5; and (b) "On a typical day when you drank, about how many drinks did you usually have? Enter Number " (Laumann, et al. 1994: 660).

For the first example, the variable marital status is a four-category nominal measure. The researchers could have created five discrete categories with "separated" and "divorced" each having its own value, or included additional categories such as "partnered with someone of the opposite sex" and "partnered with someone of the same sex." Regardless of the number of values, the variable marital status remains nominal since there is no order to the categories. Even if the responses were numbered with "married" coded 1, "never married" coded 2, and so on, these are arbitrary numberings that do not have numerical or mathematical properties. "Never married" could just as easily have come first, with "married" coded 2, and so on. There is no order, so don't let any coding of the categories with numbers fool you! You cannot perform mathematics with these numbers: a 4 assigned to "widowed" does not make it twice that of "never married" coded a 2, even though actual numbers would suggest that 4 is twice that of 2, or two points higher than 2. That is only true with ratio measures. Nominal measures do not have "higher" or "lower" properties.

The second item includes the variable "age," measured in years, making it a continuous ratio measure. Those who are 40 are twice as old as those who are 20. The numerical values given to the variable are actual numbers that can be added, multiplied, subtracted, and divided to calculate an average (mean) age, for example. The other item about work is a dummy or dichotomous variable with two nominal values assigned an arbitrary numeral: 1 is for those who had previous work experience and those who didn't would be coded 0.

(continued)

BOX 3.4   CONTINUED

The third example is a discrete ordinal measure in which the numerical values are assigned in order from "no" to "yes" with two "probably" answers in between. It is arbitrary that "no" is assigned a 1; it could have been a 4. However, once the numbering starts, the remaining categories must be assigned a numeral in order to represent the increase or decrease in opinions. Ordinal values can be described as "more" or "less" and "larger" or "smaller" than those below and above it. These comparative properties are central to the idea of ordinal measures. If the categories are viewed as equal-appearing intervals, that is, if the gap from "no" to "probably not" is seen as the same as that between "probably not" and "probably" and between "probably" and "yes," then this ordinal measure could be treated as interval/ratio for statistical purposes (as discussed in Chapters 6 through 9).

The final items indicate two important ways of measuring alcohol consumption. The first one assesses how frequently respondents drank during the past year using a discrete ordinal measure. Like the previous example, the answers begin arbitrarily, but then follow in order: "Daily" is coded 1 and "Not at all" as 5, although "Not at all" could have been coded as 1 and "Daily" as 5. They must, however, proceed in order once the choice of how to start the categories is made. Note that the intervals between the values are not equal and cannot be viewed as equal-appearing. The gap between "daily" and "several times a week" is not equal to the interval between "several times a week" and "several times a month" and so on. This is an example of an ordinal measure without equal-appearing intervals.

The second indicator of alcohol use asks for the number of drinks consumed on a typical drinking day. The response is measuring quantity with interval/ratio values: an actual number that can be treated mathematically. Someone could reply 4.5 drinks, others might say 10 or 1. In any case, this variable assesses quantity whereas the first item represents frequency. Both are needed to indicate alcohol use and abuse, since some people might respond "daily" but then say they have only one drink a day, compared with others who might respond "several times a month" but consume 12 drinks each time. Who then might be the moderate drinker and who might be the binge drinker?

It is always best to strive for the highest level of measurement. The levels of measurement are themselves ordinal, with nominal the least powerful, ordinal ones in the middle, and interval/ratio the best. Interval/ratio measures have all the properties of the ones below them. We can always recode an interval/ratio data into an ordinal measure, but not the other way around. For example, you can ask respondents their ages (a continuous interval/ratio measure), and then later move them into "young," "middle age," and "elderly" ordinal categories, or group them in ordinal age ranges such as "under 20," "between 20 and 30," "between 31 and 40," and "over 40." However, if you operationalize age in either of these last two discrete ordinal ways, you can never get an exact list of ages or calculate a mathe-matical mean age. If 100 respondents circle "over 40," you'll never know if all 100 are each 44 years of age, for example, or if they represent a range of ages from 41 to 99.

ACCURACY AND CONSISTENCY IN MEASUREMENT

We can construct the best measures in the world, but if they aren't accurate and consistent, our findings cannot be trusted. One of the major sources of error in studies is poor quality of the measurements. Operationalizing vari-ables requires attention to two core concepts of research methodology, namely validity and reliability. Often these cannot be determined until we have already completed data collection, unless we do pilot studies that test our items first before developing a final version, or use with permission items previously written for other studies that already have demonstrated validity and reliability.

Validity

We all need to be validated, as we say in "everyday speak"; that is, we all need to be recognized and taken for who we really are. So, too, with mea-surements. They need to be taken for what they really are: are the opera-tionalizations measuring what they are intended to measure? *Validity* is about *accuracy* and whether the operationalization is correctly indicating what it's supposed to. A ruler would be a valid measure to assess height, but a scale used to weigh yourself would not be a valid measure to assess height. Validity depends in part on what is being studied; the scale becomes an accurate tool when assessing weight in another study. There are several ways of determining if the measures you use are valid: face, content, con-struct, and criterion validity.

Face and Content Validity.   A legitimate, but not very scientific, way of assessing validity is to see if the measure seems to be getting the desired result. Usually a consensus develops among researchers as to whether a measure is doing what it's supposed to be doing. Take it on "*face* value" and ask, for example, does the questionnaire item about zodiac sign seem like an accurate way of indicating someone's height? It's not likely to be an accurate measure of that variable, so just on the face of it, it's not valid for assessing height. On the other hand, a question such as "how tall are you" on its face appears to be a valid way of measuring height. Of course, the respondent might not answer truthfully, so face validity is not a perfect way of deter-mining the validity of an item.

Content validity is an equally subjective way to understand how well a set of items is measuring the complexity of a concept or variable we are studying. Does the content of the items cover all the dimensions of the idea? For example, does the content of the driving test required to get a license include the range of things necessary to be a safe driver? A driving test that only asked questions about hand signals or did not require a parallel parking demonstration would not be a very accurate measure of driving skills. Its validity would be called into question. Again, consensus among researchers evaluating the measures is used to determine content validity.

Construct Validity. A better way of assessing the accuracy of a measure is to determine its *construct validity*. A construct is an abstract, complex characteristic or idea that typically has numerous ways to measure it. Take, for example, an idea of measuring student satisfaction with the university. This is not as concrete a concept as asking respondents their height.

We develop several ways of assessing satisfaction and based on the fact that there appears to be a statistical connection among these various measures (such as finding out that those who are dissatisfied with the quality of the teaching are also dissatisfied with the classrooms, sport and other recreation facilities, and the relationship with the local community surrounding the campus), we conclude that the items developed are measuring the abstract concept of satisfaction with some degree of accuracy. And if we found out that disliking the food in the cafeteria was strong among both those who were satisfied with college and those who were dissatisfied, that item would not be as accurate an indicator of overall college satisfaction, and therefore would have lower construct validity.

Construct validity is based on actual results; sometimes it is not achieved until after the data have been collected and statistically analyzed. Then this information is available for the next time someone proposes research on this topic and is operationalizing similar variables.

Criterion Validity. Another good way of determining validity, especially for constructs not easily measured, is to see if the results from an item or set of measures (a scale) are similar to some external standards or criteria. If these other criteria are available at the same time (concurrently) as the new measures are being used, then we establish *concurrent validity*.

For example, results from an item asking respondents their grade point average are compared with the official information stored by the school. Or take a more abstract variable, such as religiousness. We develop a set of questions we feel measures how religious respondents are. We give the items to a group known to be very religious already and statistically assess whether the measure indicates high religiousness for this group. If so, we have established that the items we wrote accurately clarify people's level of religiousness, and we can now use them with more confidence in our own study. The items are measuring what they were developed to measure, that is, they are valid.

Another type of criterion validity assesses how accurately our measures predict some future, rather than current, outcome. This is usually referred to as *predictive validity*. Imagine we have written a few items for a questionnaire that we feel indicate motivation to succeed in the workplace. We later track respondents to see if indeed they have successfully been promoted, received raises, and been productive employees. We can then statistically determine if the motivation items were accurate predictors of success and, if they are, declare that they demonstrate predictive validity. We or others can now use them with some confidence and accuracy in another study on this topic, or to screen potential employees, because we have established their validity.

Reliability

Just because a measure is valid doesn't necessarily mean it is reliable, and validity means little if the measure used is not reliable. Cars are a valid tool to get from one point to another around town; yet, if you've had cars like mine, they have not always been the most reliable. We want to be sure that when we turn the key, the car starts every time. We want some stability. *Reliability* is about consistency; it is the expectation that there won't be different findings each time the measures are used, assuming that nothing has changed in what is being measured. For example, we would expect our height to change over time as we grow from childhood to adolescence, so repeated measures should indeed demonstrate a consistent change. However, if the measurement tool we use to evaluate height yields inconsistent results when there aren't any changes in growth (say, within a few hours, or in thirty-year-olds) then that measure is not very stable or reliable. There are several ways of determining if the measures we use are reliable: test-retest, parallel forms, split-half, and interrater reliability.

Test-Retest Reliability. Consider a ruler made of rubber and a 25-inch long desk. You can use the rubber ruler to measure the length of the desk; it seems to have face validity as a measuring tool because it has inches marked off along the ruler. Because the desk length does not change, repeated measures should yield the same lengths. So you try again and now the ruler tells you that the desk has grown a few inches to 28. You measure one more time and it now is 32 inches long. Either some supernatural event has just occurred or the rubber ruler has been stretched each time it has been used. Results have not been consistent each time you tested and retested with the ruler, and the reliability of the measurement tool is thus determined to be very low.

Similar methods are used to evaluate the reliability of questionnaire items and other types of scales. If we asked respondents to evaluate their

■ ■ ■ ■ ■

BOX 3.5

LOOKING AT RELIABILITY AND VALIDITY

Here are some examples from published research that discusses issues of reliability and validity in the measurements of the variables used in the various studies:

1. Psychologic distress "was assessed through a 5-item measure; items were rated on a 4-point Likert scale ranging from *never* (0) to *many times* (3). . . . A reliability analysis showed that the scale had strong internal consistency (Cronbach $\alpha = 0.75$)" (Diaz, et al. 2001: 928).
2. "To corroborate self-reported HIV status, we obtained oral HIV test specimens from a subsample of respondents. . . . All men who self-reported HIV-positive status had positive test results (100% agreement), and 99% of the men who self-reported HIV-negative status had negative test results . . . (Catania, et al. 2001: 909).
3. The Columbia Mental Maturity Scale, published by Harcourt Brace Jovanovich, estimates the general reasoning ability of children from 3.5 up to 10 years of age, and assists educators in selecting appropriate curriculum materials and learning tasks (ERIC 2001): "Split-half reliability across all levels approaches .90 and test-retest reliability is approximately .85. Concurrent validity with the Stanford Achievement Test, the Otis-Lennon Mental Ability Test, and the Stanford-Binet Intelligence Test ranges from the .30s to the .60s."

The first example describes a very typical application of reliability. It combines five items on a questionnaire, each item assessed with an ordinal measure ranging from zero to three, to form a scale indicating psychological distress. The use of the Cronbach statistic (where perfect reliability is 1.0 and no reliability is 0.0; see Chapter 7) indicates that the five item scale is fairly reliable in terms of internal consistency. A *split-half internal consistency* procedure establishes the reliability of the items.

The second example in which self-reports of HIV status are compared to an orally administered biological test measuring the presence of HIV confirms that the self-report measure is valid. This is *concurrent* or *criterion validity* since another established measure (in this case a biomedical one) is used to assess the accuracy of the self-report one.

The last item presents reliability and validity information about a commercial standardized test available for schools to purchase for developmental assessment purposes. Note that two types of reliability were measured: *split-half* and *test-retest*. Both demonstrate high reliability (correlations approaching 1.0 are considered high). By comparing scores on this standardized test with scores on three other achievement, mental ability, and intelligence tests, researchers were able to demonstrate concurrent validity, although the correlations were moderate.

fear of crime and a few days later asked them again only to find different results—and assuming nothing major has occurred in the media or their neighborhoods to alter those feelings in just a few days—we may be dealing with unreliable measures of fear. Many commercial and other standardized scales, such as the Rosenberg Self-Esteem Scale, the SAT, and the Stanford-Binet Intelligence Test, report their test-retest reliability using statistical measures of correlation (discussed in Chapter 7).

Parallel Form and Inter-Item Reliability.   We can also determine how consistently a concept or construct is being measured by comparing it to some equivalent measure or set of items, either externally or internally. Many commercial and standardized tests have two versions and if the same people score approximately the same on both form A and form B, we can say there is some parallel reliability between the alternate versions. This is what you expect when a professor gives a make-up test: you hope it is the same level of difficulty as the original test!

When we compare responses to similar items within a questionnaire to see if there is consistency in the parallel measurements, it is called *inter-item reliability*. This technique is especially useful when evaluating whether several items go together to make up a scale. For example, we might ask respondents how many hours they study on average in a typical week and compare this to their answers somewhere else on the questionnaire about the number of hours they study on average in a typical month and other related items. If the number of hours per month is about four times the previous answer, then we can demonstrate some reliability with these measures.

This also illustrates that the more ways we ask something, the more the potential for reliability increases. Imagine using just one question to indicate how happy people are in the workplace, as opposed to asking them to respond to multiple items, each indicators of happiness. Reliability is obtained when you can demonstrate consistency among these multiple measures of happiness.

Split-Half Reliability.   A popular way of statistically determining consistency is to look at internal stability by selecting a group of items developed to measure some construct or variable (a scale or index) and then comparing answers within this group. Consider a set of items you wrote to measure the political values of respondents. Let's say there are ten items. You would split the number of items in half—for example, either the first five and the last five, or the odd-numbered ones and the even-numbered ones, or randomly select two sets of five—and compare the scores of the two halves. If five of the items indicate low political involvement, then the other five should be consistent and also show low political involvement. If so, you can say the scale developed to measure political involvement is a reliable one. A statistic called Cronbach's alpha (α) is often used to assess internal consistency: the closer the correlation coefficient is to 1.0, the more reliable it is.

Interrater Reliability.   When researchers use open-ended items on questionnaires or gather information using interviews and other techniques, it becomes important that the data collected are interpreted in consistent ways. Content analysis and observation field research require some degree of agreement among those who are reading the data or observing. If those coding the data agree, then we can claim there is intercoder or interrater reliability. When different members of the Florida election board agreed that a particular chad was pregnant or hanging in the 2000 presidential election, they showed a high degree of interrater reliability.

Achieving reliability and validity is part of the process of operationalizing the variables in research questions and hypotheses. And operationalization is ultimately accomplished by the process of writing a questionnaire. The reliability and validity of items and scales in a questionnaire are affected by the skill, creativity, and techniques we employ when designing everything from the survey's format to the wording of the questions. The next chapter takes you through these next steps of the research journey.

REVIEW: WHAT DO THESE KEY TERMS MEAN?

Coding	Likert scales	Reliability: test-retest,
Constants	Nominal measures	parallel form, split-
Constructs	Null hypothesis	half, interrater
Continuous measures	One-tailed, two-tailed	Research design
Dependent variable	hypotheses	Scale
Dichotomy	Operationalization	Units of analysis
Discrete measures	Ordinal measures	Validity: face, content,
Hypothesis	Positive and	construct, criterion,
Independent variable	negative (inverse)	predictive,
Indicators	relationships	concurrent
Interval measures	Ratio measures	Variables
Levels of		
measurement		

INTERPRET: WHAT DO THESE REAL EXAMPLES TELL US?

1. What *levels of measurement* are used for each of the variables described in the following excerpt from a published study on minority stress and mental health?

"Demographic characteristics. Included were age, ethnicity, education, income, and religious affiliation. *Age* is age in years; ethnicity is coded 1 for White men, O for non-White men; *education* is a scale of highest grade completed [number of years such as 8 for elementary school or 14 for two years of college, etc.]; *income* is a scale of annual income clusters in varying sized increments ranging from 1 (less than $3000) to 19 (more than $150,000); *religious* is coded 1 = yes, 0 = not religious . . ." (Meyer 1995: 44).

2. Here are some *hypotheses* from a study on the adoption of Internet technologies in U.S. organizations (Guthrie 1999). For each one, label the independent and dependent variables and describe what kind of hypothesis it is: positive or inverse one-directional, two-directional, or null.
   a. "younger organizations would be more likely to adopt this type of technology"
   b. "organizations with larger proportions of managers and staff with technical backgrounds may be more likely to be early adopters of technology"
   c. organizational size and complexity "will be significantly associated with the use of new information technologies"

3. Here is a report on the *validity* and *reliability* of a standardized measure. Describe what has likely been done and what you would conclude about this test's validity and reliability. Would you consider using it? "The Language Proficiency Test (LPT) is a criterion-referenced English language test for students from grade 7 though adulthood which assesses a wide range of language ability yet uses materials that are not demeaning to the older student. The test is especially suited to students who use English as a second language, learning handicapped students, and others with low-level language skills. . . . The test-retest reliability estimate for a sample of 46 students was .87, and concurrent validity with the Barnell-Loft Series [reading program for at-risk students] was established as .77 using the same sample" (ERIC 2001).

CONSULT: WHAT COULD BE DONE?

You are asked to serve as an advisor on a project that the local high school is starting. Administrators want to know whether students' self-esteem affects their grades and plans to go on to college. The administrators intend to use some published standardized self-esteem scale and develop new questions about grades and future plans for a survey.

1. What steps would you suggest they take? What should they do first? Begin consulting with them on a research design.

2. What would you advise them to consider when developing items for their questionnaire and when choosing a standardized scale? See if you can find some information for them about a few standardized self-esteem scales.

3. What are some ethical concerns that need to be considered?

DECIDE: WHAT DO YOU DO NEXT?

You are asked to do a study looking at the relationship between people's television viewing habits and their opinions about racial and ethnic issues and stereotyping, and their actions toward people from diverse backgrounds. Does TV viewing have an impact on their attitudes and behaviors toward diversity?

1. Write five hypotheses using ten different variables. Include a one-directional (one-tailed) negative (inverse) hypothesis, a positive one, and a two-directional hypothesis. Use both null and alternative hypotheses.

2. Make a list of all the variables in your five hypotheses and label each one as independent or dependent.

3. Say how you could operationalize each variable in your hypotheses and what level of measurement would be used.

■ ■ ■ ■ ■

CHAPTER FOUR

DEVELOPING A QUESTIONNAIRE

LEARNING GOALS

In this chapter you will read about the strengths and weaknesses of different types of survey methods. You will also learn how to design a questionnaire: how to write attitude, behavior, and demographic questions and format a survey. Coding responses and preparing data for computer analysis are important skills discussed as well. By the end of the chapter, you should be able to critique poorly written questionnaires, write a good questionnaire for distribution in a small study, and understand the different ways of designing questions and formats for surveys.

Some years ago a solicitation letter (i.e., junk mail) arrived in the mail asking for money to "clean up television." I strongly agree that there's much on TV that I would like to see changed, but my list would be to eliminate stupid sitcoms and idiotic local news shows. This letter had a different focus, though. Attached to the donations card was an "official poll" asking the following questions and expecting only a "yes" or a "no" answer:

- Are you in favor of cable television now bringing hard-core pornography into America's living rooms?
- Are you in favor of television programs which major in gratuitous violence such as murder, rape, beatings, etc.?
- Do you favor the showing of obnoxious and edited R-rated movies on network television?
- Are you in favor of America's children being subjected to the presentation of homosexuality as an acceptable lifestyle in prime-time television?

You don't have to believe that the content of contemporary television shows is problem-free to acknowledge that these four questions are slanted in a particularly biased direction. The wording all points to the answer "no" with little room for disagreement. Who would say "yes" to *gratuitous* murder (are other kinds of murder then OK?) or favor *obnoxious* movies on TV? You can readily see the problems in orienting the questions in a certain direction through the use of specific words and phrases. This "survey" is a prime example of the kinds of biases that often show up in questionnaires, sometimes even in the most professional kind. The reliability and validity of information gathered with questions like these would be highly questionable.

USING QUESTIONNAIRES IN SURVEY RESEARCH

A key element in the achievement of reliable and valid information in survey research is the construction of well-written and manageable questionnaires or interview schedules. Sometimes we are asked to fill out a survey that barely asks enough questions to make clear what we really believe, or limits the way we can respond. Other times we get a questionnaire that is pages and pages too long, and inquiring about too many personal behaviors or private thoughts. No one form or set of guidelines is going to meet everyone's goals, but there are steps that can be taken to minimize the frustrations and noncompliance that can result from biased, wordy, and poorly designed questionnaires.

Before discussing the techniques and ideas that contribute to a reliable and valid questionnaire, let's first consider the pros and cons of using a questionnaire format for collecting data. As mentioned in the previous chapters, a research topic and set of questions or hypotheses, along with the costs and time frame, must determine the choice of methods. Survey research using questionnaires is not ideal for every kind of study. Whether the questionnaires are designed for self-administered surveys, face-to-face interviews, telephone surveys, or computer-assisted forms on the Internet or sent by e-mail, raises additional considerations in deciding to use survey methods.

Self-Administered Questionnaires

Designing questionnaires for respondents to complete on their own is one of the most common methods. Questionnaires can be mailed and returned at a later time in person or by mail; distributed to large groups of people in one location at one time, such as in a classroom or at a meeting; or can be sent through e-mail or placed on a web page on the Internet.

Self-administered questionnaires are best designed for (a) measuring variables with numerous values or response categories that are too much to read to respondents in an interview or on the telephone, (b) investigating attitudes and opinions that are not usually observable, (c) describing characteristics of a large population, and (d) studying behaviors that may be more stigmatizing or difficult for people to tell someone else face-to-face. The anonymity of self-administered questionnaires permits respondents to be more candid, yet researchers do not always know if those responding are who they say they are and if they are answering honestly.

Questionnaires are more efficient tools for surveying large samples of respondents in short periods of time than interviews or other research methods, and with less expense than interviews or telephone surveys. And because they are more suitable to probability sampling (see Chapter 5), generalizing to a larger population is one of the strengths of survey research. However, response rates tend to be lowest for mailed questionnaires and it is not unusual for researchers to receive only 20 to 30 percent of the questionnaires. Low response rates seriously affect how accurately researchers can generalize the results to a larger population. Follow-up postcards or phone calls, reminder slips in mailboxes, e-mail messages, monetary or gift incentives, and other techniques increase the percentage of people who return their questionnaires (see Dillman 2000). Chapter 5 provides more discussion about sample size and techniques for distributing self-administered surveys.

It is less likely that researchers would affect the outcome of a self-administered survey when respondents read the items on their own, compared to a face-to-face interview. This allows for more standardization of the questions and an increase in reliability than other qualitative methods, because the researchers are not influencing the responses by clarifying or explaining the items in varying ways to different respondents. However, respondents can answer the questions out of order, jump to the end, or skip around, and thus alter the results by knowing what comes later or by allowing later questions to suggest answers to earlier ones.

Uniform questions and fixed responses (called *closed-ended* items) also limit how much researchers can adjust for cultural differences in respondents, clarify misunderstood items, or explain ambiguously worded questions. How many times have you tried to respond to a question that has response categories that do not reflect how you really behave? Are you being asked to agree or disagree about a controversial topic for which you don't really have an opinion or even know anything about? How valid then are these items in measuring what they are intended to measure?

Minimally, respondents must be able to read the survey, so self-administered questionnaires are not suitable for young children, the visually impaired, or anyone with learning and reading disabilities. In such cases, face-to-face interviews are preferable.

Computer-Assisted and Web-Based Surveys

An increasingly popular way of creating and distributing self-administered questionnaires is with computers. Marketing researchers and others find that response rates increase with this method. Questionnaires (especially short ones) can be sent to respondents by e-mail or respondents can be directed by an Internet link to a web site which hosts the survey. Researchers may create their own web page or hire one of many emerging commercial companies to host surveys (such as *www.hostedsurvey.com*). Often the programs used to construct the questionnaires are set up to allow for instant coding of the data, thereby eliminating a source of error that often occurs when researchers or their assistants enter data from a questionnaire by hand.

In addition to knowing how to write a good questionnaire, researchers who do not have the funds to hire outside computer consultants must also become familiar with programming computers or learn software designed to create online surveys. The added time to do this, or the fees charged by commercial companies, may be offset with no costs for duplicating and mailing surveys or paying people to code and enter data.

However, one major limitation of computer-based surveys is the question of access. Variations in computer ownership based on race/ethnicity, age, gender, income, and education can dramatically affect the generalizability of findings from computer surveys. In addition, many people who have computers cannot afford or choose not to subscribe to an Internet service provider (ISP). Issues of access are a problem if the goal is to make inferences about larger populations. On the other hand, if your goal is to find out who uses a particular web site, as marketing researchers do, or if you are interested in assessing satisfaction levels of workers at an organization in which everyone has free access to a computer and the Internet, then using online surveys or e-mail questionnaires is less of a problem.

Interviews

Surveys are often conducted by interviewers who read the questionnaire items to respondents in a face-to-face situation or over the telephone. One version is an *unstructured* or *in-depth interview* which is ideally suited for exploratory research. These can be conducted with one person at a time or in *focus groups,* which involve multiple people being interviewed simultaneously in a group discussion. Although there may be a set of queries used to initiate the unstructured interview, interviewers tend to create questions in reaction to respondents' comments in an interactive format. These *open-ended* questions do not allow for standardization of items with fixed responses and can result in interviewers biasing the data collection. But unstructured interviews are a good way for exploring how people respond to complex topics for which you do not yet have enough specific information. This information can be used to develop a questionnaire for a more structured interview or self-administered study.

This chapter focuses on designing questionnaires that can be used for *structured interviews*. These take place face-to-face or over the telephone using a questionnaire, often called an *interview schedule*. A central issue for interviews is the role of the interviewer whose style and personal characteristics (such as gender, race, sexual orientation, age) can affect the respondents' answers. Interviews are reactive situations of social interaction in which discussions about personal behavior and opinions with a stranger are influenced by the interview process itself.

Reading standardized items from a questionnaire involves tone of voice, body language, and other styles that may create a different meaning for various respondents. Interviewers are permitted to *probe* (ask for clarification or elaboration when a response is incomplete or ambiguous), especially for questions without a set of fixed responses. They should be trained to follow the wording and write down the responses, or record them in a computer program designed to host the survey, as comprehensively and accurately as they are capable, without adding, modifying, or deleting information.

Structured interviews are in the hands of the researchers who control the flow and ordering of the questions asked (respondents can't skip around on their own); know who is completing the survey; and can employ various visual aids such as charts, cards with lists of responses, and even some self-administered sections for the more controversial questions which are sealed in separate envelopes. One of the most respected structured interviews, the *General Social Survey* (GSS) from the National Opinion Research Center (NORC) at the University of Chicago, uses many of these methods.

Response rates tend to be the highest with face-to-face interviews. Not including interviews that occur when stopped on a street corner or in a shopping mall (those must be short and quick), respondents tolerate longer face-to-face interviews than self-administered surveys. However, finding respondents and interviewing them takes more time, results in smaller sample sizes, and costs more than it does to distribute self-administered questionnaires. Agreeing to participate in an interview varies by location (such as cities or rural area), time of day, number of people working at home or away, educational level, and other characteristics of the household and its members.

Telephone Surveys

Interviewing people by telephone is the most popular way of conducting survey research. It is less costly and time consuming than face-to-face interviews, and less subject to the characteristics of those conducting the interview. Many of these interviews are conducted with computers aiding the interviewers and creating a more standardized interview.

Phone surveys have the advantage of face-to-face interviews in probing for information and getting more details through the use of open-ended questions. At the same time, phone surveys have some of the aspects of self-administered questionnaires by creating a more impersonal interaction. On the other hand, respondents might be reluctant to answer questions to a stranger who calls on the phone, yet for some questions, they may be comfortable in providing information they would not give when face-to-face with an interviewer. Increasingly people receive more solicitations over the phone to buy products or enroll in various commercial programs making them hesitant to even agree to be interviewed. If they do consent, short phone surveys of around twenty minutes duration appear to be the maximum many will tolerate.

Regardless of the method used, questionnaires should be constructed in ways that allow respondents to provide answers candidly, accurately, and consistently. And they have to address the goals and hypotheses of the research clearly and efficiently. Although there are some differences in questionnaire design depending on the type of survey chosen, what follows in this chapter is applicable to most questionnaires.

CONCEPTUALIZING THE TASK

It often seems like a daunting task to write a questionnaire. Where do you even begin? How long should it be? What kinds of questions do you need to write? How do you go from the concepts and variables in the research questions and hypotheses to a reliable and valid questionnaire? It can be overwhelming, especially if you have never written one before.

The first steps are to list the set of research questions and hypotheses proposed and the variables in each of them. Keeping in mind the way in which others may have measured these concepts when you reviewed the literature, begin to extract the key themes, goals, and concepts of the study. Be sure you have at least one questionnaire item for each of the variables in your hypotheses. Operationalizing the concept—that is, making it into a variable and specifying how it can be measured—is the process of developing the questionnaire item. Developing clear and accurate operationalizations for your concepts and variables is the focus of most of this chapter.

Next, make an outline of what you want to cover. Begin by writing down the following categories: behaviors, attitudes/opinions, and demographics. These are the main components of a questionnaire, although your study might not require all of them. Depending on the goals of the research (describe, explain, explore, or predict), you might be interested in learning about the respondents' feelings and opinions about a set of topics (*attitudes*), what they actually do (*behaviors*), or who they are (*demographics*). Each of these main areas should generate a list of specific topics related to the variables in your research questions and hypotheses. Remember, once your questionnaire is written and distributed, it is too late to add new items, so try at this stage to think about as many ways to measure the variables and concepts as you can, even if they are not likely to make the final cut. Sometimes just writing down crazy ideas stimulates thinking about more relevant ones!

Now comes the difficult part: cutting out what you don't need and cannot measure. Is it really important to include zodiac signs in a list of demographics for a study of GPA and study hours? Can you actually measure how many times respondents drank a particular brand of soda two months ago? Do you really need to ask those questions about eye color and favorite food for a study on grades and study habits? Are these linked to any previous research or your own hypotheses?

In other words, you need to start winnowing the list down to reasonable items that are clearly relevant to the variables of your topic. As discussed in Chapter 2, a review of the literature provides ideas for important variables to consider, topics that have been underdeveloped, and ways of writing questions similar to the ones you want to ask. Take a look at Delbert Miller's (1991) *Handbook of Research Design and Social Measurement* for various scales and items used by other researchers. But don't be limited to what has been done before. Writing a good questionnaire is an art, and your task is to be creative and make an engaging survey that people are willing to fill out.

A frequent concern is how long a questionnaire should be. There is no simple answer to this, since length depends on the amount of time you have to write one, how long it takes for a typical respondent to complete a self-administered survey or for an interview to be finished in person or on the phone, how dense or clear you want the format of the form to look, how much money you have to print and distribute the questionnaires, and how many variables and concepts you are trying to measure. The survey should not appear crowded, with small typeface, and intimidating. Clear spacing and visually appealing fonts and format also affect the length.

Finally, if you have writer's block and can't seem to get beyond a blank computer screen or piece of paper, consider that what you are about to do when writing the questionnaire is similar to what goes on in any social interaction. The process of developing a questionnaire is, in a way, a conversation between you and the respondents. Before you start to write items, picture yourself in a discussion with a friend about the topic you are studying. Like a conversation, there are often misunderstandings, vague pronouncements, and confusing instructions. Your goal, of course, is to open up the channels of communication and have a clear and focused discussion.

How would you open up a conversation with someone about satisfaction with the work provided by a local social services agency? You have some research questions that guide your project, so begin with those. Perhaps you would first want to know if they use the facilities and how often (behavior). So you might begin by asking this imaginary person in your imaginary conversation if he or she is familiar with the social services agency in the neighborhood, and so on. Then you probably want to learn his or her thoughts (attitudes) about the quality of the staff, the resources, and the building. And eventually you need to know more about the person (demographics). Use this method to jot down concepts and variables that are relevant to the hypotheses you developed.

MEASURING ATTITUDES AND OPINIONS

Writing items for a questionnaire takes practice; experience eventually helps you learn what works best. Reading other surveys also provides a good source for developing surveys. While many of the tips offered in the next several sections apply to most situations, the goals of your research questions and hypotheses ultimately determine the ideal format and wording of your items.

In our everyday lives, we often ask people to tell us their opinions about a movie or the food at some restaurant, how good a particular professor's class is, or what they think the meaning of life is. We are not asking them what they actually do, just what they believe. Sometimes we are interested in evaluating the relationship between people's values and their behavior, or explaining why they acted a particular way using their beliefs about an issue. For example, lawyers may want to predict how jurors will decide a case knowing how these jurors feel about capital punishment, what they think are the reasons for crime, and their opinions about racial issues.

When we want to know what people believe about something, we construct a set of attitude questions. Questionnaires are ideally suited to assess what people report they believe because feelings and opinions are not readily observed and easily measured with other research methods. Keep in mind that what people say they believe is not a substitute for asking them what they actually do. Many times behavior is a much better indicator of what people feel or think about a subject. Respondents might say they are religious and believe in going to services on a regular basis, but when asked to indicate how often they attend, the frequency might be much lower. Which, then, is a better indicator of religious fervor? In either case, you have to ask people directly what they are thinking or doing.

Open-Ended and Closed-Ended Questions

A good way of finding out what people think is to ask them *open-ended* questions. These require the respondent to write out or, if doing an interview, to talk about their responses using their own words and ideas. For example, you can succinctly ask on a questionnaire, "Tell me what you think about the issue of gun control." A blank space is provided for their answers. Of course, you will later need to make sense out of these written comments (and the bad handwriting on self-administered written surveys) by doing *content analysis,* a technique that involves distilling key ideas, words, or phrases and coding them according to some system you developed. This raises issues about reliability and whether different people would interpret the content of respondents' answers similarly. Interrater reliability is required to establish some degree of consistency among those interpreting the open-ended responses.

Respondents often don't like to answer too many open-ended items, because it takes more time, despite the advantage of being able to put the issue into their own words. A more efficient method is to develop *closed-ended* items, although it allows for fewer variations in people's responses. These give respondents standardized answers to select from, similar to questions on a multiple-choice test. It's easier and quicker for the respondents to complete; coding responses is simpler for the researchers and more efficient than with open-ended items. However, many feel that closed-ended questions limit the responses people can give, impose on them the researchers' ideas and words, and frustrate those who prefer explaining their answers in more depth.

Filter and Contingency Questions

When we ask people to state their attitudes about a topic, we assume two things: they already have thought about the issue and they are willing to share their feelings. In many cases, we end up forcing respondents to provide opinions when they do not have any about a specific issue. For this reason, some researchers prefer using *filtering* techniques in which respondents are first asked if they know anything about the issue; if they do, they are then asked their views. This gives a more accurate portrait of those holding opinions about a subject with which they are familiar, and it eliminates those who answer the question without having thought about it before.

For example, pollsters often ask if you know who the candidates are for the presidential race. Then those familiar with the candidates are asked a set of *contingency* questions, which are answered only by those people who responded in a particular way to a previous item, that is, contingent on answering "yes" to knowing the candidates. They were filtered toward questions applicable only to them, such as how well they know the candidates' positions. Of those who are familiar with their positions, they are now asked how strongly they agree or disagree with the candidates' views. Different outcomes in political polls have resulted when people were asked for whom they plan to vote in the next election compared with results from surveys where filtering occurred by first asking if they are registered to vote and have plans to vote, and then inquiring for whom they will vote.

Intensity Measures

If you are like many people, your feelings cannot simply be characterized in some dichotomous way like "black or white," "true or false," or "yes or no." While we might indeed have a long list of clear preferences and opinions, a good deal of the time we may feel more or less strongly about them. For instance, you might solidly agree that gays and lesbians should not be discriminated against in the workplace, and you might also agree that gun control is not the solution to crime in the streets, but you may not feel as strongly about gun control as you do about equal rights. In other words, it is often not enough to have respondents choose "agree" or "disagree" or "yes" or "no" for a particular set of statements about various topics; you probably also want to know how *strongly* they agree or disagree. What we need is a measure of *intensity*.

Therefore, a good way of writing closed-ended questionnaire items is to measure people's attitudes and opinions with intensity scales. A common one is derived from the scaling technique devised in 1932 by Rensis Likert. It typically makes use of a 1 to 5 rating scale where 1 is "strongly agree," 2 is "somewhat agree," 3 is "neutral," 4 is "somewhat disagree," and 5 is "strongly disagree," or sometimes a 4-point scale without "neutral." Many researchers prefer even-numbered scales, thereby preventing respondents' tendency to select the middle neutral ground. Others like to mimic the original Likert format but with 3, 7, or even 10 point scales. *Likert-type scales* could also include response categories of "strongly approve" to "strongly disapprove" or "highly favor" to "highly disfavor" or any such range of positive to negative opinions.

Regardless of the scale's size, remember to be consistent with the direction of the choices throughout a questionnaire: If 1 is "strongly agree" for one set of items, do not later on make 1 "strongly disagree" for another set of items. If 10 is to represent "high" or "very favorable," then 1 should not be equal to a high ranking for other questions. Keeping the direction the same throughout the survey minimizes errors and confusion.

Whether it is a 3, 5, or 10 point scale, respondents are answering not only in terms of agreement or disagreement (sort of a "yes/no"), but also in terms of how intensely they agree or disagree. By using such Likert-type scales, we minimize the number of times we fall into the trap of writing "do you" questions which simply result in "yes/no" or "disagree/agree" responses. They often don't tell us as much as we would like to know. For example, "do you believe that television engages in gratuitous violence" or "do you agree or disagree that grades should be eliminated on our campus" tend to yield simple either/or answers. To get much better information inquire about how strongly respondents "agree or disagree" or "believe" in some statement.

On a scale from 1 to 7, where 7 is the highest and 1 is the lowest score, evaluate your supervisor in terms of the following:

My supervisor provides many opportunities for me to learn.

1   2   3   4   5   6   7

FIGURE 4.1   One-Directional Intensity Scale.

Some researchers prefer intensity scales that are in one direction, rather than the "disagree to agree" range which allows three directions of positive, negative, and neutral feelings to be reported. Instead they might ask respondents to evaluate a statement on a 7 point or 10 point scale where 1 = low and 7 or 10 = high. The scale goes in one direction without allowing negative or neutral responses. See Figure 4.1

Indexes and Other Scales

Often one item just isn't enough for assessing a particular concept, especially more abstract or complex ideas. Reliability increases when a concept is assessed with multiple items. In such cases, additive or cumulative *indexes* are used in which various items are equally combined to get a total score on the measure. For example, a summated index for happiness might include ten items, none of which by itself would indicate whether the respondent is happy or not. Rather, the score for each item (perhaps using a 1 to 4 Likert measure) is then added to the score for the next item, and so on through all ten items. Those who scored closest to 40 points (a maximum of 4 points for each of the ten items when the respondent answers in the direction of the item that demonstrates happiness) would be the most happy and those closest to scoring 10 (a minimum of 1 point for each of the ten items) would be the least happy respondents.

Some researchers reserve the word *scale* to refer to a composite set of measures in which some items are weighted more, or contribute more, when combined to achieve an overall total score. The Likert one just described is an example of an intensity scale. Scales developed by Guttman, Bogardus, and others are discussed in more comprehensive statistics and methods books, because scale construction requires knowledge of advanced statistics like factor analysis, item analysis, and reliability coefficients.

Technically, scales are defined as multiple indicators combined in a complex weighted measure to assess some construct or abstract concept. However, most researchers use "scale" and "index" interchangeably, and

Evaluate the candidate for mayor of your city using the following ratings:							
(a) Strong	1	2	3	4	5	6	7	Weak
(b) Lazy	1	2	3	4	5	6	7	Ambitious
(c) Traditional	1	2	3	4	5	6	7	Modern

FIGURE 4.2   Semantic Differential Scale.

single items on a questionnaire are sometimes even referred to as "scales," for example, when you ask on a "scale" of 1 to 10 to provide a response, or when you create a "nominal scale" listing a range of religions, or use a "scale" to measure weight. Miller's (1991) resource book offers many different scales and indexes that can be used for your research project.

One example of a popular scale is the *semantic differential* (Figure 4.2) where respondents evaluate something along a continuum of opposing values or attributes. An overall score is calculated by adding the points according to what indicates a favorable or unfavorable view of the candidate. In this example a 1 or 2 on strong-weak continuum, a 6 or 7 on lazy-ambitious, and a 6 or 7 on traditional-modern illustrate a positive reaction to the candidate. However, the low score on strong-weak must be recoded to represent a higher number before adding. None of the items by itself would be enough to make a conclusion, but the impact of the items together provides a more accurate and reliable indicator of how the candidate is perceived by potential voters.

Matrix Format

Once you select the topics, writing and grouping attitude items in a suitable format are the next steps. Rather than asking each item as a question, consider providing statements about which you want people to give their feelings. Instead of asking "how strongly do you feel about . . ." over and over again, try a matrix format, which groups several statements together that all require the same responses. Figures 4.3 and 4.4 show two different examples, the first using a one-directional intensity measure, the other using a more typical Likert scale.

Wording Items

Sometimes the answers to an item depend on whose opinions are under scrutiny. If you ask respondents to agree or disagree with "Merit raises

On a scale from 1 to 7, where 7 is the highest and 1 is the lowest score, evaluate your immediate supervisor on each of the following:

My supervisor...

a. encourages me to do my best at all times.   1   2   3   4   5   6   7

b. is too demanding with my time.   1   2   3   4   5   6   7

c. is easy to work with on projects.   1   2   3   4   5   6   7

FIGURE 4.3   **Matrix Format for One-Directional Intensity Scale.**

Indicate how strongly you agree or disagree with the following statements by circling the number that best represents your opinion. My supervisor...	Strongly Agree	Somewhat Agree	Somewhat Disagree	Strongly Disagree
a. allows me to set my own goals.	1	2	3	4
b. needs to develop better communication skills.	1	2	3	4
c. gets along well with his/her employees.	1	2	3	4

FIGURE 4.4   **Matrix Format for Two-Directional Intensity Scale.**

should be eliminated for all workers" you will get different results than if you asked "I feel that merit raises should be eliminated for all workers." The first wording is more about a general belief, the second puts the spotlight on the respondent who might personally disagree with it and be more reluctant to express his or her own particular view. While there is no simple solution to resolving this, try writing an occasional item in different ways and compare the results. In any case, be consistent throughout the questionnaire: If you start writing items with "I" or "you" don't switch later to more general, impersonal ones, unless you have a good reason to do so. If one goal is to compare your findings to what others have discovered in other surveys, then you should write your items using the same wording as they used.

Try to avoid *negatives* in sentences. It becomes difficult for people to know whether agreeing with a negatively worded statement might actually mean they are disagreeing with it. For example, "It is not good to stay up late studying before an exam." Disagreeing that "it is not good" means you probably agree with getting a good night's sleep before an exam, but trying to get your head around disagreeing with a negative statement can lead to errors in responses.

Direction of Statements

Mix the *direction* of your statements so that not all the answers for a particular set of opinions lead to "agree" or all lead to "disagree." For example, if you want to learn people's opinions about study habits, word the questions so that they must disagree with some and agree with others: "Getting a good night's rest before an exam is helpful" and "Staying up late studying the night before an exam helps a lot" are both worded without negatives but capture two different viewpoints. A respondent could not really agree, for example, to both of these items. This is often better than wording the second one in the same direction such as, "Staying up late studying the night before an exam can hurt your chances for doing well." Both items would be answered "disagree" if the person believes in cramming for exams.

Mixing the direction of the wording is a good technique to eliminate *response bias* which is a tendency for respondents to answer most questions in the same way, such as simply checking "disagree" for all the questions. It also cuts down on the possibility of respondents providing answers that are *socially desirable;* that is, giving an answer perceived to be culturally acceptable and positive.

Always and Never

Always avoid the use of the word *always* and never use the word *never.* This statement is a good way of remembering the guideline. Unless you wanted to trap a respondent as someone who exaggerates or lies, do not use such loaded words in your questionnaire items. Very few people "always" do something or "never" feel something about a statement. How many people do you know who "never" or "always" feel happy when they enter a crowded room or believe in "never" telling a lie? Even if we are someone who does, there are many circumstances or situations in which our opinions change. It is much better to phrase questions with such words as "most of the time" or "approximately" or "rarely" or "infrequently." For example, "Approximately how often in the past month have you felt in control of your time?" 1 = almost always, 2 = frequently, 3 = rarely, 4 = almost never.

Double-barreled Items

Avoid writing items that actually measure two things at the same time. These *double-barreled* questions often contain the word "and." When you ask people how much they like ham and eggs, it may be difficult to answer if you like one and not the other. In the fund-raising survey discussed at the start of this chapter, how do you answer whether you approve of obnoxious *and* edited R-rated films if you are opposed to the editing of movies for television, but don't mind obnoxious content?

Leading and Loaded Questions

It is not uncommon to start inadvertently writing items for a questionnaire in the direction of particular biases. If you ask, "Do you agree that grades should be abolished on our campus?" you are leading respondents in a particular direction and suggesting that they should agree with you. This kind of *leading* question can be eliminated by writing it as a statement and, as mentioned above, by including it in a set of items that have a range of viewpoints. Or if you want to keep it as a question, ask "Do you agree or disagree that grades should be abolished on our campus?"

Another version of biasing is to write a *loaded* question, one in which you are pushed in a particular direction by weighing it down with specifically charged or biased words. Invoking authorities or majorities is one such technique to gain agreement: "Most doctors feel that a high fiber diet is healthy. How strongly do you agree or disagree that we should be eating more fiber on a daily basis?"

People can be led to give more positive answers by loading the response categories in different ways. In one study, when researchers asked respondents how strongly they approve or disapprove of specific political candidates, the candidates received different evaluations compared to when they asked respondents to rate the candidates excellent, good, fair, or poor (Budiansky 1995). People were more likely to call someone "fair" than to say they "disapprove" of a candidate. Approval ratings tended to be higher when using the excellent-poor scale.

Language

The wording of items should reflect the educational level and reading language abilities of those filling it out. Avoid jargon, acronyms, technical terms, and obscure phrases. For example, if you were to ask students: "How effective is the SSC in meeting your needs on campus?" not everyone will know what the SSC is. Write the item using the acronym as well as the full name: "How effective is the Student Senate Council (SSC) in meeting your needs on campus?" Similarly, an opinion question such as "Does the student newspaper obfuscate the truth?" might lead to lots of blank answers or incorrect responses, even though college students should know the meaning of "obfuscate."

For many respondents, English may not be their first language. How central to your research is attracting diverse respondents? Perhaps translations are needed, or clarification of words that may be too difficult for those with limited English language ability.

Ranking

Sometimes it may be interesting to ask people to *rank,* or put into an order of preference, a set of items. A list of movie genres could be presented and the task is to rank order the most favorite to the least favorite by placing the number 1 next to the type a respondent most likes and continuing to the ones least liked. Be aware, though, that asking people to rank more than five to ten items can be a difficult task. Furthermore, intensity is not measured, since ordinal measures only tell you which comes before another one, but they do not indicate how far the gap is between the ranks.

Knowledge Questions

Many times the goal of a research project is to uncover how much people know about certain issues, and not just to find out their attitudes. One of the objectives of using filter questions is to discover who is more familiar with particular topics and then to proceed in asking them for more detailed opinions.

However, be careful in trying to get people to answer questions that you yourself could only find out with a larger survey of the population. Avoid "quiz" questions. Do not expect accurate answers when you test people about what others do or feel, unless it is the goal of your project to uncover what people perceive to be the extent of some particular opinions or behaviors. Usually the purpose is to see how familiar people are with various issues or to assess their knowledge about some information. So it is not appropriate to ask such things as "How many people at work drink beer weekly?" or "What percentage of the employees supports gun control?" unless you want to know respondents' perceptions of how many people they think drink or what they believe to be the gun control views of their colleagues. These "quiz" questions are not substitutes for surveying the attitudes of the population directly.

MEASURING BEHAVIOR

Knowing how people feel about the next major election, for example, or what their opinions are of the latest political candidates is usually not enough. We might also want to know if these opinions translate into action

■ ■ ■ ■ ■

BOX 4.1

RANKING VERSUS RATING

Asking people to rank items seems like a good idea. We often go around telling people our favorite foods, movies, or books. But ranking tends not to tell you how intense someone feels about a particular topic, only the order. It's the difference between an ordinal measure and an interval/ratio one. The latter always gives you additional information.

For example, if a questionnaire is filled in as follows, you might learn which is the favorite movie genre in your sample, but you don't learn how strongly they feel about each one. Respondents might enjoy comedies but hate all their other choices, even though Mystery and Drama are ranked second and third:

Please *rank* the following movie types beginning with 1 to indicate your favorite:

1	Comedy
3	Drama
6	Action
2	Mystery
4	Horror
5	Western

A better approach is to *rate* each item on a scale of intensity. Then the respondents would circle a number indicating how strongly they like or dislike each of the movie genres. When completed you not only know which one is the most favorite and the least favorite (just compare their ratings to get rankings), but you also know how intensely they liked or disliked it.

For each of the following movie types, indicate how much you like or dislike them by circling the relevant number:

	LIKE VERY MUCH	LIKE SOMEWHAT	DISLIKE SOMEWHAT	DISLIKE VERY MUCH
Comedy	1	2	3	4
Drama	1	2	3	4
Action	1	2	3	4
Mystery	1	2	3	4
Horror	1	2	3	4
Western	1	2	3	4

and whether people actually vote what they feel. For many researchers, figuring out how to measure what people do is of major importance when attempting to make policy, improve working conditions, or evaluate the outcomes of different innovative programs. In many cases, finding out what people do tells you as much about their values and beliefs as asking them to report their opinions.

We need to remember that measuring behavior using a questionnaire is actually a measurement of what people *say* they do. Unlike research methods that involve observations or other field methods techniques, a questionnaire can only indicate what people remember and what they are willing to tell you about their behavior. Selective memory and perception, and a willingness to be candid all play a role in the validity and reliability of the data collected.

Frequency and Quantity

When inquiring about behavior, it is essential that we develop questions people are willing to answer with accuracy and consistency. Many of the same suggestions for assessing opinions apply to measuring behavior: Avoid double-barreled questions, minimize the use of "always" and "never," be attentive to language barriers, and reduce the number of negatives in a sentence.

Your research goals and hypotheses provide direction for what you want to measure. For example, are you interested in the frequency of a behavior or just that it occurred? Do you want to know how many times in the past week your respondents studied, and/or do you want to know how long they studied each of those times? You might erroneously conclude that someone saying he studied seven times this past week, in comparison to someone else saying she studied only twice, is preparing better and a more serious student. But what if you found out that the person studying seven times a week only read for ten minutes each of those times while the person studying twice put in two hours at each sitting? Who then prepared better for the exam?

Behavior could be assessed not simply for frequency but also for quantity. Similar to the Likert scales used for attitudes, measuring behavior can employ intensity measures. For example, "Approximately, how often in the past week did you eat in the employees' cafeteria? 1 = frequently, 2 = sometimes, 3 = rarely, 4 = never." You could also get the same information with a more open-ended question and allow for a true interval/ratio measure, by providing a blank space instead of the Likert-type scale with its ordinal categories.

Another version might inquire how many times employees ate in the cafeteria this past week according to an ordinal scale of values, where 1 = six or more times, 2 = three to five times, 3 = once or twice, 4 = never. Note that the options are no longer an interval/ratio measure and you could not calculate a mean number of times since the only data you have are numbers 1 through 4 which do not represent actual number of times. A 4 is not eating four times, and 1 could represent as many as six, seven, ten, or fourteen times in a week. What you have created is an ordinal measure not useful for some of the more advanced statistical analyses which require interval/ratio data for their calculation (see Chapters 6 through 9).

Mutually Exclusive and Exhaustive

It is important to make the values on closed-ended items mutually exclusive and exhaustive. They are *mutually exclusive* when it is not possible for a respondent to select more than one category or value as an answer to the question. They are *exhaustive* when all possible values or categories are provided as responses to the item. All the choices for any given question or item on your questionnaire should offer the full range of possible answers and not overlap, unless the object is to find out, for example, "How many of the following activities have you participated in during the past year?" in which case, you would ask the respondents to "Circle all that apply." But even in such cases the list of items should be mutually exclusive and not include, for example, "Played sports" and then later on "played basketball."

Or consider the following typical error: "How many times in the past week did you go to the library?" 1 = daily, 2 = four to seven times, 3 = one or two times, 4 = never. Both 1 and 2 could be selected if someone went to the library once each day for a week, so the options are not mutually exclusive. "Daily" in this case is the same as "seven times." If students went three times, which choice should they circle? Notice that these values are not exhaustive either; they do not provide all possible answers.

Forced-Choice

One type of question that is sometimes used to get people to make a selection is called the *forced-choice* question, in which respondents are asked to choose between two options. For example, "Do you go to action films or comedies?" Note that the choices are not exhaustive and they are not an indication about how intensely someone likes them or how frequently they see movies of these types. Since a choice is forced, you'll never know if respondents attend another type of movie more frequently or how strongly they like the one they did select. Some respondents may hate both choices, but they were forced to choose the lesser of two evils, not unlike many political elections! You wouldn't know this with a forced-choice format.

Recalling Behavior

Some behavior is not easily remembered, so it is important to ask questions that respondents can actually answer. Do you really remember what you wore two weeks ago Tuesday, or how many times in the past three months you ate

French fries? Unless you wore an unusual costume, never ate fries, or indulged everyday, it's not likely that you can recall details about ordinary events.

One technique is to give a reasonable time frame in which the typical behavior occurred. Is it likely for respondents to remember how often in the past six months they did something that happens regularly, such as eating pizza or going to the movies? Does it make sense to ask respondents how often in the past week they did something that occurs occasionally, such as going to the dentist? In other words, choose a time frame that makes sense for the behavior you are studying. A good test is whether you yourself can recall the number of times you did that particular activity in the time frame you decide to use. Pilot testing questionnaires is also an important step for uncovering problematic time frames.

Response Bias

As with attitudes, some respondents are prone to exaggerating the truth or giving socially desirable answers about what they do or how they acted in particular situations. In order to assess whether there is a response bias, researchers often build in "trap" questions that are likely to pick up those who tend to exaggerate or lie. Using words like "never" and "always" is one way to catch social desirability. Another is to include unlikely choices among the closed-ended items. For example, if you are asking respondents how many of the following books they have read, be sure to include the name of a book that doesn't exist:

"During the past year, which of these books have you read?" (Check all that apply):

[ ] The Catcher in the Rye
[ ] Lord of the Flies
[ ] The Scarlet Sweater
[ ] Silas Marner

DEMOGRAPHICS

Critical to understanding human behavior is knowing how opinions and behavior vary across different categories of people. Demographic items are those that provide information about the respondents completing the survey. Typical are questions about gender, race and ethnicity, age, income, education, and occupation. Other relevant questions can include political beliefs, religious upbringing, sexual orientation, and religion now practiced.

Many people have the tendency to ask for personal demographic information at the start of a questionnaire. But professionals recommend that these questions and any other easily answered ones come at the end of a self-administered questionnaire. After some fatigue or impatience in having to

■ ■ ■ ■ ■ ▬▬▬▬▬▬▬▬▬

BOX 4.2

**EXAMPLES OF ITEMS FROM THE GENERAL SOCIAL
SURVEY (GSS) INTERVIEW**

The National Opinion Research Center at the University of Chicago conducts one
of the most important ongoing studies of social behavior. Here are two examples
from their interview schedule:

1. Are you currently—married, widowed, divorced, separated, or have you
never been married?

Married . . . .(ASK A, B)	1
Widowed . . . .(ASK A)	2
Divorced . . . .(ASK B)	3
Separated . . . .(ASK B)	4
Never married . . . .(GO TO Q.18)	5

ASK ONLY IF CURRENTLY MARRIED OR WIDOWED:

A. Have you ever been divorced or legally separated?

Yes	1
No	2

**IF CURRENTLY WIDOWED, SKIP TO Q.18; IF CURRENTLY MARRIED,
SEPARATED OR DIVORCED, ASK:**

B. Have you ever been widowed?

Yes	1
No	2

2. How often do you attend religious services?

NEVER	00
LESS THAN ONCE A YEAR	01
ABOUT ONCE OR TWICE A YEAR	02
SEVERAL TIMES A YEAR	03
ABOUT ONCE A MONTH	04
2–3 TIMES A MONTH	05
NEARLY EVERY WEEK	06
EVERY WEEK	07
SEVERAL TIMES A WEEK	08

▬▬▬▬▬▬▬▬▬▬▬▬▬▬▬▬▬▬

fill out a survey, most respondents prefer to end the session just checking
boxes that are simple to answer.

Relevant Questions

Any list of possible demographic characteristics could get fairly long, so it is
important to limit items to the ones most relevant for the project and for
investigating the specific variables in your research questions. If you are

researching the number of hours students study and their grades, are political views really important to know? Do Democrats and Republicans study at different rates? While that might be a fun and unusual thing to learn, is it central to your project, or have others found such a relationship in the past that needs replication? If not, then focus on the most important items as a way of maintaining a questionnaire of reasonable length.

When developing a list of relevant questionnaire items, be clear about what aspects of the characteristic you need to know. For example, asking respondents what their religion is does not tell how religious they actually are. Do you want to know their religious opinions (such as belief in a higher being), their religious behaviors (how often they attend religious services), the religion they were raised in, or their current religion? These are four different questions that result in four different ways of characterizing a sample. Similarly, questions about political views (conservative, moderate, or liberal), political behavior (voting, signing petitions, etc.), and political party affiliation (Democrat, Republican, Independent, Green, etc.) do not result in the same information.

The range of choices for a particular question should be appropriate for the sample. If a survey were being given to high school students, a measure of age that has the following values would no longer be a variable because everyone would circle the first option: 1 = Under 18, 2 = 18 to 25, 3 = 26 to 33, 4 = 34 and over. Or a study of retirement could also result in a constant, because almost everyone would select the last choice. In these cases, the goal of describing or explaining differences in attitudes and behaviors by age could not be achieved.

Choosing Levels of Measurement

As with behavioral and attitudinal items, you can decide to word some questions as interval/ratio measures or as ordinal ones. For example, asking respondents' ages can be done in several ways. An open-ended question would result in an actual number that can be used to calculate a mean: How old are you? _____ . During the data analysis phase, you could create an ordinal measure from this and collapse the ages into category ranges. This is called *recoding* when you instruct the computer program to take, for example, the numbers under 21 and assign them to category 1; take the numbers 21 to 25 and recode them 2; and so on. But ordinal data cannot go the other way and be made into interval/ratio data.

You could also ask people to provide their birthdate and have the computer calculate the exact age to the day, resulting in a very specific interval/ratio measure. On the other hand, an ordinal version would have category ranges like this: 1 = under 21, 2 = 21 to 25, 3 = 26 to 30, 4 = 31 to 35, 5 = 36 and above. Notice in this last version that the categories are mutually exclusive and exhaustive, and the intervals are of equal size. When providing categories of numbers, such as age, weight, income, or height, each response should contain the same range. This is better than writing the item in the following way: 1 = under 21, 2 = 21 to 25, 3 = 26 to 28, 4 = 29 to 33, 5 = 34 to 52, 6 = above 52. When the categories are of equal size, you can treat them as equal-appearing intervals and thus use some of the more advanced statistics that are normally restricted to interval/ratio measures.

Sensitive Items

People feel more comfortable answering certain sensitive questions if they are written in categorical ranges rather than as specific interval/ratio numbers. Some might not want to tell you their exact ages, but would prefer saying "between 30 and 40" instead of 39; and others might be more candid about how much money they earned last year if they could choose "between $45,000 and $55,000" than filling in a blank line with "$53,250." The more sensitive the demographic questions (and this depends on who is in the sample), the better it might be to measure these items using ordinal categories rather than trying to achieve specific interval/ratio numbers, even if these allow for more sophisticated statistical analyses. The ultimate goal is to minimize the number of people leaving answers blank, and the trade-off needs to be evaluated before constructing the final wording of the questions.

Mutually Exclusive and Exhaustive

Demographic questions also need to be mutually exclusive and exhaustive. Be sure to include the category "other" in questions for which you cannot anticipate all possible answers. It is not practical to list every religion, for example, but it is important to list those that you think will be most represented in your sample. Buddhism, Islam, or Hinduism might be relevant for some locations, but elsewhere the word "other" might be sufficient. If you get very large numbers of people choosing "other," this tells you that you may have left out a major category. Including a blank line after the word "other" helps to see common answers that can then be coded. Be sure the choices are mutually exclusive; for example, including "Protestant" along with "Episcopalian" in the list of religions can result in both categories being checked.

FORMATTING THE QUESTIONNAIRE

Creating a readable, visually pleasing, and comprehensive questionnaire requires practice; this means making multiple drafts, pretesting items, conducting pilot studies, and fine-tuning the final format. And it requires making decisions and evaluating the trade-offs, such as balancing the desire to get lots of information with the need to develop a questionnaire that does not take a very long time to complete and does not seem visually crowded.

Contingency and Branching Questions

The format of a questionnaire, and the use of arrows, boxes, and other visual tricks to filter people in skipping questions or branching off to other sections, helps the respondent flow through a survey smoothly. In general, too many contingency items in a questionnaire can create confusion and missed responses, but surveys need to plan for all possible outcomes and types of respondents.

Be sure to test out the branching or skip pattern by taking the survey yourself as if you were multiple people each holding a different response. For example, the survey asks how often respondents drank an alcoholic beverage during the past month. If some answer "none" then they should not drop down to the next question asking which ones and how many. They need to be redirected around the next set of questions and told where to pick up the next relevant items.

Without branching, people automatically go to the next numbered item, so it often is not necessary to say, for example, "if yes, skip to the next question." They will go there anyway. It is more important to tell respondents who answered "no" where they should continue the questionnaire. For interviews, it may, however, be necessary to remind the interviewers what to do when respondents say "yes" or "no" even if the next step is to go to the next question. Branching directions are for the sake of the interviewer, not the respondent.

With the emergence of web-based and other computer-assisted questionnaires, branching is smoother and errors in completing not applicable items are virtually eliminated. Those filling out the forms could not erroneously answer a section inappropriate for them because it would never appear on the computer screen. But in written questionnaires, branching can be done in words, such as "if none, skip to Question 3" as in Figure 4.5.

You can also do this visually with arrows and boxes and channel the flow where items in a box are contingent on particular responses to a question, as in Figure 4-6. Those answering "none" to item 1 would go to the next question automatically, but those selecting the other choices branch out to a box applicable only to them.

Ordering of Items

Begin a questionnaire with the most interesting topics in order to pull readers into the survey and provide an incentive to complete it. In interviews, it often is better to begin with simpler, more routine questions in order to break the ice. It would be a bit abrupt to begin an interview with the most sensi-

---

1. During the past month, how often did you drink alcoholic beverages?

none.....................0 (if none, skip to Question 3)

once or twice...........1

three to five times.....2

six or more..............3

2. For each of the following beverages, please indicate approximately how many you drank during the past month.

  a) beer _____

  b) wine_____

3. How many days during the past week did you study for more than one hour?

none...........................1

one to three days............2

four to six days...............3

daily............................4

FIGURE 4.5   **Example of Branching Questions.**

tive and controversial questions. As you start to organize your items and group them accordingly, keep in mind that earlier questions can affect how people interpret or respond to later questions. The order of the response categories can also influence answers. A study found that when respondents were asked whether the country had a "health care problem" or a "health care crisis," 55 percent said "crisis." However, when another comparable sample was surveyed and the order was changed to whether the country had a "health care crisis" or a "health care problem," 61 percent said "problem" (Budiansky, 1995). The results demonstrate that order makes a difference. Similarly, if you have a set of questions asking people, for example, about their views on a variety of problems in their community (such as unemployment, street cleaning, taxation, and related items), and then follow this section with a question about how well their political leaders are doing

1. During the past month, how often did you drink alcoholic beverages?

none.....................0

once or twice...........1

three to five times.....2

six or more.............3

1a. For each of the following beverages, please indicate approximately how many you drank during the past month.

A) beer _____

B) wine _____

2. How many days during the past week did you study for more than one hour?

none........................... 1

one to three days............2

four to six days..............3

daily...........................4

FIGURE 4.6   **Example of Branching Questions Format.**

and their confidence in them, the results may be biased by having presented all the problems first. If you initially inquire about their attitudes toward local politicians, and then seek their opinions about various problems, there could be a different outcome. It is important then to be aware of the order of your questions, which sections come before others, and how these might affect the responses. With time and money, some researchers pretest the order of items to see if there is a difference, or develop parallel forms using different ordering of questions and compare the results during the data analysis phase.

Sections and Numbering

Dividing your questionnaire into sections and numbering all of your items are important formatting considerations. People will follow the numbers and know where to go next, and will overlook any items that are not clearly numbered. It helps if the survey has numbered or lettered sections, each focusing on a particular set of questions and each with its own brief instructions or description of what is being asked.

For example, Section A might include the attitude questions, Section B the behavior items, and Section C the demographics, if all of these are relevant for the project. Items could be numbered consecutively within each section or continue across the various parts of the survey. This latter style is easier to code and eliminates any confusion about which item number 4, let's say, you mean when you direct respondents in a contingency or branching question—the one in section B or C?

Questionnaires are interactions between the researcher and the respondent, and should reflect the kind of conversational style you would use when talking with someone. Just as you try to avoid wandering from one topic to another, avoid jumping around in a questionnaire. The goal is to create a smooth flow between sections that does not confuse the respondents and result in incomplete or improperly filled out surveys.

Try to place items together in sections on a questionnaire that are about the same things, or require similar kinds of responses. Respondents find it difficult to focus on a particular issue, then jump to another, only to return to the original one. However, there may be times when it is necessary to mix together various topics and formats, in order to avoid having the respondents figure out the goals of the survey, or to alleviate repetition and boredom, thereby resulting in biased answers.

Be sure not to have page breaks in the middle of an item so that the question appears at the bottom of the page while the response categories are on the top of the next one, or some responses are on one page and the rest are on the next page.

In addition, each line should have only one question. It is easy to overlook items especially if they are not numbered and they look like this:

| How old are you? _____   What is your gender? Male. . . . 1 Female. . . . 2 |

Instructions

Begin a survey and each section with a brief and clear set of instructions. Avoid giving away everything about your study, since telling too much might affect the outcome of the research. However, ethically you need to disclose enough information for the respondents to arrive at an informed decision about whether to complete the survey or not.

For example, if you disclose in the instructions to the questionnaire that you are studying the relationship between job satisfaction and salary this could lead some people to answer with that in mind—some might think, "because I have low income, I will say how dissatisfied I am." An alternative set of instructions could simply state: "We are interested in your candid responses about how you feel about your job."

Don't say "please be as honest as possible" since that implies respondents are dishonest people; the word "candid" invites people to be open and honest without the baggage of the word "honest." Be attentive to other loaded words and phrases in the instructions.

It is ethical to inform respondents whether their answers are *anonymous* (no names or identification numbers are given that might be linked to particular respondents) or *confidential* (names or numbers are given, but the responses will not be revealed about or connected to particular respondents).

If the surveys are not being completed as a group during a scheduled time and place, be sure to give respondents information about the *due date,* typically placed at the end of the survey, as you thank them for completing it. Do not make it a long time away, or the surveys might sit around for weeks and never get completed. And remind them how and where the surveys should be *returned,* such as sent back in the postage-paid envelope, dropped off at a box in front of the personnel office, or deposited in a mail slot. Each of these factors can seriously affect response rate.

Try to be consistent in what you instruct people to do with items. If you have them circle their answer in one section, do not ask them to use check marks in another similar section, or to circle the number next to their answer in a later section. Fewer errors will occur if respondents are not confronted with numerous styles and response formats. However, used sparingly, different response styles can help relieve some boredom and inattentiveness when completing surveys.

Some researchers like to have respondents use brackets (with today's word-processing programs actual boxes □ or other shapes ◇ can be created) in which an X or check mark is placed whereas others prefer to have respondents circle the precoded number. Whichever the case, be clear in your instructions and consistent in the format.

Figure 4.7 shows several different styles that can be used, but note that the third example, the one with blank lines, is more susceptible to ambiguity and should normally be avoided. A check mark on one line hurriedly done might overlap the nearby lines and responses, resulting in confusion about which answer was selected. And the second example, with the brackets to be checked, is clear and easy to complete but is not numbered for easy coding.

---

1. For each of the following questions, please circle your response.

I believe the governor is doing a good job running the state.

Strongly agree........1

Agree...................2

Disagree...............3

Strongly disagree....4

---

2. For each of the following questions, please indicate your response by placing an X in the appropriate box.

What is your current relationship status?

[ ] Single

[ ] Married

[ ] Separated/Divorced

[ ] Living with someone of the opposite sex

[ ] Living with someone of the same sex

---

3. For each of the following items, place a check mark next to those activities you did in the past two weeks.

_____ went to the movies
_____ surfed the Internet
_____ studied research methodology

FIGURE 4.7   Formatting the Questionnaire.

PILOT TESTING THE QUESTIONNAIRE

At this point, you have a completed draft of a questionnaire. Perhaps you have pretested some individual items, but now it's time to try out the entire survey. The best way of assessing whether the questionnaire flows, the instructions are adequate, the wording of the items and format are clear, and the survey takes a reasonable time to complete is to *pilot test* it—first with yourself and then with others. Like any writing, the first version is a draft and it only gets better with revisions.

Give the questionnaire to people similar to those who will make up the sample you want to study. These people, however, should not be part of your final sample because they have already seen the questionnaire and having them take the survey a second time could bias the results. Distribute the survey or conduct the interview with all the same procedures you intend to use in the actual data collection phase.

When questionnaires are returned, read over the responses to the items to see if there is any confusion by looking for incorrect answers or marks left on the page by the respondents, such as question marks or other annotations; if there are items consistently answered incorrectly or skipped; and if multiple responses are selected when only one was expected.

You can also arrange to discuss the survey instrument with the respondents, asking them as they read each item to discuss what it means to them. Or you can wait until after they complete the survey and interview them in a focus group or individually about it. Encouraging them to say what they found confusing, how they reacted to the format and questions, and what they felt was missing will help you develop a final version. Some people give instructions to those participating in a pilot test to write comments on the questionnaire as they take it, although this makes it less like the way the final sample will answer the survey.

CODING QUESTIONNAIRES

When your surveys are completed and returned, getting them ready for data analysis is the next step. Transferring information on a questionnaire to a computer program (such as the commercial software Statistical Package for the Social Sciences, or *SPSS* as it's better known) is accomplished by assigning a value to each response category of a question, that is, to *code* the variables.

Although many computer programs accept text (alphanumeric) answers for nominal and ordinal variables, it is much more efficient to enter a numeral that stands in for the answer. In addition, when using words instead of numbers, the entered text must be exactly the same for each response: Typing in "anthropology" for a major is not the same as "anthro" or a misspelled "anthrapology." These entries would be tabulated as different majors. It takes fewer keystrokes to enter numbers, which are required when calculating certain statistics for many ordinal and all interval/ratio measures.

For example, if a question is how strongly respondents agree or disagree with a statement, it's much easier to enter a single-digit number such as "5" than to type out "strongly disagree" or even to enter "SD." This is why it is recommended that a number be assigned to each response. What helps greatly is to design your questionnaire so that every response to closed-ended items is already numbered, or *precoded*. Rather than ask respondents if they are: (a) Female (b) Male, write the item as: (1) Female (2) Male.

If the responses are based on interval/ratio measures, then the answer itself is its own coding. If you asked respondents to enter their age, the number they give is the number you enter. No coding is necessary. However, if you asked for height and some respond in inches (68 inches tall) and others give you feet and inches (5' 8"), you must convert them into the same units for comparison.

In addition, a *codebook* is needed to provide a detailed list of questionnaire items with their complete wording, the names of all variables (sometimes abbreviated, for example, PAEDUC for father's education), the relevant codes for each response categories (such as female is 1, strongly agree is 5, and so on), the location of the code in the data file (usually given in terms of which column it can be found on the spreadsheet, like Col. 112), and other guidelines for skipping responses or dealing with missing answers. Not only does a codebook serve as an aid to those doing the data entry, but it also is a reference guide for others using your data set later on.

Most programs (like SPSS or Excel) use a spreadsheet-style format for entering data into a file. Each row represents a unit of analysis, typically a respondent, but it could also be a school, a newspaper, a business, depending on what the study is about. Each column is a question and what you put into each *cell* (the space where a row and column intersect) is the answer (the value) provided by the respondent.

By precoding the questionnaire and providing a codebook, fewer errors will occur during data entry. If the coder has to remember whether male is 1 or 2, it is likely that some will be entered incorrectly. When the item is open-ended, more work and training are required in order to develop a set of coding categories. Issues of intercoder reliability must be considered, so that consistency among different coders is assured.

Content analysis is necessary for open-ended responses using a list of categories to summarize answers. For example, if a question asks people to describe their favorite leisure time activities, a coder needs to know what to do with such answers as "play sports," "watch TV," "read books," and "go to movies." Researchers must decide whether to code each possible answer with a different number (1 for sports, 2 for TV, 3 for reading books, etc.) or to create fewer categories by coding similar types of activities with the same value, such as 1 for active participation activities, 2 for watching ones, or 1 for sports, 2 for entertainment, 3 for educational, and so on.

Organizing responses using categories constructed before the questionnaires are returned is helpful, especially if these variables have been

■ ■ ■ ■ ■ ▬▬▬▬▬▬

BOX 4.3

EXAMPLES FROM THE GENERAL SOCIAL SURVEY (GSS) CODEBOOK

PAEDUC
  Highest year school completed, father

RESPONDENT'S FATHER'S (SUBSTITUTE FATHER'S) DEGREE

RESPONSE	PUNCH	COL: 106
Less than high school	0	
High school	1	
Associate/Junior college	2	
Bachelor's	3	
Graduate	4	
Not applicable (no father/ father substitute)	7	
Don't know	8	
No answer	9	

26. In what state or foreign country were you living when you were
    16 years old?

REFER TO REGION CODES BELOW AND ENTER CODE NUMBERS IN BOX.

Col. 112

1 New England = Maine, Vermont, New Hampshire, Massachusetts, Connecticut, Rhode Island

2 Middle Atlantic = New York, New Jersey, Pennsylvania

3 East North Central = Wisconsin, Illinois, Indiana, Michigan, Ohio

4 West North Central = Minnesota, Iowa, Missouri, North Dakota, South Dakota, Nebraska, Kansas

5 South Atlantic = Delaware, Maryland, West Virginia, Virginia, North Carolina, South Carolina, Georgia, Florida, District of Columbia

6 East South Central = Kentucky, Tennessee, Alabama, Mississippi

7 West South Central = Arkansas, Oklahoma, Louisiana, Texas

8 Mountain = Montana, Idaho, Wyoming, Nevada, Utah, Colorado, Arizona, New Mexico

9 Pacific = Washington, Oregon, California, Alaska, Hawaii

0 Foreign

analyzed in other studies. Asking a native born American to name the state where she or he was born can easily be coded with standard regional breakdowns, such as East, West, North, and South. Consulting other studies, such as the GSS, can provide other ways of organizing states into categories. On the other hand, you can wait until the questionnaires have been completed and then read the responses to help in the creation of meaningful categories. It's likely that you did not anticipate all possible answers and by reading them through, you can develop more relevant coding schemes. Of course, you can combine both methods and have some prearranged categories and add to them as you discover new responses that don't fit those categories. For more details about doing content analysis, consult books on qualitative research methods and content analysis (such as Berg 2001 and Weber 1990).

When dealing with a check list of items for which respondents can select "all that apply," each item in the list essentially becomes a separate question. If you ask: "Which of the following activities did you engage in last week? (circle all that apply)" (1) watching TV (2) eating out in a restaurant (3) doing aerobics etc., you will be coding each item separately. Remember, you cannot enter more than one answer in a cell. In essence, you are asking a series of "yes/no" questions, so you might enter a 2 if respondents watched TV and a 1 if they did not. Then on to the next item, 2 if they ate in a restaurant, 1 if they did not. And so on. Some researchers prefer using 1 for yes and 0 for no; whether a 0 - 1 or 1 - 2 coding, many suggest using the higher number for those who check the item "yes," and the lower number for "no." Each item on the check list becomes a separate variable and a separate column in your database.

Missing Answers

Inevitably, many respondents leave some questions blank because they missed them, refused to answer the question, didn't feel it applied to them, or didn't know how to answer the question. There are several ways of dealing with missing values. One way is to leave the response blank and the computer program will treat it as simply missing and not use it to calculate any statistics. Or you can code the missing answer with a number not likely to be a real answer, such as –9 or 0 or 99. At some point, you have to instruct the computer reading the data that the code entered is not to be used in the calculation of any statistics. You can imagine what would happen if you were trying to figure out the average age of your respondents and you include –99 or 0 as answers! But by coding a missing answer instead of leaving it blank, you can later analyze which people left the question out by having the computer search for all answers coded –9, for example, and see if they are mostly male or female. You won't be able to tell, however, whether they left the question blank because they didn't see it or because they refused to answer it.

Sometimes you do know the reason for a missing value. People were asked to skip some questions through filtering and were branched elsewhere. You can code these no answers as "not applicable" and assign a number to that response. There is a difference between those who skipped over it because it didn't apply, and those for whom it did apply and who didn't answer the question. Some researchers code "don't know" responses with a number and treat them as missing for later data analysis, or use them to see which respondents were less likely to know the answers. In short, you might want to distinguish through a coding scheme those people who simply leave it out by mistake, people who refused to answer the question, those who didn't know the answer, and those for whom it wasn't applicable.

FINDING RESPONDENTS

When your questionnaire is ready for distribution, you need to find people to take it. No matter how good your survey is, poorly chosen respondents can seriously affect what you find. Hence, it is crucial to use the best possible methods for selecting a sample of participants. Although you very likely had in mind the kinds of people who will take your questionnaire in order to have written your hypotheses and construct the items, finding such respondents requires many important considerations. The next chapter describes the strengths and weaknesses of various ways of generating a good sample for your study.

REVIEW: WHAT DO THESE KEY TERMS MEAN?

Anonymous vs. confidential	Forced choice	Ordering of items
Attitudes	Instructions	Pilot test
Behavior	Intensity	Probe
Branching or skip pattern	Interview schedule	Ranking vs. rating
Codebook	Leading questions	Recoding
Coding and precoding	Likert scales	Response bias
Content analysis	Loaded questions	Semantic differential scale
Demographics	Mutually exclusive and exhaustive	Social Desirability
Filtering	Open-ended and closed-ended items	

INTERPRET: WHAT DO THESE REAL
EXAMPLES TELL US?

1. Consider these questionnaire items (from a much larger set) used in a telephone interview survey about the extent to which people are exposed to political views unlike their own, and whether media or interpersonal contacts have a greater influence in presenting conflicting political opinions (Mutz and Martin 2001: 111–112).
   - Discuss the strengths and weaknesses of the wording and suggest alternative formats.
   - How would these items be written differently if it were a self-administered questionnaire instead of a telephone interview?
   a. "During the past week, did you read one or more newspapers? Which newspaper was that?"
   b. "During the past week, did you happen to see a talk show on television or hear a talk show on radio that included some discussion of political or social issues? What talk show was that?"
   c. "Generally speaking, do you consider yourself a Republican, Democrat, independent, or what?"
   d. "Some people seem to follow what's going on in government and public affairs most of the time, whether there's an election going on or not. Others aren't that interested. Would you say you follow what's going on in government and public affairs most of the time, some of the time, only now and then, or hardly at all?"

2. Figure 4.8 shows two pages from the 1998 General Social Survey (GSS). This is a face-to-face interview survey. Notice how complicated a simple question about parents' occupation can become (in this case a father; information about mothers is asked in the same way later on).
   a. Discuss the branching and contingency question format and instructions to the people conducting the interviews.
   b. What other formats are used?
   c. Discuss the strengths and weaknesses of the wording and suggest alternative formats.
   d. How important is it to train interviewers?

7. Were you living with both your own mother and father around the time you were 16? (IF NO: With whom were you living around that time?)
IF RESPONDENT MARRIED OR LEFT HOME BY AGE 16, PROBE FOR BEFORE THAT.

BOTH OWN MOTHER AND FATHER . . . .(GO TO Q-8) 1

FATHER AND STEPMOTHER . . . .(ASK A) 2

MOTHER AND STEPFATHER . . . .(ASK A) 3

FATHER--NO MOTHER OR STEPMOTHER . . . .(ASK A) 4

MOTHER--NO FATHER OR STEPFATHER . . . .(ASK A) 5

SOME OTHER <u>MALE RELATIVE</u> **(NO FEMALE HEAD)**
(SPECIFY AND ASK A) 6

SOME OTHER <u>FEMALE RELATIVE</u> **(NO MALE HEAD)**
(SPECIFY AND ASK A) _____7

OTHER ARRANGEMENT WITH <u>BOTH</u> MALE
AND FEMALE <u>RELATIVES</u> (E.G.,
AUNT AND UNCLE, GRANDPARENTS . . . .(ASK A) 8

OTHER **(SPECIFY AND ASK A)** _____0

A. IF NOT LIVING WITH BOTH OWN MOTHER AND FATHER:
   What happened?

   ONE OR BOTH PARENTS DIED 1

   PARENTS DIVORCED OR SEPARATED 2

   FATHER ABSENT IN ARMED FORCES 3

   ONE OR BOTH PARENTS IN INSTITUTION 4

   OTHER **(SPECIFY)** _____ 5

   DON'T KNOW 8

FIGURE 4.8   Sample Pages from the General Social Survey.

**IQ-3 INTERVIEWER: CHECK Q.7 IS A FATHER, STEPFATHER, OR OTHER
FATHER SUBSTITUTE SPECIFIED?**

**YES, FATHER OR SUBSTITUTE IS SPECIFIED
(CODES 1, 2, 3, 4, 6, 8)
(ASK: QS. 8, 9, & 10 FOR THAT PERSON 1**

**NO FATHER, STEPFATHER, OR OTHER MALE IS SPECI-
FIED (CODES 5 or 7)
(SKIP TO IQ-4) 2**

8. A. What kind of work did your (father/FATHER SUBSTITUTE) usually do while you
were growing up? That is, what was his job called?
OCCUPATION: _____
_____
_____

B. **IF NOT ALREADY ANSWERED, ASK:** What did he actually do in that job? Tell
me, what were some of his main duties?
_____
_____
_____
_____

C. What kind of place did he work for?
INDUSTRY: _____
_____
_____

D. **IF NOT ALREADY ANSWERED, ASK:** What did they (make/do)?
_____
_____
_____
_____

E. **IF ALREADY ANSWERED, CODE WITHOUT ASKING:** Was he self-
employed, or did he work for someone else?
Self-employed 1
Someone else 2
DON'T KNOW 8

GSS 1998 #6
page 6

FIGURE 4.8   Continued

CONSULT: WHAT COULD BE DONE?

Figure 4.9 is an example of a poorly designed questionnaire. You are asked to review the survey and provide expert advice in making it better.

1. How many problems can you find with it?
2. How would you correct the errors and rewrite the questionnaire?

Attitudes about Cafeteria Food Questionnaire

This is a survey assessing your opinions about the food in the cafeteria, in order to improve the quality of the service and the food. Please place a check next to the appropriate answer. Your honesty in answering the questionnaire is appreciated. Your responses are confidential.

How often do you eat in the cafeteria? _____

Are you male or female? _____   How old are you? _____

Did you eat in the cafeteria yesterday? Yes ___ No ___

Did you eat breakfast, lunch, or dinner? (Circle correct answer)

Which of the following did you eat?
 _____ cereal   _____ eggs   _____fruit
 _____ vegetarian meal   _____ hot meal   _____dessert

Do you like to eat ham and eggs for breakfast? _____

What is your opinion about the new policy concerning hot meals?
Strongly Agree   Agree   Disagree   Strongly Disagree

Please rate the quality of food on a scale from 1 to 10 _____

What is your height? Under 5' ___   5'–5'/5" _____   5'/5"–6' _____ over 6' _____

Some people feel that the quality of food is just one part of what is going on in the institution and is part of a larger problem about quality of life here. What is your opinion about the organization as a place to be?
Strongly Disagree   Disagree   Agree   Strongly Agree

A recent analysis by a nutritionist from the Department of Health concluded that the food served in the cafeteria is some of the healthiest she has seen in some time. Do you think she is wrong?
                    Yes   No

Why do you think she is not wrong?

Any other comments?

Thank you for completing this survey. Please return it to Mail Slot 999.

FIGURE 4.9   A Survey of Questionable Merit.

DECIDE: WHAT DO YOU DO NEXT?

You are asked to do a study looking at the relationship between people's television viewing habits and their opinions about racial and ethnic issues and stereotyping, and their reactions toward people from diverse backgrounds. Does TV viewing have an impact on their attitudes and behaviors toward diversity?

1. Use the hypotheses or research questions that you wrote in Chapter 3 and/or develop some new ones. Suggest ways to measure the variables in them.

2. Write five attitude questions, five behavior questions, and five demographic questions that could serve as a good start for a much longer questionnaire. These items should measure some of the variables used in your hypotheses.

3. Work with another person or two and combine your questions to form a questionnaire of a reasonable length. If you are engaged in a research project, write the questionnaire you plan to use for the study.

4. Design a codebook for your questionnaire explaining how each variable is measured and coded.

CHAPTER FIVE

■ ■ ■ ■ ■

SAMPLING

LEARNING GOALS

This chapter explains random probability sampling and describes different methods for obtaining samples. You will also learn about longitudinal and cross-sectional research designs. By the end of the chapter you should be able to distinguish several types of probability and nonprobability sampling, describe various kinds of longitudinal research designs, and explain the idea of sampling error.

Go ask your friends whether they have ever been surveyed by the Nielsen company about what television shows they watch. Every week the ratings come out with a listing of the most popular shows. Yet, so few people seem to know anyone who was ever asked by a pollster what they watched on TV that week. It is probably not surprising given that only 1500 people or so were actually surveyed. How can such a small sample of people accurately represent the entire nation?

Each election year, public opinion polls are routinely published with the latest voter preferences, and immediately the losing side claims the polls are not accurate. After all, only 1500 people were surveyed and no one we know was asked. How then do we explain why the final presidential election results have almost always been within a few percentage points (the margin of error) of the last public opinion poll taken before the election when such a small sample of voters was measured? Typically polls report the margin of error and this number applies to each candidate's percentage, not to the spread between the candidates. So, if candidate A polls 45 percent and candidate B gets 49 percent and the margin of error is 4 percent, then the true results for candidate A are anywhere between 41 and 49 percent, and between 45 and 53 percent for candidate B.

Polling people for their opinions is a common practice in contemporary society. But not all polls are done accurately and their reputation can suffer greatly. For example, CNN reports the opinions of tens of thousands of peo-

■ ■ ■ ■ ■

BOX 5.1

POLLING SAMPLES AND ACTUAL RESULTS

Look at the Gallup Poll results for the winning candidate in presidential elections since the 1960s. The actual results are almost always within the usual (three or four percent) margin of error.

YEAR	GALLUP POLL FINAL ESTIMATE	ACTUAL RESULTS	DIFFERENCE
1960: Kennedy	51 percent	49.9 percent	1.1 percent
1964: Johnson	64 percent	61.3 percent	2.7 percent
1968: Nixon	43 percent	43.4 percent	–0.4 percent
1972: Nixon	62 percent	60.7 percent	1.3 percent
1976: Carter	48 percent	50.1 percent	–2.1 percent
1980: Reagan	47 percent	50.8 percent	–3.8 percent
1984: Reagan	59 percent	58.8 percent	0.2 percent
1988: G. Bush	56 percent	53.4 percent	2.6 percent
1992: Clinton	49 percent	43 percent	6.0 percent
1996: Clinton	52 percent	49.2 percent	2.8 percent
2000: G.W. Bush	48 percent	47.9 percent	0.1 percent

Adapted from The Gallup Polls: www.gallup.com

ple responding to a survey available on their web page. You would think these findings are valid given the large numbers of people who answer. However, even though the number of responses to the CNN surveys is substantially greater than the number who report their television viewing habits to the Nielsen company, these polls are not scientifically accurate or generalizable. In fact, there is a small print disclaimer at the bottom of the CNN poll stating that it "is not scientific and reflects the opinions of only those Internet users who have chosen to participate. The results cannot be assumed to represent the opinions of Internet users in general, nor the public as a whole" (*www.cnn.com*). Why this is so and how we can conduct a survey with a representative sample with minimal funding and time are the topics of this chapter.

SOME BASIC SAMPLING CONCEPTS

As mentioned in Chapter 1, the goals of research are to describe, explain, explore, and predict characteristics of a population. A *population* is the total collection of units or elements you want to analyze. Whether the units you are talking about are American citizens, schools, editorials in newspapers, or local businesses, when the population is small enough, you can easily survey every element of the population. Of course, this means you have to be able to define clearly what is part of the population. For example, if you want to study the population of all students on a campus, you need to first determine who is a student: Do you include full-time and part-time students, those on leave of absence but still officially registered as students, or those studying abroad this year? And once you determine the actual population, where do you find a complete and accurate list of them? We know that a population survey of all Americans (that is, the census) misses quite a few people.

The *unit of analysis* is the element about which you are observing and collecting data, such as a person responding to a questionnaire, a school, an editorial, or a local business. Sometimes, however, the element surveyed is not the final unit of analysis but merely a mechanism to collect information about the unit of analysis you really need to answer your research questions. For example, you might survey school principals (the elements selected from the population of all principals) in order to gather information about student-teacher ratios in their schools. The unit of analysis is now the school and its student-teacher ratio, but the element selected randomly was the principal.

Let's focus on a group in which the unit of analysis is also the element selected from the population. If you want to know how everyone at your workplace feels about a new policy, and the number of employees is small enough, go survey each person. Then you would have information about the variables in this population of workers; these findings are usually called the population *parameters.* Or consider when a professor wants to find out what every student in a class thinks about the course and the teacher. As is done in most classes, a course evaluation is completed by surveying every unit of the class population, assuming no one is absent that day. The resulting data are the population parameters.

However, the population we are often interested in is usually larger than a class and, with limited time and money, we are unlikely to survey each and every one of the elements in a population. Therefore, in order to figure out what the population parameters are, we need to make inferences from a subset of the population; that is, we need to generate some *statistics* from a *sample* of people chosen to represent the entire population. Technically, the word statistic refers to the information we have about the variables in a sample. Population parameters are what we estimate or infer from sample statistics when we collect data from a sample because we were unable to do a full population study. In most cases, there will be a difference between the information (the statistics) we gather about the sample and what the true parameters of the population are. This difference is called the *sampling error.* As with political polls, for example, the errors are often stated in press releases as "plus or minus four percentage points."

In most cases, we need to generate a sample, but we still have to identify and count every element in the population in order to do accurate sampling. Sometimes employees, for example, are on leaves of absence. Should they be included in the list of every element of the population? Is this a study of both full-time and part-time workers? Of management and executives? In short, the researcher must first define the study population from which the sample will be selected and to which the resulting statistics will be generalized.

The best rule of thumb is that you can only talk about the population that is represented in the sample. If part-time students or fraternity/sorority members or off-campus students are not part of the population list (sometimes called the *sampling frame*) from which a sample is generated, then the resulting statistics cannot be generalized to all students at the university. The findings must be qualified as only applicable to full-time, on-campus, non-fraternity/sorority students. As discussed later, if the sample is obtained using what is called a nonprobability sampling method, then the information gathered can only be used to describe, explain, or predict information about those who completed the survey, that is, those who are part of the sample. You cannot say the data are meant to represent the opinions, behavior, or demographics of all students, or all American young people, or any population of elements greater than those sampled.

PROBABILITY SAMPLING

When we go for a medical examination and get a blood test, it's not necessary to take all our blood—a sample will do, thank you very much. Because blood is homogeneous throughout our veins, any vein will do and as little as a drop or as much as a vial will suffice. Similarly, if the population we wanted to study were totally homogeneous, then any one element would do to represent the whole. But it is a very unlikely event that all elements are exactly the same on all characteristics in reality. Heterogeneity reigns and our population usually varies quite a bit in attitudes, behavior, and demographics. Therefore, we are obliged to take a sample of elements that represent what is in the population. For example, if the population we are interested in is composed of students with different majors, then our sample should reflect the range of majors in almost the same proportion that they exist on the campus. If 10 percent of the students major in sociology, then 10 percent of the sample should also be sociology majors.

In order to achieve this, we must use a sampling process that would likely result in a representative sample. This will happen if each person has an equal chance of being chosen for the sample study. The proportion of people in the final sample who are of different ethnicities, genders, sexual orientations, ages, and so on, should look pretty close to their distribution in the

■ ■ ■ ■ ■

BOX 5.2

PROBABILITY THEORY, THE CENTRAL LIMIT THEOREM, AND M&M'S®

The web page (*http://www.m-ms.com/cai/mms/faq.html#how2*) for my favorite candy, M&M's reports the following percentage of colors for their milk chocolate (plain) candies: 30 percent brown, 20 percent each of yellow and red, and 10 percent each of orange, green, and blue. Imagine you have been invited by the company to dip a huge scoop into some large barrel of these candies at their factory. Let's say you picked out exactly 100 M&M's. How many colors will you be tossing into your mouth? Based on their figures, you should have 30 brown, 20 yellow, 20 red, 10 orange, 10 green, and 10 blue ones in your scoop. And if you got only 50, you would have 15 brown, 10 yellow, 10 red, and 5 each of orange, green, and blue.

So in the interests of research only, I went to the store and bought a package of M&M's. The 1.69 oz bag had 58 candies in it. Therefore, based on probability theory, there should be 17.4 (30 percent of 58) brown ones in it, 11.6 yellow, and so on. Because it's unlikely that there will be .6 of a candy, let's round off the numbers and expect around 17 brown, 12 yellow, 12 red, 6 orange, 6 green, and 6 blue. Remember, one bag is a sample of all possible M&M's (the entire population of candies is not in my little package!), so here's what I find: 17 orange, 13 red, 10 green, 9 brown, 7 yellow, and 2 blue. Not even close, except for the red. Perhaps then it is not a random probability sample.

To make sure I take another sample and buy a second package (well, somebody has to do this kind of research!). Remember, the proportion would be exactly what the company says it is, if I took all possible samples, but I'm only doing two. Guess what. In this one, out of 58 pieces, I have 20 red ones, 14 orange, 12 green, 6 blue, 4 yellow, and only 2 brown ones. This time I got exactly the number of blue ones expected by chance and pretty close to the number of yellow ones.

Number and percent of candies by color:

	PACK #1 (*N* = 58)	PACK #2 (*N* = 58)	TOTAL (*N* = 116)	EXPECTED (*N* = 116)
Brown	9 (15.5%)	2 (3.5%)	11 (9.5%)	34 (30%)
Yellow	7 (12%)	4 (7%)	11 (9.5%)	34 (20%)
Red	13 (22.5%)	20 (34%)	33 (28.5%)	24 (20%)
Orange	17 (29%)	14 (24%)	31 (27%)	12 (10%)
Green	10 (17%)	12 (20.5%)	22 (19%)	12 (10%)
Blue	2 (3.5%)	6 (10.5%)	8 (7%)	12 (10%)

(continued)

BOX 5.2   CONTINUED

I can keep doing this until I got all the M&M's made, but for a variety of dietary and financial reasons, I don't. By increasing the number of candies with each additional bag, the percentage of each color becomes closer to the actual number produced by the company. The question becomes: Can I generalize to the entire population of M&M's manufactured based on any one sample of a 58-count pack? Theoretically, if I were to look at all possible samples, taking 58 candies at a time, the average percentage of all brown ones would be exactly 30 percent. Some packets would probably be 32 percent brown, others might be 28 percent, a few could have extremely few brown ones (like my second bag), and a few would have extremely many brown candies. But when these sample percentages were averaged together, brown ones would be 30 percent of the total because, at that point, all possible samples of 58 size would equal the total number of M&M's made. If my sample sizes were larger (that is, if I were to buy one of those jumbo bags of candy), they would even more closely follow the percentages of the true population figures.

If I were to plot these sample percentages on a graph, they would form a normal curve. But because I wouldn't be able to get all these samples, it is a theoretical distribution. This is what is called the *Central Limit Theorem* and is discussed more in Chapter 6. It helps me decide whether my particular sample is representative of the true population information or whether I have a sample so extremely different that the probability of having gotten it by chance is less than 5 percent, the traditional cut-off point used in the social sciences to declare that this was not a typical sample or finding.

Our goal, then, is to obtain a sample that is representative of the population. If I were to ask someone to put together a bag of M&M's for me, that person might select the colors he or she favored, or would try to balance out the mix, erroneously assuming that the colors are made equally by the company. It would, in either case, be a biased sample and nonrepresentative of the true population. Because there is no reason to believe that factory workers are choosing the colors for each bag of M&M's, we assume that the colors are selected randomly by the packaging machines, and therefore each bag (sample) should be close to the population figures.

However, in the case of the two packets I bought, I am beginning to wonder if there isn't something going on with the packaging machines: Maybe the colors are not mixed first before packaging and are instead put into the bags in the order they are made. Or did I just happen to get unusual samples by chance alone because I looked at so few of them? Unless I call the company to find out how they package their candies, I wouldn't be able to answer the question accurately.

population. If the population is 60 percent female, then the sample chosen should also be around 60 percent female. Unless you wanted to under- or oversample a subgroup (and this can be done by weighting or through disproportionate sampling techniques, both discussed in more advanced textbooks), probability sampling will assure approximate representation of the population.

When we can specify the (nonzero) probability of each element in the population being selected for membership in the sample, we have what is called a *probability sample*. The most common types include:

- Simple random sampling
- Stratified random sampling
- Systematic random sampling
- Cluster or multistage sampling

Simple Random Sampling

It is a mistaken everyday use of the word "random" when someone tells you she stood on a street corner and "randomly" gave out questionnaires, or walked up to people "randomly" in the mall and asked them to participate in a study. The researcher may have aimlessly wandered around finding people, but that doesn't mean every person chosen was randomly selected. Did every shopper, let alone citizen, have an equal chance of being designated a respondent? Not likely because some people were working, others shopped earlier in the day, and still others were hanging out at the other end of the mall.

Therefore, in order to achieve a true *simple random sample,* you must be able to provide a complete list of all possible units in the population from which to choose a sample. Whether you are randomly selecting ads in a magazine, students on a campus, or clients of a social service agency, somehow you must first get a complete and accurate set of elements according to the criteria you decide. For example, if you want to generate a sample of employees where you work, then you must first decide what an employee is (full-time, has worked at least six months, is not on maternity leave, etc.) and be able to get a complete list of all who fit the criteria. This becomes the sampling frame from which a sample can be chosen.

All units in the sampling frame may be identified with a number, either computer-generated or done by hand, in order to use random sampling techniques. Each ad in a magazine could be assigned a number, every student already has an ID or mailbox number, each employee has a worker or social security number. Using either a table of random numbers (found in most statistics and methods books) or computer-generated ones, the units of analysis are chosen. Or their names can be written on pieces of paper, placed in a box, mixed well, and then, like a lottery, picked out at random until the desired number of respondents is selected.

■ ■ ■ ■ ■

BOX 5.3

USING A TABLE OF RANDOM NUMBERS

Imagine this list of random numbers is part of a much larger table (usually available in most statistics books):

10570	15064	21121	15888	67710	04068	01509	64201	37714
74862	64821	63837	28633	78404	81599	35584	84476	50272
05235	92517	77904	43052	98066	48967	52408	02086	42821
78592	72486	89458	88743	81361	28906	29360	07461	24407

Although they look like 5-digit numbers, these are just arbitrary spaces to make the table more readable. You can begin anywhere and decide to go in any direction, but not because you see some numbers you like. That would be biasing it. Once you choose a starting point (close your eyes and point to any number) and decide on a direction (for example, move to the left and then up when you get to the end of a line), keep going in that direction and choose the numbers that are within the range you need. Computer programs or web based programs (such as the one on *www.random.org/nform.html*) can also randomize phone numbers, student IDs, and so on, for you, but if you are trying to get a relatively small sample from a small population, doing this by hand is not too difficult.

Let's say you had to choose 100 subjects from the 1100 students on your college campus or employees at work. You find out from the mailroom that box numbers go from 100 to 1200. A computer program can generate for you a hundred numbers anywhere between and including 100 and 1200. Or you can jump into the table of random numbers and begin looking at 4-digit numbers. Even if you need only 3-digit box numbers you must use the number of digits that are represented in the highest box number you have.

Just to make it easy, let's start at the very first number (since these are randomly generated you can start anywhere in the table) and go to the right. The first four digits reading across are 1, 0, 5, and 7. So box number 1057 gets a questionnaire. Now go to the next four: 0, 1, 5, 0; remember the space is just used to make the table readable. Box number 0150 (that is, 150) gets a questionnaire. And continue on, in any direction, taking four digits at a time until you get your hundred box numbers, worker/student ID, social security, phone numbers, or whichever numbers you are using. If you get a number already selected or out of range, in this case above 1200, keep going.

However, because response rates for questionnaires are rarely above 50 percent the first time around, you may need to give out 200 questionnaires by using 200 box numbers in order just to get back 100. Theoretically, for every person who does not respond, your sample becomes less random. What if only the women tended to complete and return the questionnaire? It doesn't matter if the original 100 or 200 were randomly chosen, the final sample is only truly random if everyone selected responds. For many researchers, it is therefore important that the sample be representative of the population.

Telephone surveys employ random sampling through *random digit dialing* techniques in which machines generate phone numbers within various area codes and then dial the numbers. Even those with unlisted numbers can be selected using this method. Only those without phones are not part of the sampling frame, and this possibility could bias the resulting sample by underrepresenting the poorest people.

Stratified Random Sampling

Let's say that you want a sample with comparison groups of equal size, even if they are not that way in the population. For example, you know that there are more female employees but you need to be sure that half of your sample is female and the other half is male. What do you do now? Based on probability theory, your final random sample will come out looking like the population with more women in it, so somehow you have to ensure a 50-50 gender split. This is where *stratified random sampling* comes in. With this method, you disproportionately stratify (categorize) your sample along the lines you want to analyze by establishing quotas for certain kinds of respondents. For example, you might want 20 percent Roman Catholic, 20 percent Protestant, 20 percent Jewish, 20 percent No Religion, and 20 percent Other Religions. Or 50 percent female and 50 percent male. You divide the sampling frame into categories, let's say males and females. Within each category (stratum), you take a simple random sample using the methods described above (computer- or hand-generated random numbers) until you get an even distribution of respondents or whatever proportion you desire for each category.

Stratified sampling can also be a way to guarantee an exact proportionate representation of the population, even if simple random sampling might yield almost similar results. If you know that the population is 60 percent female and 40 percent male, you can stratify on gender and achieve a 60-40 ratio quota in your final sample, rather than leave it to chance. You could also stratify on a combination of traits, such as both gender and height, in which you want each 25 percent of your sample to be men 5′ 9″ and under, men over 5′ 9″, women 5′ 9″ and under, and women over 5′ 9.″ Whatever strata you use, you must first be able to identify people who fit into these categories and then perform random sampling within the strata. That's the key part for a probability sample: Without randomizing respondents, you would have a nonprobability quota sample (covered more thouroughly in the section on Nonprobability Sampling) and lose the ability to generalize the results to a larger population.

If you don't know how many people in different categories responded until they completed the demographic section of the questionnaire, you can use statistical weighting techniques during the data analysis phase to adjust for under- and overrepresented groups. This is discussed in advanced statistic books and available in statistical computer programs.

Systematic Random Sampling

Another way of generating a random sample, especially if there is a large number of population members, is to use *systematic random sampling*. This involves taking every n^{th} element in the sampling frame until the total is reached. Imagine you need a sample of one hundred and you have 1100 people or any other elements such as magazine ads, schools, TV shows, and so on, to select from. If you divide 1100 by 100, you get a sampling interval of eleven. So you take every eleventh person, ad, school, or whatever from the population list.

Let's use mailbox numbers as a way of identifying each person in the population; student or worker ID numbers, social security numbers, and so on, could also be used. Imagine these begin at number 100 and go up to 1200. You must begin randomly somewhere between and including mailbox number 0100 and number 1200. Get a table of random numbers, close your eyes, and randomly point to any four adjacent digits. Keep going until you get a number from 0100 to 1200. Let's say you select 500. Mailbox number 500 gets a questionnaire, then box number 511, 522, 533, and so on, until you get one hundred, increasing in sampling intervals of eleven. If you want to distribute 200 questionnaires instead, then divide 1100 by 200 and to get a sampling interval of 5.5; you would now choose every sixth mailbox (because there is no such thing as a half mailbox) after starting randomly, such as 500, 506, 512, 518, and so on, until you select 200 mailbox numbers.

The sample resulting from this systematic method is typically quite similar to a simple random sample, unless for some reason there is a pattern to the order of the population elements. For example, consider the case where stratified random sampling selects every tenth house on a city's streets. At some point you notice that every tenth house happens to be on a corner lot containing larger houses probably with higher-income residents. The final sample could end up disproportionately composed of upper-class respondents. In this situation, a systematic random sample would not generate a representative group of people.

Multistage or Cluster Sampling

When even larger populations are used from which to select a sample, researchers use what is called a *multistage* or *cluster sampling* method. Large national polling agencies typically employ this method to generate samples. This method involves randomly selecting units beginning with larger clusters and moving to smaller ones at each stage. If, for example, you are interested in surveying Americans' attitudes toward a presidential candidate, you might begin by randomly choosing a certain number of states either stratified by region or simply taken from the entire list of fifty. Then, the next stage is to randomly select counties from within the selected states. The third stage involves randomly choosing cities within the counties now selected. The next stage is randomly generating streets, and the final stage is randomly choosing houses on those streets. At each stage, simple, stratified, or systematic random sampling can be done. This is how pollsters can get away with 1500 people representing the entire population of the country and why it is unlikely you would know anyone selected for such a survey!

Although this technique is more useful when you have very large national samples, it's possible to do something like this on a large campus. Make a list of residence dorms and fraternity/sorority houses. The first stage randomly selects from this cluster. Perhaps if the residences are large enough, you can then choose a second cluster from floors, then randomly select rooms, and finally pick roommates at random. Of course, such a sample would not include off-campus students. But if your study is about residential life, then this random multistage method allows inferences to be made about the entire population of residential students, but not about all students at the university.

These probability sampling methods can be combined; perhaps a stratified systematic random sampling is useful for some studies, or stratified sampling can be used at the various stages in cluster sampling. The key point for any of these is that every element should have a specified (usually equal) chance of being selected into the final sample.

NONPROBABILITY SAMPLING

Sometimes it is just not practical, cost- or time-efficient, or necessary to do a true random sampling. However, it must always be kept in mind that, unless there is a random selection of units from the population, you cannot generalize to the entire population. With nonprobability methods – those for which every element does not have an equal chance of being selected for the study – you are limited to making conclusions only about those who have completed the survey.

There are several kinds of nonprobability sampling, including

- Convenience or accidental sampling
- Purposive or judgmental sampling
- Quota sampling
- Snowball sampling

Convenience or Accidental Sampling

Everyone at one point fills out some sort of questionnaire, whether it's a warranty card for a product recently purchased or as part of some major academic study in a class you took in college. Perhaps you have been stopped while shopping at a mall or walking down the street and asked to answer some questions. Maybe you wasted 99 cents calling a 900 phone number to vote on whether Madonna should have another child, or answered a political poll on an Internet web site. While you may have felt like a good citizen in helping out, what you may not be aware of is that you have been part of a nonprobability and typically nonscientific *accidental* or *convenience sample*, one from which it would be difficult to generate any reliable information about a population of people, despite misleading statements by people using these data to imply that these are what *all* Americans believe or do.

All that can be reliably said is that the data resulting from these studies apply only to those who were available and attending that particular psychology class the day surveys were distributed, who had money to call the 900 number, who had access to the Internet and linked to that web page, or who were stopped on that day at that hour in that particular mall. To say anything about all college students, all listeners of a radio show, all Internet users, all shoppers, or for that matter all citizens in the country is impossible. But too often these data are misused just that way.

Convenience samples are based on whoever just happens to be available at a particular moment or accidentally walking by the person distributing the survey. Every person does not have an equal chance of getting selected. While it certainly is more convenient to go to an intro economics class and get a hundred students at once than it is to generate a hundred random numbers and stuff mailboxes with questionnaires, the results have limited generalizability.

Volunteer samples are also samples of convenience. Those who respond to a sign asking for research subjects, participate because of some incentive (a course grade or money), or hear about a survey on some web site, may be different kinds of people from those who do not even see those announcements. Again, all people do not have an equal chance to select themselves into these studies. And even if they did see calls for survey respondents, those who volunteer may be a very different type of person from those who don't volunteer, such as they need money, have extra time to participate, or are interested in the particular topic of the study.

Purposive or Judgmental Sampling

Sometimes there is a specific reason to choose a unique sample on purpose, because of some characteristics of the units of analysis. *Purposive* or *judgmental sampling* involves designating a group of people for selection because you know they have some traits you want to study. For example, you choose a particular sorority on campus for study because prior research has shown that it represented the feelings of most students on campus in the past. Many times subscribers to magazines get surveyed to find out more about the characteristics of their readers. Marketing researchers test products in a particular city because they have made the judgment that shoppers in that city represent a cross-section of potential buyers. Although people in these kinds of samples are not randomly selected, prior research may have indicated that their patterns of buying were representative of the entire population and could be purposely chosen to make inferences about all potential buyers. In all these situations, every person does not have a specified chance of being selected for the study, only those who are available and purposely chosen.

Quota Sampling

Like stratified random sampling, researchers occasionally want to be sure that there is some representation in the final sample. An accidental sample might involve researchers stopping the first one hundred people walking out of a movie theater to survey them about the film. Because it is not a random sample, the number of men and women leaving first may not be in the same proportion as they were in the theater. In order to guarantee that half are male and half are female a *quota sampling* is done in which the first fifty males and the first fifty females coming out of the theater are surveyed. It is still an accidental sample, but one using a quota system. Breaking your sample into various strata can entail any number of categories, such as race/ethnicity, gender, age, and any other characteristic used to screen respondents. Respondents are solicited until the number needed for each of the various criteria is met.

Snowball Sampling

There may be times a study needs respondents who are difficult to find or identify. What if you wanted to do a survey of gay men and lesbians? A stratified random sample or a nonprobability quota sample would require that you identify everyone's sexual orientation before getting your participants. This is a question people might not want to answer when stopped accidentally in a shopping mall! So what researchers do to get such a sample is first to identify a handful of gays and lesbians, perhaps through some personal contacts or organizations. Each person who volunteers then is asked to pass along a questionnaire to someone he or she knows who is also gay or lesbian, like a snowball rolling down the hill that becomes larger and larger as it picks up more snow. This is why this technique is called *snowball sampling.*

Let's say you wanted to study housekeepers. You survey a few chosen through various channels and then ask them to provide names of other housekeepers they know who would be willing to participate in your study. It helps if people are contacted first by their friends and then give permission to give you their names. You survey them and ask for a list of more names, and so on and on. Clearly this is not random and the final sample is made up of networks of people who tend to be somewhat similar in other characteristics (social class, race/ethnicity, etc.), since people tend to pass along questionnaires to those who are their friends. Studies of friendship demonstrate that people's friends are similar to themselves in many basic characteristics such as educational level, race/ethnicity, marital status, and income.

CROSS-SECTIONAL
AND LONGITUDINAL STUDIES

When a survey is given at one point in time and only once to a particular sample of respondents, it is referred to as a *cross-sectional* study. These are not ideal for uncovering causal relationships that require demonstration of a time sequence for the independent and dependent variables, but they are easier to do and require less time commitment than *longitudinal studies* in which samples of respondents are followed over lengthy periods. One kind of longitudinal study involves following the same people and surveying them at different points in time. This is called a *panel study*, but it has the risk that people cannot be found later on due to moving, death, changing names, or simply disinterest. What may have begun as a random sample, now due to attrition, ends up as a biased one and composed of volunteers who continue to participate.

Another version of a longitudinal study is a *cohort study*, which involves sampling, at different periods of time, different people who are similar to the first sample, usually in age. Perhaps researchers surveyed 20-year-olds in 1990, then studied a group of 30-year-olds in 2000, and will look at a sample of 40-year-olds in 2010. Even though the samples are not composed of the exact same people, they represent people who were born the same year (the same cohort) and have likely experienced similar historical events and changes in the culture.

Like public opinion polls, some studies are interested in seeing how the same behaviors or attitudes change over time. Every year since 1975, the University of Michigan's *Monitoring the Future* study continues its survey of high-school seniors inquiring about their drug and alcohol use. This is a *trend* study in which different people are surveyed about the same things at different periods of time in order to track changes. These are not the same people followed over time, and they are not those born in the same period. Figure 5.1 shows the differences in cross-sectional and longitudinal samples.

	Respondents	Time line
Cross-sectional:	One set	One time
Longitudinal: Panel	One set	Two or more time periods
Longitudinal: Trend	Different people	Two or more time periods
Longitudinal: Cohort	Different people, shared characteristics	Two or more time periods

FIGURE 5.1   **Cross-Sectional Versus Longitudinal Samples**

SAMPLE SIZE

A common worry is how large a sample should be in order to have a rea-sonable study. Although mathematical models determining sample size are discussed in advanced statistics books (they involve "power analysis" and the calculation of confidence limits based on accuracy at, say, 95 percent or 99 percent confidence levels), there are some points to keep in mind for a beginning researcher. When a population is more homogeneous, fewer ele-ments are required to get a representative sample. The more heterogeneous a population is on a variety of characteristics (let's say such things as race, gender, age), then a larger sample is needed to reflect that diversity. Strati-fied random sampling can achieve representation with a smaller number than simple random sampling would require to insure representation of the diverse population.

Sample size also depends on what is being studied. If you want to find out information about something that occurs less frequently in the popula-tion you are studying, such as marital life among 16-to 20-year-olds, then you will need a large sample in order to find enough respondents. On the other hand, if the behavior and attitudes you are interested in are much more likely to occur (like the use of cell phones) or large differences or relation-ships are expected, then a smaller sample size is sufficient.

One simple answer is the larger the sample size the better. Sampling error is greater when making inferences to a large population from a small sample, especially if the population is diverse and large (recall the M&Ms example; also see Chapter 6 for more about this and the concept of the *Cen-*

tral Limit Theorem). But remember, if you are using nonprobability techniques, it doesn't really matter whether one hundred thousand or one hundred people call the 900 phone number to voice their opinions, the results are only limited to those who called. Generalizing to the entire population is not possible, regardless of the sample size.

Another way of estimating sample size is to consider the kinds of analyses you plan to do. If you are interested in comparing subgroups, such as gender differences within five categories of ethnicity/race, then you will need enough people to fill ten different categories—five ethnicities by two genders equals ten categories: Asian/Pacific women, Asian/Pacific men, Native American men, Native American women, and so on. You are not going to be able to do much in the way of sophisticated statistical analysis if you do not have at least five people in each of those ten categories. Already you need fifty respondents, assuming they fall equally into these categories. If you use stratified random sampling you might be able to achieve this, but it may take hundreds of people selected by simple random sampling to get at least five in each category.

Given the limited time and money most of us have to do a short survey, especially for class projects or theses, consider giving out a hundred surveys using random sampling techniques with the hope that half will reply (after some reminders) in order to get a small sample size of fifty respondents. Usually 20 to 30 percent of people who receive questionnaires return them right away. Reminder mailings or calls can bring that percentage up to 50 percent or more. Response rates under 60 or 70 percent may compromise the integrity of the random sample.

Sometimes it is necessary to supplement randomly distributed questionnaires using nonprobability methods in order to increase sample size. However you must be sure to code them in some way to see if the responses from this group are different from the randomly chosen ones. In any event, once you introduce nonprobability sampling, you are limited to making conclusions only about those who filled out and returned the survey. For most small surveys, this might be all you really need.

How you distribute your questionnaires can affect the quality of the sampling. Mailing them with return postage and envelopes requires some funding, but prepaid postage increases response rates. Giving them to people and asking them to send the surveys on their own results in fewer returned ones, especially for those on limited incomes. Dropping by in person and picking surveys up from respondents later might be a better way of getting them back if this is convenient to do.

Following up with reminders (regular mail, e-mail, phone calls) one week after distribution, for example, and another reminder a week or ten days later, increases response rates. But when names or identifying numbers are not used, you have to send reminders to everyone, including those who already returned their surveys. It is essential that the reminder notice acknowledge those who already sent their forms backs.

Distributing questionnaires in large settings, such as a class, and waiting for them to be completed generates a much better response, since nearly everyone fills it out in such settings, but the nonprobability sample may not be ideal. In general, it is considered good if you get around 50 percent of mailed questionnaires returned in the first phase, but don't be surprised if the response rate is closer to 25 percent. After several reminders, it is very good if your response rate is over 70 percent.

At this point in the research journey, you should have a clear set of research questions or hypotheses guiding the development of a clearly written valid and reliable questionnaire, a sample ready and eager to take your survey, and a method for distributing and collecting the forms. Now you eagerly await their return and make preparations for coding the data for statistical analyses (see Chapter 4). The next four chapters discuss various ways of presenting results and analyzing your data.

REVIEW: WHAT DO THESE KEY TERMS MEAN?

Cohort studies	Population	Sampling frame
Convenience or accidental sampling	Population parameter	Snowball sampling
Cross-sectional design	Probability sampling	Stratified random sample
Longitudinal design	Purposive sampling	Systematic random sample
Multistage or cluster sample	Quota sampling	Trend studies
Nonprobability sampling	Random digit dialing	Unit of analysis or element
Panel studies	Random sample	Volunteers
	Sample size	
	Sample statistic	
	Sampling error	

INTERPRET: WHAT DO THESE REAL EXAMPLES TELL US?

For the following examples from actual research, discuss what sampling strategy is used and what the limitations and strengths might be with each type of sample:

1. For a study on gender stereotypes and self-image, a "systematic, random sample of names was drawn from a special listing of telephone subscribers . . ." (Mackie 1980:122).

2. The data for a study on the fear of crime, life satisfaction, and community involvement "come from a random sample of households in . . . California. Using computer-assisted telephone interview technology and random digit dialing, a household was contacted and an adult member of the household willing to be interviewed was selected. . . . The overall response rate was 71 percent" . . . (Adams and Serpe 2000: 611).

3. For a study on sexually risky behavior among gay and heterosexual adolescents, "A multistage cluster sampling design was employed to obtain a representative sample of adolescents enrolled in public high schools. . . . At the first stage of sampling, 63 of 299 schools with 100 or more students in grades 9 through 12 were randomly selected. . . . On average, 3 to 5 required classes (e.g. English, homeroom) per school were randomly selected at the second stage of sampling, yielding a total of 5370 students, 4159 of whom completed the survey (77% response rate)" (Blake, et al. 2001: 940).

4. A survey of beliefs about family responsibilities, gender, and work roles "employed a randomly selected national sample. Two thousand thirty-three married people were first interviewed by telephone in fall 1980 and then interviewed again in fall 1983, 1988, and 1992. . . . Sample attrition is relatively high at 41 percent when the 1992 group is compared to the original group" (Zuo and Tang 2000: 32).

5. For a study on pay differences between men and women, "Data were collected from a random sample, stratified by sex and major job category . . ." (Aiba and Wharton 2001: 75).

6. A study about men's and women's friendships "is based on in-depth interviews with fifteen men and six women that included questions concerning cross-sex and same-sex friendships. Using the same open-ended protocol, the men were interviewed by a male interviewer and the women were interviewed by a female interviewer. The sample was drawn from public university undergraduates . . ." (Swain 1992: 157).

7. An article on how race affects informal social encounters between people, especially those of the general category "Asian" reports that its sample of sixty-four Chinese Americans and Korean Americans was "located though the membership lists and referrals of a variety of churches, professional and social clubs, and college and university alumnae associations. The sample was expanded through 'snowballing' " (Kibria 2000: 80).

CONSULT: WHAT COULD BE DONE?

A study was completed at a university focusing on students' use of alcohol and drugs. Questionnaires were left in everyone's mailboxes and students were told to return them to a particular location by a certain date. Almost 25 percent of the students returned the surveys and the results were printed in the campus newspaper. The author of the article concluded that an extremely high percentage of students at the school drank or took drugs, despite anecdotal evidence to the contrary. You are asked to consult and explain more about the sampling.

1. What might be going on here?

2. What could you do to remedy any problems?

3. Describe several different ways of sampling and their strengths and weaknesses.

DECIDE: WHAT DO YOU DO NEXT?

You are asked to do a study looking at the relationship between people's television viewing habits and their opinions about racial and ethnic issues and stereotyping, and their actions toward people from diverse backgrounds. Does TV viewing have an impact on their attitudes and behaviors toward diversity?

1. Design a sampling strategy that involves a purposive method. Who would you survey and why?

2. How would you go about getting a random sample of people in your local community?

3. Describe several ways of getting an accidental or convenience sample for this study.

4. In each case, list the strengths and weaknesses of the sampling design.

5. If you were to do a study of racial images in television sitcoms and dramas, and you wanted to do a content analysis of the shows themselves, describe how you would go about designing a random sample of TV shows.

6. If you are doing your own research project, select a sampling method, describe how you plan to survey respondents, and generate an actual list of respondents, mailbox numbers, or other relevant information.

CHAPTER SIX

PRESENTING DATA
DESCRIPTIVE STATISTICS

LEARNING GOALS

Understanding how to describe your findings using graphs, tables, and statistics is the focus of this chapter. By the end of the chapter you should be able to decide how to use the mean, median, mode, standard deviation when presenting data. You should also understand the concept of the normal curve and z-scores. In addition, you will learn the idea of probability and statistical significance.

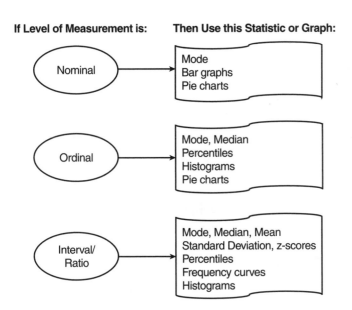

FIGURE 6.1   Statistical Decision Steps.

Finally comes the big moment: What did you discover from your surveys? You eagerly await the outcome after weeks, maybe months, of designing a questionnaire, developing a sampling strategy, distributing surveys, begging people to complete them, and coding and entering data into a computer program. Now what do you do? Where do you even begin? How are you going to make sense of all these responses to the questionnaires? Presenting data, analyzing relationships among the variables, and applying statistical tests to the findings are the focus of the next four chapters. This chapter discusses the first steps in describing the data and introduces some basic theoretical concepts about the normal curve and significance level.

PRESENTING UNIVARIATE DATA

If we want to describe, explain, explore, or predict some phenomena, we must first be sure that the variables in the study are actually variables. Imagine an extreme situation in which the only people to have completed your survey were all over the age of 45. The age variable is now a constant and you could no longer use age as a variable in explaining or predicting any other variables in the study. Hence, before any further data analysis is accomplished, it is important to do some *univariate* (one variable at a time) analysis and look at every item in the study to get a sense of the variability of responses. This is necessary in order to decide whether the variables can be used for additional statistical analysis.

In the process of doing a descriptive analysis of the variables, you also get a profile of the respondents with the demographic items and descriptive data for the other behaviors and attitudes measured. These may be all that are needed for a descriptive study, but just the start for other kinds of research. There are several ways of presenting univariate information about variables, including frequency distributions, graphs, and statistical measures.

Frequency Tables

A *frequency table* or *distribution* shows how often each response (a *value*) was given by the respondents to each item (a *variable*). Frequency tables are especially useful when a variable has a limited number of values, such as with nominal or ordinal measures. It is less useful when an interval/ratio variable has many values: If, for example, age varies from 18 to 89 in your study, the output could have over seventy rows of numbers making the table all but unreadable.

The frequency for each value is listed in absolute raw numbers of occurrence and in percentages relative to the number of total responses. Percentages can be presented in terms of both the total number of questionnaires coded and the total number of those actually responding to the question (sometimes called the *valid percent*). A percent is the proportion of responses standardized on the basis of one hundred. "Per cent" means "per 100" from the Latin *per centum* for "by hundred."

A proportion is calculated by dividing the number of responses given for a particular value by the total number of responses for the variable; then that proportion (usually somewhere between 0.0 and 1.0) is multiplied by 100 to get the percent. Sometimes if occurrences in a population are small, such as crime rates, numbers are presented "per 1000" or "per 10,000" instead of "per 100." For example, the U.S. Bureau of Justice Statistics reports that in 1999 there were 198 property crimes (such as auto thefts, burglaries) per 1000 households compared to 310.2 five years earlier. Note that the unit of analysis in this case is a household, not a person. This means that for every 1000 households in the United States, 198 experienced some property crime in 1999. This would be the same as saying 19.8 for every 100 households, or simply 19.8 percent.

Let's review a frequency table, as presented by output from the SPSS program. (Table 6.1.) Three people out of 154 in a survey of college students taking a research methods course did not report their political party affiliation. Therefore, eighty-eight respondents said they were Democrats representing 57.1 percent of the total number of people who completed the questionnaire (154), but 58.3 percent of those who actually answered the question (151); this is the valid percent. The cumulative percent is useful only for ordinal or interval/ratio measures since it requires that the values accumulate in some order.

We could conclude that there seems to be a variable here; it is not a constant. How do you decide if this is the case? What if 90 percent said they

TABLE 6.1   **Frequency Table, SPSS**

			POLITICAL PARTY		
		Frequency	*Percent*	*Valid Percent*	*Cumulative Percent*
Valid	Democrats	88	57.1	58.3	58.3
	Republicans	23	14.9	15.2	73.5
	Independents	31	20.1	20.5	94.0
	Other	9	5.8	6.0	100.0
	Total	151	98.1	100.0	
Missing	.00	3	1.9		
	Total	3	1.9		
Total		154	100.0		

were Democrats, or 80 percent, or 75 percent? When is variability evident? There is no set rule: You have to decide if there are enough respondents in each of the categories (values) of the variable to do further data analysis. Clearly in this case, only nine people have another political identity than the three most common ones, and "other" would not be a useful category for further analyses, although the variable itself can still be used. Perhaps the "other" category should be combined with the "independents" by recoding the data.

Charts and Graphs

In addition to a table of numbers, you can represent your findings visually with a graph or chart. If the variable has a limited number of discrete values, as with nominal or ordinal measures, then select a *bar graph* or *pie chart* to illustrate what you found. These graphic representations give a quick visual description of your variables but usually do not allow you to present very specific numerical results. Figure 6.2a shows a pie chart for religion. Figure 6.2b shows the same information with a bar graph.

If your data are continuous or interval/ratio measures, histograms and frequency curves (sometimes called frequency polygons) are better ways of visually presenting univariate information. *Histograms* (Figure 6.3.) are similar to bar charts but the bars are adjacent and touching each other to indicate the continuous nature of the measure. Their width and height communicate the number of responses grouped within some interval. The intervals of the values for the variable are placed along the horizontal or *x-axis*, and the frequency range, in raw numbers or in percentages, is designated along the vertical or *y-axis* of the graph.

A *frequency polygon* (Figure 6.4) is the result of connecting the mid-points of each of the intervals (bars) in the histogram with a line. Other visual ways of displaying information, such as other line graphs, stem-and-leaf displays, box plots, and stacked bar graphs, are described in more advanced statistics books and available in most statistical computer packages.

The Normal Curve.   One of the most important frequency polygons is the normal curve; it is at the core of most social science statistics and methodologies. Whether or not a variable is normally distributed in a population can affect the interpretations made about the results. By definition, a *normal curve* is bell-shaped (statistically measured by something called *kurtosis*) and symmetrical (statistically measured by *skewness*), that is, if you cut the curve in half, the right and left side have the same shape.

If there are more scores bunched together on the left side or "negative" tail of the distribution and fewer on the right or "positive" side, then the curve is said to be *positively skewed*. A few high scores skew, or distort, the sample in favor of the positive end of the distribution. A *negative skew* is

(a)

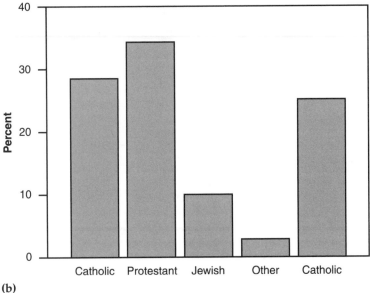

(b)

FIGURE 6.2   Examples of Pie Chart (a) and Bar Graph (b).

when few of the scores are at the left side or negative tail of the distribution and most are bunched at the higher end. A few extremely low scores distort the results in favor of the negative side of the distribution. This seems to go against intuition or the words we use when we talk about a "skewed" sample in everyday language, but think of a perfect bell-shaped curve as a piece of string and whichever end you pull and stretch out to distort the curve a

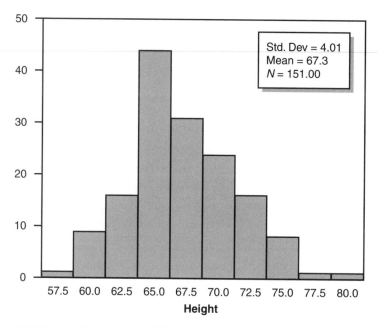

FIGURE 6.3   Example of a Histogram.

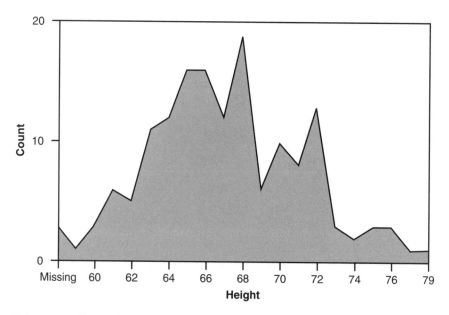

FIGURE 6.4   Example of a Frequency Polygon.

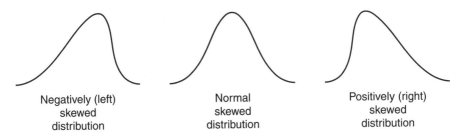

| Negatively (left) skewed distribution | Normal skewed distribution | Positively (right) skewed distribution |

FIGURE 6.5 **Examples of Skewed and Normal Distributions.**

little, tells you whether it's negatively or positively skewed. If you tug at the right side to include a few high scores, you are skewing the sample in the positive direction. (See Figure 6.5.)

Univariate Statistics

Generating statistical information about each variable in a study is another way to find out what you have and to understand more about the distribution of the variables in a sample. Of most importance is a *measure of central tendency* which provides a quick summary of where the responses are clustered. Depending on whether the variable is nominal, ordinal, or interval/ratio, a mode, median, or mean is used. These measures can also tell you something about the distribution of a variable's values. When all three measures are equal, there is a perfect normal curve. When the mean is higher than the median, there is a positive skew, because a few high scores distort the mean away from the median; a negative skew is indicated by a mean lower than the median, since a few low scores pull the mean down. Let's look at each of these measures.

The Mode.   For nominal data, the *mode* is used as a measure of central tendency. It is obtained by finding the most frequently selected value for a variable. A simple look at a frequency table, bar graph, or pie chart to see which value has the largest raw frequency or percentage of occurrence is all it takes to "calculate" this measure. Do not confuse the mode with the "majority" answer which is a response that is more than 50 percent. The most frequently occurring value could have been selected by fewer than 50 percent of the respondents and still qualify as the modal response, but a majority response is always the mode. When there are two values that are selected with equal frequency, the result is a *bimodal* distribution.

The Median.   If the values for the variable are ranked or ordered categories (ordinal data), a *median* is the ideal measure of central tendency to report in addition to the mode. The median—like the median that runs down the middle of a highway—is the halfway point, the value above which half the values fall, and below which the other half falls. It has virtually nothing to do with the actual values, just the number of values.

For example, imagine you asked five people to state their birth orders; you first list their responses in order: 1, 1, 2, 3, 3. The halfway point is the third response because this would place two below and two above that response. For these findings, the median birth order is 2. And if the fifth person actually said she was number 7 in her family of 8, the distribution would look like this: 1, 1, 2, 3, 7. Notice what happens: The median birth order remains 2. It is not affected by the size of the value, as the mean is. This is why it is a better statistic to use when you have a sample of values that include extremely low or high scores like income. Not everyone living in Seattle would appreciate being told that the average income of people in that city includes Bill Gates' yearly take!

When you have an even number of responses—for example only four people are surveyed and you found their birth order to be 1, 1, 2, 7—then you take the halfway point between the two middle values, in this case, between 1 and 2 which results in a median birth order of 1.5. How to calculate the median when the data are grouped, that is, when the ordered categories represent ranges (such as when value 1 represents ages 10 to 20, 2 equals 21 to 30, and so on) is discussed in more detail in statistic books.

Percentiles.   The median is also called the fiftieth percentile. A *percentile* tells you the percentage of responses that fall above and below a particular point. So when you receive test scores on some national exam and the results are at the eightieth percentile, it means that you scored higher than 80 percent of those taking it and lower than 20 percent.

Percentiles can be used to show the dispersion of scores for ordinal data by finding the value at the twenty-fifth percentile (called the first quartile) and subtracting it from the value at the seventy-fifth percentile (the third quartile), resulting in the *interquartile range*. Percentiles can be broken down into any number of categories, such as deciles to get the scores at every tenth percentile. A *range* indicates the spread of scores by subtracting the highest and lowest values. However, the range is affected by extreme scores unlike interquartile ranges which are better suited when there are a few very high and very low values in the distribution.

The Mean.   The most sophisticated measure of central tendency, and one that forms the basis of advanced statistics, is the arithmetic *mean*. You have calculated this many times and it follows you around school as the Grade Point Average (GPA). The mean is the sum of the values divided by the

■ ■ ■ ■ ■

BOX 6.1

BASIC DESCRIPTIVE MEASURES

Table 6.2 shows output from SPSS and the General Social Survey.

TABLE 6.2 Descriptive Statistics

STATISTICS

Age of Respondent

N	Valid	1401
	Missing	3
Mean		45.56
Median		42.00
Mode		34
Std. Deviation		16.914
Variance		286.083
Range		71
Minimum		18
Maximum		89
Percentiles	20	30.00
	25	33.00
	50	42.00
	75	56.00
	80	61.00

Only 3 people out of 1404 declined to reveal their age in the interviews. Of those 1401 valid responses, the following descriptive statistics were calculated. Because age is an interval/ratio measure, the mean and standard deviation are used. These data tell us much about one characteristic of the sample: 45.56 is the average age, 42 is the age half of the respondents are above and half are below (the median and fiftieth percentile), and the most frequently occurring age is 34. However, a frequency table needs to be viewed in order to find out exactly what percentage of the total are 34 (it's 3.1 percent of the 1401 respondents).

The data also show that the youngest person in the survey is 18 and the oldest is 89, for a range of 71 years. To calculate the interquartile range, simply subtract the age or value at the twenty-fifth percentile from the value at the seventy-fifth percentile to get 23 years. Other percentiles can be used, for example, to show that 20 percent of the sample is over 61 or 80 percent are under 61 (the value at the eightieth percentile), whereas 20 percent are under the age of 30. The standard deviation is 16.9 years; note that this is the square root of the variance 286.08. These numbers are meaningful primarily in comparison to another sample where age is used. If another survey reported that its mean age is also 46, but with a standard deviation of 20.3, then you would conclude that although it has the same

(continued)

BOX 6.1 CONTINUED

average, its respondents are more widely dispersed around that mean. The ranges indicate this wider dispersion as well.

With these data, you could tell if the distribution of ages formed a normal curve by looking at the mean, median, and mode. If all are approximately the same number, then you have a normal distribution. Although the mean and median are within four years here, note that the mode is much lower. Because the mean is higher than the median (suggesting that there are some very elderly people pulling the mean higher from the median), and given that there is a clustering of respondents around a younger age (as the mode tells us), then it's likely there is a positive skew rather than a normal distribution of age. A positive skew occurs when most values cluster at the low end and a few values at the high or positive end pull the distribution in that direction. A histogram (shown in Figure 6.6), appropriate for continuous interval/ratio measures, illustrates the skew.

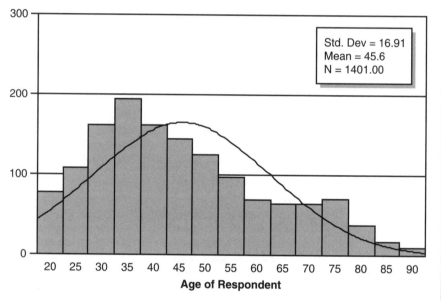

Std. Dev = 16.91
Mean = 45.6
N = 1401.00

Age of Respondent

FIGURE 6.6 **Histogram.**

number of values and is most suitable for interval/ratio variables. $\bar{X}$ (pronounced X – bar) is used for samples, and mu (μ) for population means.

$$\bar{X} = \frac{\Sigma X}{N}$$

Calculating the mean for some ordinal scales (such as Likert ones) that look like equal-appearing interval scales is acceptable. When the interval/

■ ■ ■ ■ ■

BOX 6.2

DESCRIPTIVE STATISTICS IN A PUBLISHED ARTICLE

Misra, Kennelly, and Karides (1999) studied job listings in a sociology newsletter by drawing a stratified random sample of ads and then mailing a questionnaire to the chairs of the departments advertising the job openings. About 81 percent of the chairs ($n = 200$) responded and the following descriptive statistics were reported (1999: 227).

	NUMBER OF CASES	MEDIAN	MEAN	S.D.
Average course load	188	5	5.34	1.76
Average SAT score	183	1007	1016.31	132.8
Percent of students funded	142	0	12.16	24.27
Number of graduate students	142	22	42.49	62.61

What these results say is that, out of 200 departments, 188 answered the item about the teaching load expected for the professor to be hired. The median number of courses is 5 and the mean is 5.34 with a standard deviation of 1.76. Other items ask how many graduate students there are in the program, how many of them get scholarships to attend, and what the SAT scores are for the undergraduates at the university.

We can see that the median number of graduate students is 22, although the mean is almost 43. This tells us that several of those 142 departments must have a very large number of students in order for the mean to be so much higher than the median. It is a positively skewed distribution. The large standard deviation also tells us how widely dispersed the numbers are for these departments.

A median of 0 for funding indicates that around half of the departments do not provide any funds and half provide some funds. The mean and median SAT scores are fairly close suggesting a possible normal distribution of scores for these departments. Notice also how the standard deviation is in terms of the units of measurement of the variable: SATs are in the hundreds, but course loads are single digit.

ratio measure is discrete rather than continuous, the mean often produces a peculiar number, such as the 2.3 mean number of children in families, or the 38.5 average number of books borrowed at the library per day (can you really borrow just half a book?).

Standard Deviation. Besides describing the dispersion of values using a range, such as the interquartile range, a more powerful measure of dispersion, called the *standard deviation* is available for interval/ratio data. Think of it as the average variation of all the values from the mean. With the standard deviation we can compare similar variables in different samples or in the

■ ■ ■ ■ ■

BOX 6.3

CALCULATING THE STANDARD DEVIATION

The standard deviation (s for sample statistics, σ [sigma] for population parameters) is calculated by taking each score (X) and subtracting (deviating) it from the mean. Because the mean is the perfect mathematical middle of a set of values, when you deviate the scores from the mean you notice that, when added together, these deviations always equal zero. If one score is –2 below the mean, then another one is +2 above the mean, and so on for every value in the distribution. This creates problems because to calculate a mean you have to add up the scores and divide by the number of scores. If the sum of those scores equals zero, good luck in doing any division!

$$s = \sqrt{\text{var}} = \sqrt{\frac{\Sigma(X - \overline{X})^2}{N - 1}}$$

So, the calculation for the standard deviation requires that the deviations be squared to eliminate the negative numbers, then they can be added and divided by the number of scores minus one (sometimes called *df*, or the *degrees of freedom*, a concept explained later). The resulting number is called the *variance* (s^2), a core concept of statistical analysis. A good deal of the time we want to understand why people vary in our sample. We usually want to explain the variance in our dependent variables in terms of the variance in our independent variables. We have to remember, though, that we sort of arbitrarily squared all those differences in order to calculate the variance, so just to "undo" what we did, we take the square root of the variance and the resulting number is the standard deviation.

Let's take a teacher who found that the thirty students in her third grade class had an average reading score of 75 and another teacher discovered that his thirty third graders also had an average reading score of 75. These findings wouldn't tell you much more than that both classes seemed to be at the same level of reading ability. Yet, every student in the first class might have scored exactly 75 to achieve an average of 75 (add up thirty scores of 75 and divide by 30), while in the second class fifteen of the students may have scored 60 and another fifteen may have scored 90, also resulting in an average of 75. The second class has a much larger dispersion of scores: The students range from 60 to 90. Comparing the two means by themselves wouldn't uncover this very unusual and important difference.

What we need then is the standard deviation to give us this information. In the first class, the standard deviation is zero. This is obtained by subtracting all thirty scores of 75 from the mean of 75 resulting in lots of zeros, and when zero is squared you still get zero. The sum of zero divided by 30 remains zero even after you take the square root of zero. See what happens when you use zeros in multiplication or division!

On the other hand, in the second class, when you subtract fifteen scores of 60 from 75, you get many scores of –15 and when you subtract the other fifteen scores of 90 from 75 you see many scores of +15. Square all those numbers and you now have thirty values of 225 to add together. Divide that total by 29 (n–1) and take the square root of the new number to get the standard deviation of 15.26. This is a much larger number than zero.

When comparing the two classes' reading scores, the standard deviation tells us that the students in the second class are more widely dispersed in their reading ability than the students in the first class. For the first class, reading scores are a constant, not a variable, as a frequency table or histogram would have also illustrated. But for the second class, reading scores represent a variable that can now be used for further data analysis.

same sample at different points in time. The larger it is from zero, the more dispersed the scores are in the sample for that particular variable.

The standard deviation number itself is in the units of the values of the variable, for example, scores on a 100-point reading test, and cannot be compared to a standard deviation calculated on a different variable, like inches for height. They are most useful when comparing similar measures between two different groups, or two sets of similar measures for the same group. For a quick sense of whether a particular interval/ratio variable in your study is indeed a variable, this statistic provides that information. The further away the number is from no deviation of zero, the more dispersed the scores are for that variable in your sample.

THE NORMAL CURVE AND Z-SCORES

Standard deviations are also important when figuring out where exactly a particular value or a sample of scores is relative to the mean. If the distribution of scores form a normal curve—indicated by the frequency polygon or by looking to see if the mean, median, and mode are the same number, as they are when the distribution is normal—you can compare any score with others by standardizing them using *z-scores*. These are used to locate a particular value in a distribution of values, to get its percentile rank, or to compare it with a score measured in different units. For example, when you want to compare respondents' grades on a reading test with their verbal aptitude scores, because they are measured in different units, you must first translate the values to z-scores.

■ ■ ■ ■ ■

BOX 6.4

CALCULATING Z-SCORES

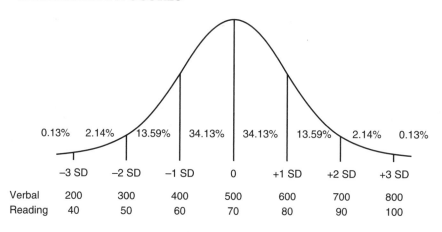

FIGURE 6.7 **Normal Curve Distribution.**

Imagine that a student scored 600 on a verbal aptitude test that goes from 200 to 800 points. Let's assume the mean for that test is 500 and the standard deviation is 100. Now let's also imagine that a student has a score of 80 on a reading test where 70 is the mean and the standard deviation is 10. Assume that both distributions form a normal curve (see Figure 6.7). Is the student consistent in how she stands within each of these normal distributions? To answer that question, z-scores are calculated. A z-score is obtained by subtracting the mean of the distribution from a score and dividing the result by the standard deviation, in order to "standardize" it.

$$Z = \frac{x - \bar{x}}{s}$$

For the verbal aptitude score, $600 - 500 = 100$, then $100/100 = 1$. This student has a z-score of 1 for a test score of 500. For the reading test, $80 - 70 = 10$, then $10/10 = 1$. We now know that a verbal score of 500 and a grade of 80 on the reading test are comparable standardized scores even though they are in different units of measurement. Both are one standard deviation unit above the mean. If it were a minus result, it would tell us the score is below the mean.

A z-score also gives us the *percentile* for the score. Based on the mathematics in the formula for the normal curve (available in advanced statistics books), a normal distribution of values has a mean of zero and a standard deviation of one. Approximately, 99.7 percent of all the scores in a distribution (the area under the normal curve contains all the scores) fall within three standard deviations above and three standard deviations below the mean; approximately 68 percent of all scores fall within plus or minus one standard deviation of the mean; and 95 percent fall within two standard deviation units of the mean. Using this information and a table of z-scores and percentages available in most statistics books, we can figure out the exact percentile of each score in the distribution.

For example, 34.13 percent of all the scores fall between the mean and one standard deviation above or below the mean. Since the curve is symmetrical, we also know that 50 percent are below the mean; therefore, a z-score of 1.0 tells us that 84.13 percent of all the scores are below that one (50 + 34.13). In other words, a verbal aptitude score of 600 has a percentile rank of 84.13. Conversely, 15.87 percent of all the scores are higher than 600. We can also say that approximately 68 percent of all the scores fall between 400 and 600, since 34 percent fall between the mean (in this case, 500) and one standard deviation unit (in this case, 100 points) below the mean and another 34 percent fall within one unit above the mean.

If the score is exactly the same as the mean of the distribution—in this case, if someone scored 500 on the verbal test—then the z-score would be zero. In this case, 50 percent of the scores are above and another 50 percent are below 500. You can see that the mean is also the median in the normal curve.

Statistical Significance, Confidence Intervals, and the Central Limit Theorem

Z-scores are not reported too often but are used for calculating the percentiles of individual scores. Therapists, guidance counselors, and others working with data about individuals can see if a client, for example, is significantly different from the norm on a psychological test. You could also see how you stand in comparison with others who took the same test, especially if your teacher is "grading on the curve," that is, using a normal curve to determine grades.

Besides giving us a percentile, z-scores assist in determining confidence intervals for understanding probability levels of significance, and determining sampling error. A z-score tells us the probability of obtaining a score by chance. If 50 percent of the scores are above the mean in a normal distribution, then the probability of finding someone with a verbal aptitude score above 500 is 50 percent or, conversely, for finding someone below 500. If the percentile is 84 percent then the odds of finding someone with a score above 600 is 16 percent and 84 percent for finding someone below 600, and so on.

Statistical Significance.   One of the conventions in social science research is to declare that a finding is *statistically significant* if the probability of obtaining a statistic by chance alone is less than 5 percent. This can be either 5 percent at one end, or tail, of the normal distribution for one-directional tests, or 2.5 percent at the low or negative end *plus* 2.5 percent at the high or positive tail of the distribution for two-directional tests. A *two-tailed* or *two-directional test of significance* exists when we allow two chances in our hypothesis for the outcome to be different: Either differently high or differently low from what is expected. For a score to be significant, then, it must be lower or higher than the z-score at which 2.5 percent of the scores fall above or below. The top 2.5 percent of values in a normal distribution have a z-score higher than +1.96 and 2.5 percent would be lower than –1.96, or approximately above a z-score of 2 and below a z-score of –2.

If we set our significance level (often called the *alpha level*) to the probability of obtaining a statistic by chance 1 percent of the time, that is, in the top 0.5 percent or the bottom 0.5 percent for two-directional hypotheses (.5 + .5 = 1), then we would use a 2.58 z-score (plus or minus) as the point above or below which significance would occur. For example, if there is a distribution of verbal scores where 500 is the mean and 100 is the standard deviation, then a verbal score of 758 or higher would be in the top 0.5 percent. Each z-score unit in this distribution is "worth" 100 standard deviation points so 2.58 times 100 results in 258 points above the mean of 500. A score of 242 or lower would be in the bottom .05 percent (500 minus 258) of the distribution of all verbal scores. The probability of randomly selecting someone whose verbal score is above 758 or below 242 would be less than 1 percent, and would be a statistically significant outcome if we selected someone with those scores. Notice that we get two chances to be significantly different from the norm: Either very high scores or very low ones. That's what is meant by a two-tailed test of significance.

Alpha significance levels are usually represented in tests of significance as $p < .05$ or $p < .01$ or $p < .001$, meaning the probability of obtaining that statistic (or score) by chance is less than 5 in 100 (5 percent) or 1 in 100 (1 percent), or 1 in 1000 (0.1 percent) respectively. A single asterisk (*) often appears in tables of data to signify that the .05 significance level has been reached, two asterisks for .01, and three for the .001 level.

If we want to see whether a particular score is significantly *higher* than the average —that is, it would be significantly different only if the score were higher, but not lower than the average—then we would apply a *one-tailed* or *one-directional test* of significance. In this case, to be statistically significant, the score should be higher than 95 percent of the values and in the top 5 percent with a z-score of 1.64, or –1.64 if looking for scores significantly lower than the average and in the bottom 5 percent. In short, when the probability of obtaining a particular statistic by chance is less than the cut-off point established, we can state that the hypothesis or research question being tested is statistically significant.

■ ■ ■ ■ ■

BOX 6.5

UNDERSTANDING PROBABILITY AND SIGNIFICANCE LEVELS

When calculating probability and using "or" as the criteria, you *add* the odds. When you use "and" as the criteria, you *multiply* the odds. For example, if you were asked to pick a red card from a deck of cards (26 chances out of 52 or $26 \div 52 = .50$) *or* a black card (also .50), then the probability of being successful (significant) is $.50 + .50 = 1.00$. In short, you have a 100 percent chance of picking a red or black card. This should come as no surprise!

But if you asked what the odds are of picking a black card (.50) *and* an Ace (4 chances out of $52 = .077$), then the probability of picking a black Ace is $.077 \times .50 = .038$. There is a 3.8 percent chance you will pick a black Ace from a deck of cards. Another way of figuring this is to calculate the odds of getting the Ace of Spades *or* the Ace of Clubs using the additive rule. The odds of picking the Ace of Spades is 1 out of 52, or .019. The odds of picking the Ace of Clubs is also .019. Therefore the odds of picking either the Ace of Spades *or* the Ace of Clubs is $.019 + .019 = .038$. In short, you have two chances out of 52 to pick a black Ace, or $2 \div 52 = .038$.

The key point to remember here is that when we are testing to see what the odds are of obtaining a statistic or value by chance that is significantly higher *or* lower than the mean at the .05 alpha level (a two-tailed hypothesis), then we are looking for a value that is either in the top .025 area of the normal curve (the top 2.5 percent) *or* in the lower .025 area in order to get an added probability of .05, that is, $.025 + .025 = .05$. When we do, we can declare that the statistic or value is a significant finding, just as we would in randomly pulling an Ace of Spades from a deck of cards, because the odds of doing so are certainly less than .05. As we just saw, the probability is .038 and therefore $p < .05$.

Here's another easy way of remembering significance levels: Think about 1000 people standing around flipping coins. Let's say you ask them to flip a coin ten times. At what point do you accuse some of them of using a phony coin? If they get five heads or tails. Nah, that's a pretty likely outcome. If they get three or four heads or tails, or six or seven or what? Those seem fairly reasonable outcomes as well. However, the odds of getting ten heads or ten tails by chance when you flip a coin ten times is .001. That is, only one person in that group of 1000 is likely to do so by chance alone. Any more and you might be suspicious that some people have magic coins.

The odds of getting nine heads or tails is around .01, or one in every hundred people flipping a coin ten times. You wouldn't expect many more than ten people in your sample of 1000 to get nine heads or tails. And the chance of flipping eight heads or tails is approximately .044, or less than .05 using our criteria of significance.

In other words, you would say that it would be a statistically significant event if someone got eight ($p < .05$), nine ($p < .01$), or ten ($p < .001$) heads flipping a coin ten times since the odds are so low that these could occur by accident. So when you see significance levels, translate them into coin flips and ask yourself if the statistical findings are as rare as these coin flip results. If they are, you have a statistically significant finding.

Type I and Type II Errors.   Because a decision to declare statistical significance is based on probability, it means we could be wrong some of the time. We might incorrectly conclude there is a relationship between an independent and dependent variable in the population from which the sample was chosen when there really isn't one. Finding a relationship when there isn't one could occur the percentage of time established by the alpha level of significance. For example, if we wanted to declare a statistic significant at the .05 level, then the probability of the statistic occurring by chance is less than 5 percent or, put another way, we are 95 percent confident it is not due to chance but instead to a real finding.

This could be one of those chance times that a statistic of the magnitude calculated happened accidentally and was not due to actual findings and relationships in the population. The likelihood, then, of declaring a relationship statistically significant when it is not, is the value of alpha; this is called a *Type I error*. In words of the null hypothesis, a Type I error is rejecting a null hypothesis that is truly null. There is no relationship between the independent and dependent variable but we rejected that by mistake and declared there is a relationship. Normally, when a statistic's significance level is less than .05, or whatever other number was selected, we say that we have a statistically significant finding and we reject the null hypothesis. That is, we reject that there is no relationship and declare the alternative hypothesis that there is a relationship. In this case, we should have accepted the null of no relationship.

We hold a press conference to announce our findings; yet we should be aware that our outcome could be the result of chance, and not due to the independent variable, as the statistical calculations have led us to believe. By setting a probability strict enough to limit the number of Type I errors, we become more reassured that our results are genuine and not likely due to chance alone. Thus, many researchers choose .01 or .001 as levels of significance. The odds of making a Type I error and declaring a relationship when there really isn't any, is in these cases less than one in one hundred (1 percent) or one in one thousand (0.1 percent).

On the other hand, we might be making a *Type II error* instead and accept a null hypothesis that should be rejected, that is, declaring that there is no relationship between our variables when in fact there really is a statistically significant one. These two errors are intertwined: Decreasing a Type I error increases the possibility of making a Type II error. The goal of testing hypotheses is to minimize errors when making inferences about a population from a sample, but convention encourages us to use at least .05 as the level of significance ($p < .05$) when testing statistics, depending on what is being tested and for what reasons. Exploratory research may allow a lower standard, while predictive research looking at the outcomes of a new kind of drug or intervention program, for example, might require a more stringent test, such as $p < .01$.

The key point to remember is that any results and statistics never prove a hypothesis or question. Statistics suggest a finding that is tentative; we just never know for sure whether what we found occurred by chance or is due to actual influence of the independent variable on the dependent variable. All we can say is that the probability of a relationship happening by accident is less than a certain standard we set.

Central Limit Theorem.   Making inferences about a population and stating probabilities assumes a normal distribution. What happens though when the distribution of the variable is not normal as is usually the case? There are other distribution shapes and appropriate statistics that can be used for other models, but these are beyond the scope of this book. Luckily, though, the distribution of statistics (like sample means) is assumed to be normally distributed. If you were to plot on a graph the reading test means of all possible samples of people taken from a population, the distribution would approach a normal curve, especially the larger the sample size is. This is something in reality you wouldn't do, because if you had the time and money to gather all possible samples of a certain size, you would end up with a survey of the entire population. If the population were small enough for you to survey, then you wouldn't have a need to sample in the first place.

What we are talking about is a theoretical idea known as the *Central Limit Theorem* and something useful in understanding sample size, sampling error, and confidence limits. It states that a distribution of sample means— again, not to be confused with the distribution of individual sample scores— will approach a normal curve, the larger the sample size and the larger the number of samples taken. And the mean and standard deviation (here called the *standard error of the mean*) of all the sample means will be the true population mean (μ) and population standard deviation (σ).

Consider a situation in which we know what the population parameters are for a group of people. Imagine that the entire population of some small village is 1495 people and has an average age of $\overline{X} = 46.23$, and a standard deviation of $s = 17.42$. As illustrated previously, the distribution of age is not normally distributed; it has a slight positive skew. Now, let's take random samples from that population of size five (see Table 6.3). If we were able

TABLE 6.3   Samples of 5

	SAMPLE SIZE (n)	MEAN ($\overline{X}$)	STANDARD DEVIATION (s)
Sample 1	5	44.8	19.15
Sample 2	5	35.2	17.21
Sample 3	5	56.0	16.51
Sample 4	5	40.0	10.07
Sample 5	5	53.8	15.51

to take all possible combinations of samples of size five, calculate the mean age for each of those samples, plot them on a graph, and then calculate a mean of all those means, the graph would begin to look like a normal curve and the mean of all those means would be equal to 46.23, the true population mean.

Because the sample size is so small (only 5 out of 1495), many of the samples are way off from the true mean of 46.23. Yet, even without showing all possible samples of size five from the population, a mean of 45.96 for just five of these sample means gets pretty close to the true population parameter. What if the one random sample of five we actually generated ended up being sample three? The odds are great that with small sample sizes, the sample statistics (in this case the mean and standard deviation) will be further away from the true population parameters and we are more likely to end up with a sample that does not represent the population. There would be greater sampling error, hence the justification to gather samples of larger sizes.

The central limit theorem argues that larger sample sizes will result in a distribution of sample statistics that is closer to a normal curve with most of the values close to the mean (a curve that is narrow and peaked) and therefore we would be more confident in the accuracy of predicting the population information and make fewer errors doing so.

Now consider random sample sizes of fifty from the same population in Table 6.4. Here, the mean of the five means is 46.44, almost exactly the true population mean of 46.23. And that is with only five samples. In other words, any one of these samples would be a much better estimate of the true population mean than any one of the samples that had only five people in it. Still not convinced? Then take a look at random sample sizes of 100 in Table 6.5.

The mean of the sample means is 46.76, pretty close again to the actual population mean of 46.23. Also note how close the standard deviations are to the true population standard deviation. Any one of these samples would provide a more accurate estimate of the population parameters than any of the samples with sizes of five. Remember, in actual research we only survey one sample. Notice that the increase in accuracy from samples sizes of fifty to one hundred may not be worth the extra time and money; doubling the sample size did not increase the number of samples that were closer to the true population. As we increase the sample size, more of the samples' means tend to be closer to one another and the true mean.

In Chapter 5 we discussed how large a sample should be for a good study. One of the points made was that the larger the random sample size, the more likely it will capture the diversity that exists in the population. This idea is based primarily on the concepts just described about the central limit theorem. Similar calculations are made by professional research organizations when determining sample size. Choosing a sample size depends on the population size, its heterogeneity on a variety of key characteristics being studied, and the amount of money and time available to do the research.

TABLE 6.4 Samples of 50

	SAMPLE SIZE (n)	MEAN ($\bar{X}$)	STANDARD DEVIATION (s)
Sample 1	50	46.0	16.37
Sample 2	50	46.8	16.79
Sample 3	50	46.5	16.38
Sample 4	50	44.6	13.80
Sample 5	50	48.3	17.16

TABLE 6.5 Samples of 100

	SAMPLE SIZE (n)	MEAN ($\bar{X}$)	STANDARD DEVIATION (s)
Sample 1	100	46.4	17.14
Sample 2	100	46.5	17.59
Sample 3	100	47.2	17.70
Sample 4	100	44.6	16.05
Sample 5	100	49.1	17.67

Confidence Intervals. The central limit theorem is a theoretical concept because in reality no one takes all possible samples from a population. However, it does help in determining whether the one sample we actually have is representative of the population, that is, whether the sample mean and standard deviation are fairly accurate estimates of the true population mean and standard deviation. Using *inferential statistics,* we infer (arrive at some conclusion about) the population parameters from the sample statistics with some degree of confidence. We can do this since the normal curve tells us with z-scores and percentiles how far off the statistics are from the mean. Not unlike political polls which present results in terms of plus or minus four percentage points of the true population percentage, what we also do is determine how confident we are that the true mean of the population is within a range of plus or minus certain number of points.

This range is referred to as the *confidence interval* and the numbers at the beginning and end of the interval are often called the *confidence limits.* You see this range in the output results performed by most computer statistical programs. If we use the traditional cut-off point for significance of .05, we can state that we are 95 percent confident that the true population mean—or whichever other statistic from the sample we are using to infer the population parameter—is within this confidence interval range. It states that if we were to complete 100 samples of the same size as the one we just did and calculate the confidence limits for each one of them, 95 of those confidence limits would contain the true population mean. We could also set the alpha level at .01, or 1 percent, and use a z-score of plus or minus 2.58 to calculate the confidence interval if we want to be 99 percent confident that the true population mean is within that range. In any case, we will never know the true population parameter unless we did a survey of every element in the population, so our results are always an estimate and subject to some sampling error.

What the central limit theorem provides us with, then, is proof that even when a variable is not normally distributed in a sample, if large enough sample sizes are taken, the distribution of statistics from those samples would be normal. This fact allows us to use probabilities in making conclusions and inferences about the population from which the one sample we actually have comes. Our inferences have fewer errors, the more confident we are that the true number is within a particular range. And we make many more errors the smaller the sample size is, because the distribution of statistics from small random samples has a standard deviation (standard error) that is larger than the true population's dispersion.

The central limit theorem tells us that larger sample sizes produce distributions that have more limited dispersions, ones in which the normal curve is narrow and peaked. We will make fewer errors in estimating the population parameters if we have a sample from a theoretical distribution of all samples that is normally distributed this way since we know that the odds of obtaining a sample that is statistically very different from the norm (the mean, for example) are 5 in 100, 1 in 100, 1 in 1000, or whatever alpha level we set as our standard of statistical significance.

Practically speaking, what we need to be aware of when reviewing the output from various statistical procedures is the information about probability or significance levels, confidence intervals, standard error, and sample size, as described in the next three chapters. These numbers are our guide to making more accurate inferences or generalizations about the characteristics of the population from which we drew our random sample. Without a random sample, however, generalizations about a population are not possible, and inferential statistics cannot be calculated. Yet, we can still use many of these statistics and graphs to describe what we have in our study.

Displaying and describing the basic statistics for each of our variables is the first step in analyzing data. These univariate statistics help us determine if the items from our questionnaire are actually variables and useful for later data analysis. They also allow us to describe the characteristics of the sample through displays of the demographic findings. Once we determine which items are variable enough for further analysis, we can begin to evaluate the research questions and hypotheses we developed using concepts of inferential statistics and probability levels. To do this we need to explore relationships between two or more variables at a time. The next chapter discusses the many ways to assess whether variables are correlated.

REVIEW: WHAT DO THESE KEY TERMS MEAN?

Alpha levels
Bar graphs
Central Limit
  Theorem
Confidence limits and
  interval
Frequency polygons
Frequency tables
Graphs and charts
Histograms
Inferential statistics
Interquartile range

Mean
Measures of central
  tendency
Median
Mode
Normal curve
One- and two-tailed
  tests
Percentiles
Pie charts
Positive and negative
  skews

Range
Standard deviation
Standard error of the
  mean
Statistical significance
Type I and Type II
  errors
Univariate analysis
Values and variables
Z-scores

INTERPRET: WHAT DO THESE REAL EXAMPLES TELL US?

1. In a published academic article on the importance of racial/ethnic identity and how it might vary in four different social settings (home, work, neighborhood, in public) among whites, blacks, and multiracials, Jaret and Reitzes (1999: 723–724) report the following descriptive information about the variables in the study. Identity is measured in each of the four settings with a high score of 4 = "very important" and 1 = "not important at all")

	BLACK		MULTIRACIAL		WHITE	
	Mean	S.D.	Mean	S.D.	Mean	S.D.
Racial-ethnic identity importance when "at work"	2.89	1.22	1.82	0.98	1.95	1.06
Racial-ethnic identity when "at home"	2.42	1.29	2.02	1.10	1.92	1.10

   a. First of all, why are means and standard deviations (S.D.) calculated?
   b. How would you put into words what this table of means and standard deviations says?

2. The National Health and Social Life Survey asked respondents to indicate how many sexual partners they have had in their life since the age of 18. According to the findings (Laumann, et al. 1994: 180), the minimum number reported by the 3126 respondents was 0, and the maximum was 1,016. The researchers found the median number was 3 and the mode was 1.
   a. Why did they use the median for the level of central tendency and not the mean?
   b. Put into words what a median of 3 and a mode of 1 tell us.
   c. What is the range for these data? What else would you need to know to interpret these findings?

3. Here are some results using data from 151 students who reported their height (in inches):

Mean 67.3   Median: 67   Mode: 68

a. How can you tell if this is approximately a normal curve?
b. The Standard Deviation is 4 inches. Assume a normal curve and calculate:
   i. What percentage of the sample is between 63.3 and 71.3 inches?
   ii. What height would put you in the shortest 16 percent of the class?
   iii. What percentage of the respondents are taller than 67 inches?
   iv. If you set the significance level at 5 percent ($p < .05$), and you were to randomly select one respondent from the sample to find someone "significantly different from the mean," approximately what height would it take for this respondent to qualify as statistically taller or statistically shorter than the mean? Is this a two-tailed or one-tailed research question?
   v. Assume this is a random sample from a population: Between approximately what heights would you be 95 percent confident that the true population mean was?

CONSULT: WHAT COULD BE DONE?

You've been hired to do the data analysis for a survey conducted at a local business. The questionnaire contains the following variables and you need to advise the business which ones are good for further analysis in its study.

1. What do you do first? Describe the steps needed to be taken at the start of data analysis.

2. Which measures of central tendency and what kinds of graphs would be best to use to describe the following variables:
a. type of job performed in the organization
b. hours worked per week
c. seniority ranking (oldest employee to newest)
d. monthly salary
e. a checklist of employee benefits (health plan, dental insurance, child care, etc.)

DECIDE: WHAT DO YOU DO NEXT?

You are asked to do a study looking at the relationship between people's television viewing habits and their opinions about racial and ethnic issues and stereotyping, and their reactions toward people from diverse backgrounds. Does TV viewing have an impact on their attitudes and behaviors toward diversity?

1. For each variable in the questionnaire you developed in the previous chapter, describe which measures of central tendency, other statistical descriptions, and graphs would be best to use during the first phase of data analysis.

2. If you have actually collected data, now is the time to code and enter the data into a statistical program and begin data analysis with descriptive statistics.

CHAPTER SEVEN

ANALYZING DATA
BIVARIATE RELATIONSHIPS

LEARNING GOALS

Understanding bivariate statistical analysis is the focus of this chapter. Central to this is learning how to read and construct cross-tables of data and deciding which statistics to use to measure association and correlation. By the end of the chapter you should understand how to reject or accept a hypothesis using the appropriate statistics to assess bivariate relationships. You should also be able to put together cross-tables and interpret them clearly in words.

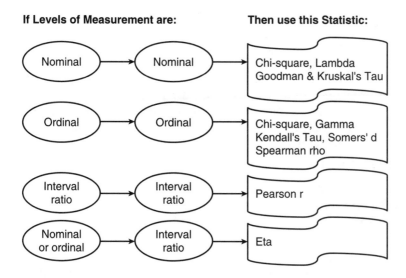

FIGURE 7.1   Statistical Decision Steps.

After you evaluate your univariate data analysis and feel confident that you have variables with good distributions, it is now time to begin investigating the bivariate relationships you proposed in your research questions and hypotheses. *Bivariate* data analysis assesses the association between two variables at a time. If you are interested in studying three variables or more, then multivariate analysis is required (see Chapter 9). Remember, if for some reason, any of your variables approximate a constant—that is, almost everyone has selected only one or two of the values for that variable—then you must eliminate them from further analysis. For example, when 90 percent of the people who completed the questionnaire agree or strongly agree that they are satisfied with their current job, then job satisfaction is no longer a variable in your study.

Keep in mind what the objective is: To demonstrate whether the independent variable is exerting significant influence on the dependent variable in order to infer something about a population from which your sample was selected. You want to see if the variation that exists in the dependent or outcome variable among the respondents can be explained or predicted by the variation that exists in the independent variable. For example, you might want to establish whether studying more leads to higher grades. If there is some relationship, you have fulfilled one of the three aspects required to establish cause and effect. Once you have eliminated alternative explanations and can show that the independent variable occurred prior in time to the dependent variable, then you hold a press conference and declare you have found a cause for the occurrence of the dependent variable.

Another objective may simply be to describe how the dependent variable varies according to different categories of the independent variable. You might be interested in showing whether political party affiliation differs between men and women, or among Latinos, Asian/Pacific Island people, and African Americans. Or you would like to report how many respondents in your study are young, middle-aged, and elderly and who are from rural and urban areas, such as young urban, young rural, elderly urban, elderly rural, and so on. This chapter focuses on developing skills for accomplishing these objectives through bivariate data analysis and for understanding measures of association.

PRESENTING NOMINAL AND ORDINAL DATA IN TABLES

Using your research questions and hypotheses, begin by making a list of the variables in them. Next, label each variable in terms of its level of measurement (nominal, ordinal, or interval/ratio), and—based on what follows in this and the next two chapters—decide the appropriate way of presenting the data visually with tables or graphs. Finally, select the most relevant statistics to assess what you have found.

Similar to the way you show the distribution of a single variable, constructing frequency tables for both variables simultaneously is a good way to start analyzing the variables in your hypotheses. What is the occurrence of one variable in terms of the other one? Is one variable's distribution contingent on the other's variation? Is the dependent or outcome variable associated with the independent or predictor variable in any way? To answer these kinds of questions visually, a table crossing the two variables is made. These are usually referred to as *contingency tables* or *cross-tabulations* (*crosstabs,* for short). They illustrate the number and percentage of occurrences in the sample of each value of one variable simultaneously with each value of the other variable.

Crosstabs are ideally suited to variables that are nominal or ordinal measures, or interval/ratio data with a very limited number of discrete values. Each value (or category) of one variable constitutes the columns in the table, and each value (or category) of the other variable makes up the rows of the table. It is easy to remember which is which: Just as *columns* hold up a building, they hold up a table; just as you move across the *row* to get to your seat in the movie theater, you move across the rows in a table. These are similar to the concepts used in a spreadsheet.

Ideally, the number of rows and columns in a table should be small enough to see all of them at the same time, thereby restricting crosstabs to mostly nominal or ordinal measures. Interval/ratio data with a limited number of values can also be used, but imagine a table that has a row for every age that exists in your sample of 18 to 89 year olds! The size of a table is referred to in terms of its rows and columns, in that order, such as a 3 by 2 table (or 3×2, three rows and two columns). *Cells* are the locations where each row's values and each column's values intersect, and the number of them is quickly calculated by multiplying the number of rows by the number of columns: A 3×2 table has six cells, for example. A cell's location is also given in terms of its row and column number (in that order), so you can refer to the data in a cell as being "in row 3, column 3."

Another convention is that the percentages for each value (or category) of the independent variable should add up to 100 percent; if the values of the independent variable are columns, as is recommended, then each column should total 100 percent. In this way you standardize the responses when the numbers of responses for each value of the variable are not equal. This allows you to make a fair comparison about the frequency of occurrence of each value of the independent variable in terms of each value of the dependent variable.

Let's say you are interested in seeing if there is some relationship between gender and political party affiliation. Your hypothesis is two-tailed, so you simply state that there is a relationship between the two, or using the null form, there is no relationship between gender and political party affiliation. It seems logical to see if political party choice is an outcome of gender (clearly, choosing a party doesn't result in your gender); in other words, political party affiliation depends on the independent variable of gender. The values for gender (male and female) compose the columns, and the values for party (Republican, Democrat, Independent, Other) become the rows.

Table 7.1, a bivariate frequency table, or cross-tabulation, shows that there are 68 women who are Democrats in this sample (the cell at row 1, column 1). Or, we can say that 69.4 percent of all the women who answered both questions on the survey are Democrats and 77.3 percent of all Democrats are female. Remember, data are based on valid responses and, to be included, the respondent had to answer both questions, no blanks or missing values. Because percentage is standardized, we can compare 69.4 percent with 37.7 percent in the next cell (row 1, column 2). Notice that although there are sixty-eight women and twenty men who are Democrats, it would not be correct to say that over three times as many women are Democrats than men. This would assume there was the same number of men and women answering the questions, but as you can see, the total sample is ninety-eight women and fifty-three men. To make up for the unequal totals for each value of the independent variable, a percentage is used instead to make the comparison. It would be more accurate to say that approximately twice as many women than men are Democrats, in terms of the percentage that is relative to their sample sizes.

The total numbers at the bottom of the columns and at the right end of the rows are called *marginals*, because they appear at the edges or margins of the table. They essentially provide you the same information you would have gotten if you had constructed two separate univariate frequency tables. Notice also that this table includes percentages in terms of the dependent, or row, variable. For example, the thirteen respondents who are male and registered as Independents (row 3, column 2) can be read either as 41.9 percent of the men are Independents, or you can say that 24.5 percent of all Independents in your study are male.

These are two different things; it all depends on how you want to report your data. If someone from the Republican Party wanted to know the breakdown of men and women in the party, then you would use the row percentages (percent of Political Party). If, on the other hand, you wanted to know whether there was a difference between men and women in terms of Republican affiliation, then use the column percentages (percent of gender). Sometimes there is no clear-cut independent and dependent variable because both can occur at the same time. These are often referred to as *symmetrical* relationships because either can be seen as the predictor for the other and either one can be the outcome needing explanation.

TABLE 7.1   Bivariate Cross-table Example, SPSS

POLITICAL PARTY BY GENDER CROSS-TABULATION

			GENDER		
			Female	Male	Total
Political Party	Democrats	Count	68	20	88
		% of Political Party	77.3%	22.7%	100.0%
		% of gender	69.4%	37.7%	58.3%
	Republicans	Count	8	15	23
		% of Political Party	34.8%	65.2%	100.0%
		% of gender	8.2%	28.3%	15.2%
	Independents	Count	18	13	31
		% of Political Party	58.1%	41.9%	100.0%
		% of gender	18.4%	24.5%	20.5%
	Other	Count	4	5	9
		% of Political Party	44.4%	55.6%	100.0%
		% of gender	4.1%	9.4%	6.0%
Total		Count	98	53	151
		% of Political Party	64.9%	35.1%	100.0%
		% of gender	100.0%	100.0%	100.0%

This can be confusing, so think aloud what you really want to know and figure out how to show the percentages according to your objectives. It is not the same thing to say that 20 percent of women on campus major in political science and that 20 percent of political science majors are women. These are two different meanings and it is crucial to make the distinction when presenting your findings in bivariate cross-tabulations.

The categories or values of a variable that you want to compare should each add up to 100 percent. If you want to compare men with women and which majors they choose, the categories of gender should each add up to 100 percent. Then you can say what percentage of men select political science compared to what percentage of women major in it, and so on. But if you want to compare the majors and find out how many men and women are in each major, the categories for major (political science, sociology, psychology, etc.) should each add up to 100 percent. Then you can find out what percentage of political science majors are female and male compared to the percentage of sociology majors who are female and male, and so on.

TESTING BIVARIATE RELATIONSHIPS

With crosstabs you see whether some relationship is occurring with your data. There seems in this table to be some difference in political party affiliation between men and women. Sometimes, however, the percentages and frequencies are so close that it is not possible to tell if there is a meaningful difference at a glance. Even when there appears to be a difference, you still need a more objective assessment than your own, perhaps selective, perspective to tell you whether the relationship is a significant one.

Chi-Square

Rest assured, there is a way of testing whether there is a significant relationship between your variables! One of the most important and frequently used statistics to assess the association between ordinal and nominal measures is called *chi-square* (χ^2, pronounced "kie square"). This measures how independent your two variables are and asks whether what you found (observed) is significantly different from what you would have expected to get by chance alone. The calculation looks at each cell and measures the difference between the actual frequency you got and the frequency that would have been expected by chance. For example if half the sample is male and half are female, and half are Latino and half are Asian, then you would expect 25 percent of the sample to be in each cell in that 2 by 2 table by chance, that is, 25 percent should be Latino men, 25 percent should be Asian women, and so on.

■ ■ ■ ■ ■ ▬▬▬▬▬▬▬▬▬▬▬▬▬▬▬▬▬▬▬▬▬▬▬▬▬

BOX 7.1

CALCULATING CHI-SQUARE AND DEGREES OF FREEDOM

$$\chi^2 = \Sigma \frac{(O-E)^2}{E}$$

Calculating a chi-square by hand is fairly simple. For each cell in the table, take what is actually found in the study or the Observed value (O) and subtract from it the Expected value (E). Figuring out what is expected in each cell is the tricky part. This is calculated in several steps: (1) take the total number of people in a column and divide that by the total of all respondents answering the questions in order to get what percentage of the entire valid sample holds the value of the variable in the first column; (2) then use that percentage and multiply it by the total row value for each row associated with the first column. Next go on to the second column, take its total and divide by the grand total, and use that percentage and multiply it by the row total for each row in the second column, and so on. Using a formula, it's:

$$\frac{\text{Column Total}}{\text{Total total}} \times \text{Row Total}$$

Imagine these are your results in raw numbers:

	MEN	WOMEN	TOTALS
Psychology	28	56	84
Sociology	26	35	61
Political Science	67	27	94
Totals	121	118	239

1. Take the column total for Men and divide by the total of all those answering the questions: 121/239 = .506 or 50.6%
2. Multiply that percentage by the row total for each row in the Men column to get the expected:

   50.6% × 84 = 42.5

   50.6% × 61 = 30.9

   50.6% × 94 = 47.6

Note these numbers add up to 121, the column total. All we did was to say that if men make up 50.6 percent of the total number of people answering these two questions, then we would expect 50.6 percent of Psychology majors to be men, and 50.6 percent of Sociology majors, and 50.6 percent of Political Science

(continued)

BOX 7.1 CONTINUED

majors. Since there are 84 Psych majors, we would expect 50.6 percent of 84 to be men, that is, 42.5, and so on for each major.

In each cell, the expected frequency is then subtracted from the observed one, that number is squared, and the result is divided by the expected frequency. Do this for each cell and sum all those numbers to arrive at chi-square.

In our example, the observed for the first cell is 28 and the expected is 42.5. Already we can see that there is a deviation from the expected. There is an under-representation of men who are psych majors.

1. First we subtract the expected from the observed:

   $28 - 42.5 = -14.5$

2. Then we square the difference; recall how we did something similar to get the standard deviation – we squared the deviations of each score from the mean which is the expected:

   $-14.5^2 = (-14.5) \times (-14.5) = 210.25$

3. Next, we divide this number by the expected:

   $210.25 / 42.5 = 4.95$

4. We continue to do this for each cell:

   $26 - 30.9 = -4.9$

   $4.9^2 = 24.01$

   $24.01 / 30.9 = .78$ and so on for each cell.

5. We add up all the calculations for each cell to arrive at chi-square:

   $4.95 + .78 + 7.91 + 5.07 + .80 + 8.11 = 27.62$

The chi-square value is compared to a distribution of chi-squares to find the probability of achieving that chi-square by chance. Should it be less than .05 (or whatever standard was set such as .01 or .001), then you declare a statistically significant finding and hold your press conference!

Remember the size itself tells you nothing unless you know the number of cells. In this example, 27.62 is not necessarily statistically significant just because it is a particular value. A chi-square with a value of 8.5, for example, might be significant and one of 30 might not. It all depends on the number of cells and the size of the sample.

DEGREES OF FREEDOM

In this example, we have a 3 by 2 table, or six cells. Probability levels make use of a concept called degrees of freedom. *Degrees of freedom* (df) are the number of values that can vary in any calculation. When there is a fixed outcome (such as the sum of deviations around a mean always equals zero), it limits how many numbers can contribute to that outcome, usually by one ($n - 1$). For example, consider the following: The total number of seats in a theater row was ten, and three groups wanted to be seated. A party of four enters, then a group of two; only four more people can now be accommodated. The first two numbers, four and two, could have been anything—they were free to vary. Once established, however, the next number is fixed. If a party of five came first, then three more came along, there is now only room for two. Out of three groups of people, two are free to vary, one is fixed, or $n - 1$.

For cells in a crosstab, the degrees of freedom are the number of rows minus one times the number of columns minus one or $(r - 1) \times (c - 1)$. In this example, it would be two rows ($3 - 1$) and one column ($2 - 1$), for a total of 2 degrees of freedom.

In fact, if you calculated the expected frequencies for the first cell (row 1, column 1) and then for the second cell in the example (row 2, column 1), you didn't have to calculate any more. All you had to do was subtract the expected in the first cell (42.5) from the row total of 84 to figure out the expected for the cell in row 1, column 2. It has to add up to 84 so the expected for that cell must be 41.5. That cell's value is not free to vary once you calculated the first cell's. Notice that with two numbers adding up to 84 one is fixed and one is free to vary ($df = n - 1$).

Similarly, add up the expected frequency from cell 1 with the one below it (30.9) and subtract that number from the column total of 121 to get the expected value of the cell at row 3, column 1: $42.5 + 30.9 = 73.4$, then $121 - 73.4 = 47.6$. In short, only two cells are free to vary and had to be calculated; the rest are not free to vary. Again the degrees of freedom are $n - 1$, in this case three rows minus one results in two. Out of six cells, there are two degrees of freedom and four are fixed. Degrees of freedom are also used as a correction when estimating a population parameter from a sample statistic, as was seen in Chapter 6 when discussing the formula to calculate the standard deviation with its denominator of $n - 1$.

Like the concept of the standard deviation, a mean deviation for each cell is calculated and these are added together to produce a number called chi-square. Obviously, when there are many values for both variables, the larger the final number will be since there are many more cells to add together. This number is compared to a sampling distribution of chi-square values; the chi-square distribution approaches a normal curve, when the number of cells increase, or more accurately when the degrees of freedom increase. The chi-square number in itself is not a measure of strength or magnitude; it must be compared to a distribution of chi-square values not to other chi-squares unless the sample sizes and number of cells are the same.

Its value depends on the size of the sample and the number of cells: The more cells there are, the larger chi-square is going to be.

The probability of obtaining a chi-square value by chance for a particular number of cells in a table is determined by the computer program or by comparing the value to a normal curve table of probabilities. If the probability is less than .05 (or whatever alpha level you set), then you can declare there is an association between your two variables by rejecting the null hypothesis of no association.

Consider Table 7.1 on political party and gender. In Table 7.2, a chi-square value of 17.361 was calculated for these data. Notice there are three degrees of freedom (df) since there are four political party rows (4 − 1 = 3) and two gender columns (2 − 1 = 1), resulting in 3 × 1 = 3. What this statistical test tells us is that for a table with three degrees of freedom and 151 respondents, a chi-square value of 17.361 is significant at .001 level for a two-tailed hypothesis: There is no difference in political parties between men and women. The odds of obtaining a value of 17.361 by chance alone is less than one in one thousand. We therefore reject the null, accept the alternative that there is a relationship between gender and political party preference, and conclude that women in this sample are more likely to be registered Democrats than are men. It's not enough just to say there is a relationship, you must also say what it is, or else the press conference will be fairly dull!

The value of the chi-square statistic is also affected by cells with low frequencies, hence the information provided in footnote "a" which lets you know how many cells have small numbers. A rule of thumb is that every cell should have at least five expected respondents; you can see now how the size of the sample can make a difference when you have a table that is large, say five racial/ethnic groups and five religions, resulting in a 25-cell table. If your table has small numbers in its cells, there are statistical corrections, such as Fisher's Exact Test. If you have a 2 by 2 table, Yate's Correction should be used to adjust the calculation of chi-square. More information about these statistics can be found in advanced statistic books and in most computer statistical programs.

TABLE 7.2   **Example of a Chi-Square Test, SPSS**

CHI-SQUARE TEST		
Value	*df*	*Asymp. Sig. (2-tailed)*
Pearson Chi-Square 17.361[a]	3	.001
N of Valid Cases 151		

[a]One cell (12.5%) has expected count less than 5. The minimum expected count is 3.16.

Correlation Coefficients

Chi-square is not the best statistic to use if you want to compare the results with other data because it is not a measure of comparative strength. If you are interested in the *strength* of an association, then correlation coefficients must be calculated. There are many available depending on the level of measurement for the variables being assessed. *Coefficients* range in value from 0.0 to 1.0. Like all coefficients, the closer a coefficient is to 1.0, the stronger the association. The closer a coefficient is to 0.0, the weaker the relationship. Except for nominal data where there is no order, coefficients also have either a negative or positive direction. A relationship is an *inverse* or *negative* one when an increase in one variable goes along with a decrease in the other; it's a *positive* relationship when a decrease in one variable goes along with a decrease in the other, or an increase in one goes with an increase in the other.

The strength of the correlation is not weakened in any way with the appearance of a minus sign. A correlation of –.54 is stronger than a positive correlation of .45, for example. Sometimes the direction is due simply to the way the variables were measured, that is, if one variable is measured with 1 = strongly agree and 5 = strongly disagree, and another variable has 1 = strongly disagree and 5 = strongly agree, then a negative correlation between two variables measuring similar traits could result.

An easy way to understand coefficients is to think about them as the amount of change you have in your pocket. The closer the number is to $1.00, the more you have. If your coefficient is .83, then you have 83 cents, almost a dollar. If you get a coefficient of .17, then you have small change. Typically coefficients below .30 are considered weak, those between .30 and .70 are moderate, and those above .70 are fairly strong. But it's all relative in comparison to other studies and the size of the sample: If most research has found a coefficient of .14 between religious affiliation and political party choice, and you get .35, then yours might be considered pretty strong.

When evaluating a coefficient and its significance level, be sure to make a distinction about which numbers you are reading. Coefficients range from 0.0 to 1.0 with the larger number meaning a strong and, very likely, statistically significant relationship. On the other hand, for probability levels which also range from 0.0 to 1.0, smaller numbers mean low probability of chance occurrences. Because the goal is to get a statistic that did not happen by chance a good deal of the time—it is a finding due to the actual influence of the independent variable on the dependent variable, not due to chance—then the objective is to have a probability level that is low, smaller than .05, .01, or .001, the typical numbers used as cut-off points for significance levels. The closer the probability is to 0 (that is, no probability the statistic occurred by chance), the more likely that what you found did not occur accidentally. The closer the coefficient is to 1.0, the stronger it is; the independent variable explains almost all the variation in the dependent variable. You will make fewer errors in explaining or predicting it.

It is important to know, though, that low correlation coefficients can be significant with large sample sizes; thus, it is better to look at the strength of correlations rather than to focus only on their significance levels.

Measures of Association: Nominal Variables

When you are interested in evaluating relationships between two *nominal* level variables, then use such statistics as the *Phi* (Φ) *Coefficient* (for 2 × 2 tables), the *Contingency Coefficient* (for larger than 2 × 2 tables), *Cramer's V* (for tables without the same number of columns and rows), *Goodman and Kruskal's Tau* (T), and *Lambda* (λ). These are discussed in more detail in advanced statistics books. For our purposes, the goal is to understand how to interpret correlation coefficients.

Consider the results of the correlation between political party and gender found in Table 7.1. Note in Table 7.3 that the Phi, Cramer's V, and Contingency coefficients are all fairly similar around .32 to .34 (rounding off) and all are statistically significant (p < .001). Chi-square told us that there is a relationship, but these statistics communicate that it's a moderate one in strength. Chi-square does not let us know how strong or weak the relationship is, only that there is one.

Lambda and Tau.   Many researchers prefer to use coefficients that determine the *proportional reduction in error*, or *PRE. Lambda* and *Goodman and Kruskal's Tau* are two statistics best suited for this when you have nominal variables. What PRE means is that the values of Lambda and Tau tell us approximately how many fewer errors we will make when predicting the outcome values of the dependent variable when we know the values of the independent variable. Be aware, though, that Lambda is based on modes, so it is possible to obtain a Lambda of 0. This simply means that a prediction of the dependent variable mode is not helped by knowing the modes of each category of the independent variable, yet there may still be a relationship.

TABLE 7.3   **Example of Statistics for Nominal Variables, SPSS**

	SYMMETRIC MEASURES		
		Value	*Approx. Sig.*
Nominal	Phi	.339	.001
Measures	Cramer's V	.339	.001
	Contingency Coefficient	.321	.001
N *of Valid Cases*		151	

Because it is calculated using modes, the value of Lambda is a function of which variable is the dependent one. Note that several values are calculated depending on whether the association you are assessing is symmetric or asymmetric. *Asymmetric* (or directional) measures assume that one of the variables is definitely dependent on the other; *symmetric* measures allow for the possibility of either one being dependent. If your goal is one direction, than asymmetric Lambda or Tau is more appropriate. If you are interested, for example, in the relationship between gender and race/ethnicity in your sample, then you would look at symmetric Lambda because neither one comes before the other in time or is being used to predict the other.

Because political party is the dependent variable, the value of Lambda is .000, the second one in Table 7.4. According to these statistics, there is no correlation between gender and political party, hence there is no significance level given. With most of the output, focus primarily on two items: The value of the statistic and its significance level. The other information provided is useful for those with more advanced statistical training.

Lambda is calculated using the mode, and the modal political party for men in this sample is Democrat and the modal political party for women is also Democrat. Knowing respondents' genders does not improve or reduce

TABLE 7.4   Example of Lambda and Tau Statistics for Nominal Variables, SPSS

			DIRECTIONAL MEASURES			
			Value	*Asymp. Std. Error*[a]	*Approx. T*[b]	*Approx. Sig.*
Nominal Measures	Lambda	Symmetric	.069	.046	1.424	.155
		Political Party Dependent	.000	.000		
		Gender Dependent	.151	.098	1.424	.155
	Goodman and Kruskal Tau	Political Party Dependent	.057	.028		.000[c]
		gender Dependent	.115	.053		.001[c]

[a]Not assuming the null hypothesis

[b]Using the asymptotic standard error assuming the null hypothesis.

[c]Based on chi-square approximation

our errors when predicting their political preference. Your best guess in either case is Democrat, regardless of the gender. And that is your best guess in general because the mode for the overall sample is Democrat as well.

Here is how you interpret a PRE if there is some correlation coefficient greater than 0. Let's say you get a value for Lambda of .45 between gender and religious affiliation. This coefficient tells you that errors in predicting the religion of the respondents in your sample are reduced by a proportion of .45 (or 45 percent) when you know what their genders are. Imagine you and your friends go to a "Guess Your Occupation" carnival booth. Suppose the person guessing your jobs knew nothing about you; you hide behind something and don't even speak. The guesses will be all over the place because there are no hints or clues to help the guesser. So you help out and you and your friends disclose your genders. There will be fewer errors now since many men tend to have different kinds of jobs than many women. By how much does the guesser improve? The PRE tells you that. So, for nominal level data, Lambda and Tau provide you with this information. Not only do you get a sense of the strength of the relationship and can compare the results to other relationship coefficients, you also know how well you will be reducing errors in predicting and explaining the dependent variable.

Because the goals of research include explaining and predicting as much as we can about our outcome variables, it is important to calculate statistics that determine how well we are doing with our independent variables. Chi-square tells us whether our two variables are independent of each other, or to put it another way, whether they are associated. Once we know that they are related, coefficient measures like Tau and Lambda tell us how strongly the variables are associated and how much error reduction we have when we predict the dependent variable values knowing the independent variable values.

Measures of Association: Ordinal Variables

In addition to chi-square, several other statistics are appropriate when the categories of the variables are ordered. If you wish to assess the association of two ordinal variables, such statistics as Gamma (γ), Kendall's Tau-b and Tau-c, and Somers' d can be used to determine the strength of the association. These coefficients also range from 0.0 to 1.0 but, unlike the ones for nominal data, they can be negative or positive depending on the order of the categories. Each of these has sampling distributions that are used to determine the probability of obtaining that statistic by chance. So, if the probability of obtaining the value calculated for Gamma or Kendall's Tau-c by chance is less than the level you set (minimally .05), then you reject the null hypothesis and declare there is an association between the independent and dependent variable.

Gamma.   A popular statistic to use is *Gamma* which is based on a concept of evaluating pairs of responses and whether the respondents' relative order on both the independent and dependent variables is similar or dissimilar. Gamma is a symmetric statistic (only one coefficient is calculated because it doesn't matter which is independent or dependent) and a PRE measure. This means that the coefficient itself not only tells you the strength of the relationship but it also indicates the proportion of reducing error in predicting the dependent variable once you have information on the independent variable. See Table 7.5, which shows the results of a study that found a Gamma of .191 between two ordinal variables: Political views (liberal, moderate, conservative) and attending religious services (several times a year or less vs. once a month or more). Although statistically significant, this could be interpreted as a weak relationship in which 19 percent of the errors in predicting religious attendance are reduced by knowing respondents' political views.

Kendall's Tau.   Kendall's Tau-b (not to be confused with Goodman and Kruskal's Tau for nominal level variables) uses different methods for calculation than gamma and assumes there are the same number of rows and columns in the table. *Kendall's Tau-c* can be used for tables of data in which the number of rows and columns is not equal. In this example, because there are three categories for political views and two for religious attendance, Tau-c could be used. These are symmetric statistics and the same coefficient of .127 would result if we decided political views depended on religious attendance. But Kendall's statistics are not PRE measures. The coefficient calculated can only be interpreted in terms of strength (weak to strong) and direction (positive or negative/inverse relationship). In this case, it is positive but weak.

TABLE 7.5   Example of Kendall's Tau and Gamma Statistics for Ordinal Variables, SPSS

SYMMETRIC MEASURES				
	Value	*Asymp. Std. Error[a]*	*Approx. T[b]*	*Approx. Sig.*
Ordinal by Kendall's Tau-b	.111	.026	4.298	.000
Ordinal Kendall's Tau-c	.127	.030	4.298	.000
Gamma	.191	.044	4.298	.000
N *of Valid Cases*	1316			

[a]Not assuming the null hypothesis.

[b]Using the asymptotic standard error assuming the null hypothesis.

**TABLE 7.6   Example of Somers' d Statistic
for Ordinal Variables, SPSS**

DIRECTIONAL MEASURES

			Value	Asymp. Std. Error[a]	Approx. T[b]	Approx. Sig.
Ordinal by Ordinal	Somers' d	Symmetric	.110	.025	4.298	.000
		Religious Services Attendance Dependent	.096	.022	4.298	.000
		Political Views Dependent	.128	.030	4.298	.000

[a]Not assuming the null hypothesis.
[b]Using the asymptotic standard error assuming the null hypothesis.

Somers' d. Similar to Gamma in the way it is calculated (that is, based on comparing the similarity or dissimilarity of ranking on pairs of responses on the two variables), *Somers' d* differs in that it can be an asymmetric statistic where two values are calculated depending on which is the dependent variable. However, it does not have a PRE interpretation.

In Table 7.6, the correlation between political views (in order: liberal, moderate, conservative) and attending religious services (several times a year or less vs. once a month or more) is .110, when you assume it is symmetrical and one variable is not predicting the other. If you feel that political views precedes religious attendance, then the value of Somers' d is .096. In either case, it is statistically significant (p < .001) but a weak positive coefficient. This means there is some relationship between those who are conservative (a high value on the political views measure) and attending services once a month or more (a high value on the religious services measure), or conversely, those who are more liberal in this sample seem to attend religious services less frequently than those who are conservative. It is statistically significant at such a low level of strength because it is from a large sample of over 1300 respondents.

The differences among all these ordinal statistics are the way they deal differently with pair rankings that are tied, something discussed in more detail in advanced statistics books. Yet, notice how similar they are in terms of the actual coefficient values. However, if you want a statistic that not only provides a measure of the strength of the association but also indicates how much error reduction occurs, then Gamma is ideal for ordinal measures.

Spearman's rho. Sometimes both the independent and dependent variables consist of rank ordered numbers. For example, you want to compare the rank order of people in terms of their grades on the first research methods exam with their rank order on the last exam taken. So, student A might be ranked third on the first test and fifth on the last test, student B might be twelfth on the first test and second on the last test, and so on for each of the 100 students in your study. Note that you are not comparing actual grades, but rather their rank order number. In such cases, *Spearman's rank order correlation coefficient* or *rho* (ρ) provides a measure of association.

Spearman's rho is a symmetrical statistic that results in a coefficient between 0.0 and 1.0 to indicate the strength of the relationship and a plus or minus to show the direction of the relationship. In addition, it's a PRE measure when you square the value of rho. For example, if the correlation coefficient is .65 between the first set of grades and the last set, then you can

■ ■ ■ ■ ■

BOX 7.2

CORRELATIONS IN PUBLISHED RESEARCH

Here are some excerpts from articles in academic publications.

1. Baumann (2001) studied audiences' shift in perceptions about movies from a form of entertainment to cultural art. One argument is that seeing film as an art form was partly due to changes in how critics wrote about movies over time. Consider these findings (Baumann 2001: 414):

NUMBER OF "HIGH ART" AND "CRITICAL" TERMS USED IN TWELVE FILM REVIEWS FOR EACH YEAR FROM THE NEW YORK TIMES, NEW YORKER, AND TIME MAGAZINE	Year
19	1925
18	1930
21	1935
5	1940
21	1945
9	1950
12	1955
31	1960
32	1965
107	1970
69	1975
103	1980
78	1985

(continued)

BOX 7.2 CONTINUED

The researcher tests the one-directional hypothesis that over time there is an increase in the number of artistic and critical words used in film reviews. Since year is already in rank order, the author decided to use Spearman's rho to test the correlation. This requires ranking the dependent variable (number of artistic words), and the rank order for artistic words is then compared with the rank order of years. The results are rho = .88, $p < .001$ (one-tailed test). This is a very strong positive correlation, leading to the conclusion that in the late 1950s through the late 1960s, movies became valorized as an art form. Year of the review explains more than 77 percent of the ranking variation in the number of artistic and critical words (Spearman's rho is a PRE measure that must be squared to calculate the error reduction).

2. Jobes (1999) studied felony convictions in small rural towns in Montana. Among many other things, he was interested in seeing whether migrants (short-term residents) committed more crimes in small towns whose economy was primarily agricultural compared with small towns dependent on recreational tourism. Here are the crime rates by migrants per 1000 residents (1999: 515):

	AGRICULTURAL TOWN	RECREATIONAL TOWN
Large town (2500+)	3.0	8.8
Medium town	5.7	8.7
Small town (< 1000)	26.6	34.3

In other words, in large agricultural towns, the crime rate committed by short-term residents is 3 for every 1000 residents, compared with 8.8 for every 1000 residents in large tourist towns, and so on.

To test the relationship, Jobes (1999: 504) used gamma "as the measure of association because of its proportional reduction in error interpretation." For this table, $\gamma = .49$ is a moderate to strong correlation. The PRE tells us that errors in predicting crime rates are reduced by 49 percent knowing the size and type of town. It appears that smaller towns have more crime committed by short-term residents than larger ones, and tourist towns have higher rates than those whose economy is primarily agricultural. Small tourist towns have the highest overall crime rates committed by short-term, migrant residents.

---

conclude that there is a strong positive relationship between the two, and that error in predicting rank order on the last exam is reduced by around 42 percent (.65 squared). If for some reason the coefficient were −.65, then you would conclude that those who rank higher on the first exam, tend to rank lower on the last exam, and those who rank lower on the first, rank higher on the last.

Measures of Association: Interval/Ratio Variables

Ranking scores on a test, as in the previous example, loses information. The person with the best grade could be only one point higher than the next one, or twenty points higher. Ordinal measures also do not give you enough information like the distance between the ranks. Certainly, if you have interval/ratio measures, then make use of them, because they represent the best level of measurement for the more sophisticated statistical analyses. There are several ways you can evaluate a relationship between interval/ratio variables.

Scatterplots.   Although you are not likely to put interval/ratio variables into cross-tabulations when there is a large number of values for each variable, you can visually assess the relationship with a graph. Most common are *scatterplots*. As with frequency polygons for univariate data, scatterplots assume interval/ratio measures. The horizontal x-axis is usually for the values of the independent variable, and the vertical y-axis for the units of the dependent variable. A mark is placed at the point where each surveyed person's responses to the two variables intersect, not unlike the idea of a cell in a contingency table for nominal and ordinal variables. When all the responses are plotted, a pattern emerges.

If it looks as if the points are scattered everywhere in the graph with no apparent pattern, it is signifying no relationship, that is, an association close to 0.0 coefficient. If the points tend to fall along an almost straight line, then there is a perfect relationship close to 1.0. If it looks like an uphill line, then it's a positive linear relationship; if it looks like a downhill line, it's a negative/inverse linear one. If the points tend to form a curve, then it's called a curvilinear relationship.

Take for example the relationship between height and weight. Usually, taller people weigh more, and shorter people weigh less. But as we all know, this is not a perfect guide; there are many short heavy people and tall thin people. We would expect then a scatterplot that looks like an uphill slope, but not all the points would fall in a perfect straight line.

As you can see from the scatterplot in Figure 7.2, there is a tendency for those who are shorter (the x-axis marks the height in inches) to be lighter in weight (the y-axis marks the weight in pounds). Each point on the chart represents one person's height and weight. If you were to draw an exact straight line from any point to the x-axis you would find out the height for that respondent, and a line from the same point to the y-axis would indicate the weight. Notice that there are some *outliers*, that is, respondents who fall beyond an imaginary straight line that could be drawn through the middle of the points. For example, there appears to be three people around 60 inches tall but one of the points is closer to 175 pounds or so on the y-axis. That person's data falls outside the general pattern.

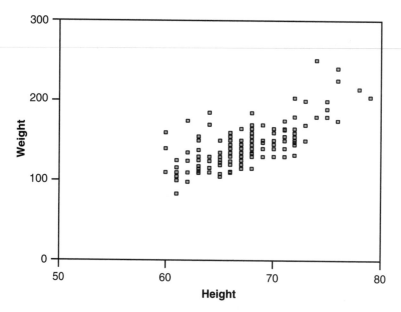

FIGURE 7.2   **Example of a Scatterplot, SPSS.**

Pearson r.   Although scatterplots are not as precise as a table of numbers, they do provide a rough indication of the kind of relationship that exists between two variables. However, for a more specific assessment of the magnitude (weak to strong) and direction of the relationship (positive or negative/inverse), *Pearson's product-moment correlation coefficient,* a symmetric statistic known simply as *Pearson r,* is calculated. Similar to the other coefficients discussed, it has two components: A number ranging anywhere from 0.0 to 1.0 to indicate strength, and a plus or minus sign to show direction. Like Gamma, Lambda, and Goodman and Kruskal's Tau, it is also a PRE measure, but like Spearman rho, it must be squared to establish the proportion of error reduction.

Pearson r is one of the most used statistics in social science research and central to path analysis, linear regression analysis, and other statistical methods. Its calculation is based on means, standard deviations, and z-scores. In order to compare variables with two different units of measurement, such as height and weight, respondents' answers are transformed into z-scores (as described in Chapter 6). What Pearson r does is measure how much change in the z-scores of one variable is related to change in the z-scores of the other variable. Is the variation from respondent A's z-score for height to that of respondent B's similar to the variation from respondent A's z-score for weight to respondent B's, and so on throughout the sample of respondents? Every change in an independent variable z-score (a standard

TABLE 7.7   Example of Pearson r Statistic for Interval/Ratio Variables, SPSS

		CORRELATIONS	
		Height	*Weight*
Height	Pearson Correlation	1	.714**
	Sig. (2-tailed)	.	.000
	N	151	149
Weight	Pearson Correlation	.714**	1
	Sig. (2-tailed)	.000	.
	N	149	150

**Correlation is significant at the 0.01 level

deviation unit) is related to a change in a dependent variable z-score. That is why it is called a correlation. If those changes vary at the same rate and with the same incremental units, then you have a perfect 1.0 correlation coefficient which looks like a straight line in a scatterplot, either going up if positive / or going down if it's a negative/inverse relationship \ .

The data correlating height and weight results in a Pearson r of .714 (Table 7.7.) For every change of one standard z-score unit in height (independent variable) there is a .714 standard unit change on the outcome or dependent variable (weight) in the same direction. Those who are taller tend to weigh more, and those who are shorter tend to weigh less. If it were an inverse relationship of −.714, then we would conclude that taller people weigh less and shorter people weigh more. The correlation does not tell you about any one person, so it is not accurate to say that any one short person weighs less. This is aggregated data and is only interpretable in terms of the entire sample, not in terms of one person at a time. Because the goal is to predict variation across the sample on the dependent variable, you can also say that you have reduced errors in predicting the weights of all respondents by 51 percent (r^2), knowing information about their heights.

The properties of this statistic also allow you to say it another way: You have determined 51 percent of the variation in weight (the dependent variable) through your knowledge of height (the independent variable). This is why r^2 is called the *coefficient of determination*. In this particular example, of all the variation that exists in your sample for weight (after all, not everyone is the same weight), you account for 51 percent of it with the respondents' heights. Height is only one cause or explanation or predictor, albeit a major one, of the outcome, namely weight. The remaining 49 percent of the variation (sometimes referred to as the *residual*) must be explained or predicted by other reasons such as genetics, food habits, and amount of exercise.

As with the other statistics, Pearson r has a sampling distribution and we can use it to ask what the probability of obtaining a particular coefficient is by chance alone. If the probability is less than .05, we reject the null hypothesis and declare there is a statistically significant association between the independent and dependent variables. However, when sample sizes are large, small coefficients tend to be statistically significant, and for this reason, many people look primarily to the strength of the relationship and not its significance level.

Eta.   Pearson r also requires that the relationship between your variables is linear, that is, it is not a curve. As one variable increases or decreases, so too does the other. An example of a nonlinear relationship might be age and muscle strength. As you grow older, you get stronger, but then after a certain age, your muscles get weaker. Strength does not continue to grow linearly as you get older. Pearson r would not be an adequate measure of the relationship between age and physical strength. It would be more appropriate to use *eta* (η) which is designed for nonlinear associations. It requires an interval/ratio dependent variable, and the independent variable should be in nominal or ordinal categories. When squared, eta is a PRE measure and can be interpreted similarly to r^2. So, if you find an eta of .50 between age and muscle strength, then you can say that you can reduce your errors in predicting physical strength by 25 percent knowing different categories of age such as younger people are stronger, older people are weaker.

The Purposes of Measuring Relationships

Remember that the main goals of doing research are to describe, explain, and predict. The objective is to account for the reasons why the dependent variable varies among the respondents in your study, to predict future occurrences, and simply to describe any relationships among your variables. Measures of association are a good way of evaluating these relationships, to see if they exist at all and, if so, how strong they are and in what direction they go. It also becomes necessary sometimes to elaborate on the original relationship, to control for alternative explanations, and to test for spurious relationships. Chapter 9 discusses how to elaborate your findings by introducing a third or control variable into the analyses.

When we analyze relationships and generate PRE information, we answer some of the research questions or hypotheses we began with, thereby contributing to theory building, to the assessment and evaluation of programs, and to descriptions of some social phenomena. However, sometimes we are interested in describing, explaining, or predicting differences among various categories of people and not just uncovering associations between variables. Ways of analyzing data for differences are discussed in the next chapter.

REVIEW: WHAT DO THESE KEY TERMS MEAN?

Bivariate analysis	Eta	Outliers
Cells	Gamma	Pearson r
Chi-square	Goodman and	PRE
Coefficient	Kruskal's Tau	Rows and columns
Coefficient of	Kendall's Tau-b and	Scatterplots
determination	Tau-c	Spearman's rho
Contingency tables	Lambda	Symmetric and
Cross-tabulations	Marginals	asymmetric
Degrees of Freedom		

INTERPRET: WHAT DO THESE REAL EXAMPLES TELL US?

1. Table 7.8 shows some SPSS output from the General Social Survey.
   a. Which is the strongest correlation in this matrix? Note that the table is symmetrical because the correlation of "Hours Watching TV" with "Highest Year of School Completed" is the same as "Highest Year of School Completed" with "Hours Watching TV" and that correlations of variables with themselves always equal a perfect 1.0 correlation.
   b. How would you put into words the relationship between these two variables of education and TV viewing? What does the minus sign tell you?

TABLE 7.8   Pearson r Correlations

		Highest Year of School Completed	Hours Per Day Watching TV	Age of Respondent
			CORRELATIONS	
Highest Year of School Completed	Pearson Correlation	1	−.225**	−.186**
	Sig. (2-tailed)	.	.000	.000
	N	1396	1380	1393
Hours per Day Watching TV	Pearson Correlation	−.225**	1	.098**
	Sig. (2-tailed)	.000	.	.000
	N	1380	1388	1385
Age of Respondent	Pearson Correlation	−.186**	.098**	1
	Sig. (2-tailed)	.000	.000	.
	N	1393	1385	1401

**Correlation is significant at the 0.01 level (2-tailed).

c. The correlation between age and hours viewing TV is statistically significant. Yet almost 1400 respondents answered these questions. How would you interpret this significance level in comparison to the strength of the correlation?

2. Hansen and Mitchell (2000) published results of their study on the political activity of Fortune 500 corporations. They compared companies which have political action committees (PAC) that make donations to election candidates with those that don't on several variables, including whether they engage in lobbying the government with consultants and how much they give in charitable contributions. Here are a few results (2000: 896):

TABLE (A)	NO PAC	PAC
No lobby	67%	25%
Lobby	33%	75%

$\chi^2 = 97.95$, df = 1, p < .001

TABLE (B)	NO PAC	PAC
No charity	80%	45%
Charity	20%	55%

$\chi^2 = 75.32$, df = 1, p < .001

a. State the hypothesis being tested in each of these tables.
b. Put into words what is going on in each of these two tables. How do you read the tables? For example, 67 percent of what is what, and so on.
c. What does the chi-square tell you? How was *df* determined? What does the *p* value mean?
d. What do you conclude?
e. Which other statistics could you use to assess the strength of the relationship?

CONSULT: WHAT COULD BE DONE?

You are hired to do a marketing research analysis for the local newspaper. The publishers want to find out which kinds of people read their paper, how often, and which sections and features are most read and liked.

1. Preliminary data analysis suggests that men and women read different sections of the paper. What would you do to see if this is statistically significant?

2. Frequency of reading the paper seems to vary based on such characteristics as income, educational level, age, and size of family. How would you statistically test each of these possible relationships (income and frequency of reading the paper, education and frequency, age and frequency, and size and frequency)?

3. What other relationships would you recommend be studied to provide the newspaper owners more information about readership?

DECIDE: WHAT DO YOU DO NEXT?

You are asked to do a study looking at the relationship between people's television viewing habits and their opinions about racial and ethnic issues and stereotyping, and their actions toward people from diverse backgrounds. Does TV viewing have an impact on their attitudes and behaviors toward diversity?

1. In order to construct a bivariate cross-tabulation evaluating the association between hours of watching TV and attitudes toward racial equality, what do you need to do first with these two variables if hours is measured using an interval/ratio item? What categories would you develop for both the independent and dependent variables?

2. Review your bivariate hypotheses and list the variables.

3. Describe the statistics you would use to evaluate the relationships and why you would use these.

4. If you have actual data, begin to analyze the hypotheses which are best suited for statistical measures of association and correlation.

CHAPTER EIGHT

ANALYZING DATA
COMPARING MEANS

LEARNING GOALS

This chapter shows you how to assess differences between means using t-tests and analysis of variance. As with other bivariate data analysis, knowing when to use these statistical procedures and how to interpret them is central to testing hypotheses. By the end of the chapter you should be able to understand what t-tests and ANOVA are and when they are suitable for data analysis.

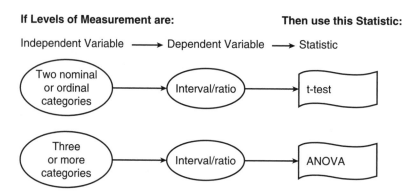

If Levels of Measurement are: **Then use this Statistic:**

Independent Variable ⟶ Dependent Variable ⟶ Statistic

FIGURE 8.1 Statistical Decision Steps.

Every day it seems people are making comparisons among groups of people. Women are from Venus, and men are from Mars, or something like that. Young people drive differently than the elderly; African Americans don't vote for the same candidates as whites; and certain cities have higher crime rates than others.

One of the fundamental questions asked in research is whether there are differences among respondents. All questionnaires ask demographic information that can provide useful ways of breaking the data into interesting comparison categories. For example, you might be interested in the differences in amount of television viewing among racial/ethnic groups, or comparisons between men and women in attitudes toward the death penalty.

If the data you want to compare are interval/ratio measures, or at least ordinal measures with equal-appearing intervals, then there are several basic statistical techniques that can be used to answer the question of meaningful differences. For example, if you wanted to compare the average number of hours studied per week between males and females, it is unlikely that the means would be identical for both men and women. Hence, the question is whether the difference that exists in hours studied between men and women is a statistically significant one, as opposed to just any difference that could easily occur by chance alone.

When seeking to evaluate differences in means, we can use two very important and popular statistics: the *t-test* and *analysis of variance (ANOVA)*.

T-TESTS

When what you want to know (the dependent variable) is a ratio/interval measure, an ordinal measure with equal-appearing intervals, or a dichotomy, and a mean and standard deviation can be calculated for two categories of comparison (usually values of the independent variable), you can select a *t-test* for data analysis. T-tests ask whether the difference between two means is significantly different from zero. If both means were identical, then their difference would be zero. When data come from a sample of respondents, you are technically asking whether the difference in the true means in the populations from which these samples are derived is zero. To put it another way, you are asking a null question: There is no difference between the two sample means; they are the same and are from the same population; hence, subtracting them to find the difference results in zero.

Remember you are comparing information that you collected from just one set of respondents. If all possible samples of a certain size were taken from the population and all possible differences in means between every two samples were calculated and plotted on a graph, the figure would approximate a normal distribution, as discussed in earlier chapters. Actually they would form a t-distribution, slightly different in shape from a perfect normal curve, or so "Student"—the *nom de plume* for W. S. Gosset, an employee in Ireland's Guinness brewery who developed the "Student's t"—realized.

What we are asking is the core question of statistical research in the social sciences: How much do our sample means deviate from the norm? Is the difference in means we found between two categories significantly different from zero, so that we would conclude the sample differences are on the outskirts of that t-distribution? Where on the distribution of all possible mean differences is our mean difference? If it is 1.96 standard deviation units away (actually called *the standard error of the differences between means* when discussing distributions of mean differences), then you can conclude that the results are significant at the .05 level using a two-tailed or two-directional hypothesis. If we wanted to see whether one of the means was significantly larger than the other, or conversely one was smaller than the other, we are asking a one-directional question, and we would see whether the mean difference was 2.58 units away from the norm of zero difference in order to be significant at the .05 level.

Let's take an example in which we want to learn if older or younger people watch more television. First, we have to create two categories in order to make the comparison suitable for a t-test, if there does not already exist a dichotomy as with male and female. In this case, what is probably an interval/ratio measure (age) needs to be made into a simple dichotomy by deciding what constitutes "younger" and "older." We can look at the frequency distribution and cut the sample at the median, so that half the respondents are now above the median (older) and half are below (younger). Or we can decide ahead of time, based on previous research or theory, and make forty or less the "younger" respondents and those forty-one and above the "older" people, even though we may not get a 50 percent split this way.

Now we have two groups and we can calculate the average number of hours each watches television in a typical week. Remember, the questionnaire item has to be written as an interval/ratio measure, or an ordinal one with equal-appearing intervals, so we can accurately generate a mean and standard deviation. We hypothesize that the difference in average number of hours watching TV between the younger and older people is zero and, since we have no preconceived idea about which group is more likely to be heavier viewers, we proceed with a two-directional t-test to assess the differences in means. We will definitely get some difference in means because it is unlikely the two groups watch exactly the same average number of hours of TV, but we want to know if that difference is *statistically significant.*

The computer calculates a t-test value and presents us with the significance level. If the probability of obtaining that t value by chance alone is less than .05, then we conclude that the category with the higher mean watches more TV on average than the group with the lower mean. The difference between these two means is declared to be significantly different from zero; that is, if we wrote a hypothesis in the null form, we would reject no difference between the two groups and hold a press conference to declare a significant finding. Rather than use the double negative of rejecting a null, we can more easily say that we are accepting a finding of difference between the two categories and then state which group watches more or less TV than the other.

Understanding T-Tests

When I was a kid, I often got frustrated when I did not reach the special line on the sign at the entrance to a really cool ride at the amusement park. I was too short to get on. I was sure I was shorter than everyone else in the world. But I guess I did not have it as bad as my sister and all her girlfriends who were shorter than I. After all, we all know that girls are shorter than boys! Let's take a look at this and see if indeed there is a significant difference between the average height of women and the average height of men in a survey of 151 college students.

Because height is an interval/ratio measure, you can calculate a mean and standard deviation for each category. And because you are comparing means between two groups, the t-test is the most appropriate statistic to use. You are testing to see if the difference between the two means is significantly different from zero. Let's just assume for the moment that you do not have any preconceived ideas about which group is taller or shorter. You are just interested in seeing if there is a difference and do not have any real interest in which group is taller or shorter. Therefore, you employ a two-directional test of significance.

Independent Samples T-Test

Because the two subsamples are independent of one another, that is, it is unlikely that someone selected both the female and male categories on the questionnaire item, we use the *independent samples t-test*. The first part of the SPSS output tells us that the average height of the ninety-seven women who answered the question is 65.39 inches (approximately 5′ 5″) and 70.72 inches (approximately 5′ 11″) for the fifty-four men. There definitely is a difference in height, but is it a statistically significant difference? What is the probability that this difference could have happened by chance and not be a result of real differences between men and women? Is five or six inches a meaningful difference given the way the sample of men and the sample of women are distributed, and the size of the samples? If the male and female samples each are widely dispersed, smaller differences will be less meaningful. If the distributions are closely dispersed, that is, a lower standard deviation, then a small difference will be much more meaningful.

The standard deviations in the first part of Table 8.1 tell us that the heights for the men in the study are more dispersed than those for the women (3.36 versus 2.94), and that the distribution of all possible means for men is wider than it is for women (the standard error of the means show that). The calculation of the t-value is affected by these distributions.

The SPSS output for independent samples includes the results of the calculations for two different t ratios, depending on which standard error formula is used in the denominator. To determine which t-test to look at, you first

TABLE 8.1 Example of Independent Samples t-test, SPSS

GROUP STATISTICS

	Gender	N	Mean	Std. Deviation	Std. Error Mean
Height	female	97	65.3918	2.9353	.2980
	male	54	70.7222	3.3614	.4574

INDEPENDENT SAMPLES TEST

	LEVENE'S TEST FOR EQUALITY OF VARIANCES		T-TEST FOR EQUALITY OF MEANS					95% CONFIDENCE INTERVAL OF THE MEAN	
	F	Sig.	t	df	Sig. (2-tailed)	Mean Difference	Std. Error Difference	Lower	Upper
Height Equal variances assumed	1.148	.286	-10.148	149	.000	-5.3305	.5252	-6.3684	-4.2946
Equal variances not assumed			-9.764	97.817	.000	-5.3305	.5459	-6.4139	-4.2470

■ ■ ■ ■ ■

BOX 8.1

EXPLAINING THE T-TEST

Just as we can tell how far away an individual score is from the group mean in terms of standard deviation units (that is, z is a score minus the mean divided by the standard deviation), so too t is a mean minus another mean divided by the standard error of the differences in means.

$$t = \frac{(\bar{x}_1 - \bar{x}_2) - (\mu_1 - \mu_2)}{s_{\bar{x}_1 - \bar{x}_2}}$$

In this formula, the two sample means are subtracted to find a difference, and the two population means are subtracted to find their difference. But because the null hypothesis is that the two population means are the same, the difference between them is zero. Hence, the second part of the numerator (where the μ are being subtracted) becomes zero and is not used in the calculations. The formula essentially is asking how different the difference in the two sample means is from zero, but all you need to know are the two sample means. It doesn't really matter what the real population means are since they are hypothesized to be the same, and therefore equal to zero when subtracted. Besides, if we knew what they were, we wouldn't be doing a sample survey in the first place!

The denominator is the *standard error of the differences between means* and it is calculated differently depending on whether the variances of the two samples are the same or different and whether the data come from paired samples and how correlated they are, that is, the same people measured twice. Advanced statistics books provide the formulas for the denominators. The main thing to remember is that the t is a ratio of the difference between two means (the numerator) divided by the standard error (the denominator).

When calculating the t value for the difference between a sample mean and some known population mean, the formula is similarly a ratio of the mean differences divided by the standard error or deviation:

$$t = \frac{\bar{X} - \mu_0}{s_x}$$

must take a side trip and look at the Levene F-test for Equality of Variance (hereafter called the F value). The second part of Table 8.1 shows whether the two variances (that is, the standard deviation squared) are equal to one another. If the F value calculated is significant ($p < .05$), then you conclude there is a difference and reject the null hypothesis of no difference in variances; equal variances are not assumed. If the significance level for the

F value is not significant ($p > .05$) then you accept the fact there is no difference and assume equal variances between the two categories. In the second part of the table, you can see that the significance level for the Levene F value is greater than .05 (it is .286), so you assume that the variance of height for our sample of men and the variance of height for women are approximately equal.

But you're not done yet. You just took a side trip and finished figuring out if there was a difference in *variances*. Now you have to decide if there is a difference in *means*. Note that there are two t values calculated: The one following the phrase "equal variances assumed" is –10.148 and the one following "equal variances not assumed" is –9.764. Because variances are assumed equal, you follow the t value in the first line and see that its significance level is less than .05. In fact, it is so small, it's below .000, so you don't see all the other digits, which could be something like .00059 for example. You can say that the probability of obtaining a t-value of 10.148, with samples of this size and with these standard deviations, by chance alone is less than one in a thousand ($p < .001$).

This is certainly good enough for you to hold a press conference and state that indeed men are taller than women in your sample. The difference between means is –5.33 inches. The minus signs are simply a function of which mean was subtracted first. Because the men's mean was subtracted from the women's, it results in a minus sign. If women's mean height were subtracted from the men's, then the result would still be 5.33 inches, but positive. The number is important for determining the significance level, not the minus or plus sign.

Confidence Interval.   If you were to draw one hundred samples of the size of the sample in Table 8.1, ninety-five of them would have a mean difference in heights somewhere between 4.29 and 6.37 inches; this is called the *confidence interval.* In other words, you are 95 percent confident that the true difference in mean heights between men and women in the population from which you drew this particular sample is within that range. Remember you are inferring population information based on what you found in one particular sample, so there is likely some error and a range within which the true information lies.

Paired Samples T-Test

This analysis was based on the assumption that the two categories being compared do not have any overlap: No one in the survey responded both "male" and "female" to the question. These are independent samples. Sometimes, however, you need to compare two means for the same sample of people. For example, you might want to compare the graduating seniors' average grades with their own first year grade averages. Or you might want to look at the before and after effects of a new diet plan and compare the subjects' weights when they first started the diet with their current weights.

■ ■ ■ ■ ■

BOX 8.2

T-TESTS IN ACADEMIC ARTICLES

In their study of academic employment for sociology graduates, Misra, Kennelly, and Karides (1999:233) analyzed whether there were any differences in the quality of undergraduate students and the support of graduate students in universities where men got academic jobs versus women, and where whites got jobs versus ethnic/racial minorities.

		MEAN	t	SIGNIFICANCE LEVEL
SAT scores of undergraduates				
In universities hiring:	men	1024.04	−1.20	.23
versus	women	997.38		
Number of graduate students				
In universities hiring:	men	35.19	−.53	.59
versus	women	42.22		
Percent graduates funded				
In universities hiring:	nonwhite	13.54	−.90	.36
versus	white	9.07		

For example, the SAT scores of the universities that hired men averaged 1024, while the universities hiring women averaged 997. Those departments hiring minorities funded 13.54 percent of their students on average, compared to 9.07 percent of grad students who were being funded by departments hiring whites. The authors concluded, based on the results of t-tests, that there were no significant differences in the quality of the undergraduate students, the gender diversity of grad students, and funding of grad students between the departments where men and women were hired, and where whites and nonwhite minorities got the jobs.

Because comparisons are being made for means (interval/ratio measures of SAT scores, number of graduate students, percent funded) between two categories of gender and between two categories of race/ethnicity, then independent sample t-tests are appropriate. Notice that none is statistically significant; the *p* levels are all above .05. It usually takes a t value of 2 or so to be statistically significant at the .05 level and all are below a value of 2. It's easy to remember: It takes "t for two" to be significant!

When you do this, you must also take into account that there is a connection or correlation between the two measures; after all, it is the same pool of people being studied at two different points in time. You need to use a t-test formula that assesses the difference in means while taking into account the correlation between the two measures. In such cases, we calculate a *paired samples t-test.* Consider the following two measures: Starting salary and current salary. (Table 8.2.)

TABLE 8.2 Example of Paired Samples t-test, SPSS

PAIRED SAMPLES STATISTICS

		Mean	N	Std. Deviation	Std. Error Mean
Pair 1	Current salary	34419.57	474	17075.66	784.31
	Beginning salary	17016.09	474	7870.64	361.51

PAIRED SAMPLES CORRELATIONS

		N	Correlation	Sig.
Pair 1	Current salary & Beginning salary	474	.880	.000

PAIRED SAMPLES TEST

		PAIRED DIFFERENCES							
					95% CONFIDENCE INTERVAL OF THE DIFFERENCE				
		Mean	Std. Deviation	Std. Error Mean	Lower	Upper	t	df	Sig. (2-tailed)
Pair 1	Current salary—Beginning salary	17403.48	10814.62	496.73	16427.41	18379.56	35.036	473	.000

The same 474 employees were sampled at two different periods of their employment. The average beginning salary was $17,016.09 and the average current salary is $34,419.57. Certainly there is a difference, but is it significant? Or should the employees complain more about their low salary increases using the null hypothesis that there is no significant difference between their current salary and what they started out with? Remember this is not about any one person's change in salary, but change in the *average* salary of all these 474 employees together.

According to the results of the SPSS analysis, the difference in average salaries of $17,403.48 is statistically significant. The probability of obtaining a t value of 35.036 by chance, with a standard error of the mean of 496.73 and 474 subjects, is less than .001. And we are 95 percent confident that the true difference between average beginning and current salaries in the population from which this sample is drawn is somewhere between $16,427.41 and $18,379.56.

One-Sample T-Test

There are also a few occasions in which we might want to compare a mean to some standard that already is known. For example, you wonder if the average grade of a group of students is really different from the average grade of all students at the university. In this case, you would calculate a *one-sample t-test*. (See Table 8.3.) In a survey of 151 undergraduates, the grade

TABLE 8.3 **Example of One-Sample t-test, SPSS**

ONE-SAMPLE STATISTICS				
	N	Mean	Std. Deviation	Std. Error Mean
GPA	150	3.1013	.4171	3.4E–02

ONE-SAMPLE TEST						
TEST VALUE = 2.95						
					95% CONFIDENCE INTERVAL OF THE DIFFERENCE	
	t	df	Sig. (2-tailed)	Mean Difference	Lower	Upper
GPA	4.444	149	.000	.1513	8.4E–02	.2186

point average is 3.10 (out of 4.0). According to the registrar's office, the average grade for the entire college is 2.95 so this number is entered as the one to compare with the sample average. But is that difference of .1513 grade units statistically significant? The probability of obtaining a t value of 4.44 by chance is less than .001 and is therefore statistically significant. You can conclude that the sample of 151 has a larger mean grade point average than the college as a whole. There's something special about this group—they must be sociology students!

ANALYSIS OF VARIANCE (ANOVA)

A good deal of the time we find ourselves wanting to compare more than two means at a time. For example, we might be interested in studying racial/ethnic differences in the amount of television viewing. When there are more than two categories for race/ethnicity, which is typically the case, we should use analysis of variance (ANOVA), a technique that asks whether the differences *within* a category are larger or smaller than those *between* (or, more grammatically, *among*) three or more categories. Like the t-test, ANOVA requires that the dependent variable be an interval/ratio, a dichotomy, or an ordinal measure with equal-appearing intervals, so that a mean and variance can be calculated. The categories of the independent variable (sometimes called a *factor* in ANOVA) should be mutually exclusive in order to perform a one-way ANOVA. When there are multiple factors or independent variables, and interactive effects among those factors need to be assessed, or there are repeated measures on the same sample to be compared, use more sophisticated versions of ANOVA as discussed in advanced statistic books.

Understanding ANOVA

ANOVA works by looking at the dispersion of scores around various means: The overall total dependent variable mean and the individual means for each of the categories of the main factor or independent variable. The computer program calculates an F value which, if significantly high enough, suggests that there is indeed a difference among the three or more means. In short, it tells you that the independent variable or factor has some effect on the dependent or outcome variable.

Consider the example in Table 8.4: Your hunch is that students in different years of college have different grade point averages. Everyone likes to think that their class is smarter than the others! Because grade point average is an interval/ratio measure, you calculate a mean and standard deviation for students in each level of college. As can be seen, there is some difference,

TABLE 8.4   **Example of Analysis of Variance, SPSS**

DESCRIPTIVES		
GPA	Mean	Std. Deviation
1.00 Freshmen	3.0714	.53763
2.00 Sophomores	2.9130	.46251
3.00 Juniors	3.1361	.40867
4.00 Seniors	3.1424	.38201
Total	3.1013	.41708

ANOVA					
GPA	Sum of Squares	df	Mean Square	F	Sig.
Between Groups	.995	3	.332	1.942	.125
Within Groups	24.925	146	.171		
Total	25.920	149			

but you need to be sure that the difference is not one that could have occurred merely by chance alone more than five times out of every hundred samples (p > .05). If it is, then those differences are not statistically significant and we accept the null hypothesis of no difference.

The first part of the ANOVA output is descriptive data that show that seniors have higher GPAs (3.14) than others and higher than the overall average for all 151 students answering the questions (3.10). Staying in college must make you smarter. But you clearly can't make any causal conclusions until you can first demonstrate that there is a relationship and rule out alternative explanations (those with lower grades were kicked out). Since you are comparing means for more than two categories of the main factor (four levels of the independent variable are measured), you use ANOVA which calculates an F ratio comparing the variation between the four categories relative to the variation within categories.

According to the second part of the table, the F value of 1.942 is not significant at .125 which is greater than the minimum .05 we require for statistical significance. Therefore, we accept the null hypothesis of no difference and conclude that students' average grades cannot be attributed simply to what year of college they are in.

As a rule of thumb, if the Between Groups variation is the same as the Within Groups variation (a null hypothesis of no difference), then the F statistic will be 1, since dividing a number by itself always results in one. In

■ ■ ■ ■ ■

BOX 8.3

EXPLAINING THE F-TEST FORMULA

The F is based on a formula that breaks down the *total sum of squares* (which is the sum of squaring each score subtracted from the overall mean) into the *within groups sum of squares* and the *between group sum of squares*. Within groups sum of squares is calculated by taking each score, subtracting its category (or subsample) mean from it, squaring the difference, and summing those numbers:

$$\sum_{i=1}^{k}\left[\sum_{j=1}^{n_i}(X_{ij} - \overline{X}_i)^2\right]$$

Or it can be calculated by subtracting the between sum of squares from the total sum of squares:

$$SS_W = SS_{tot} - SS_B$$

The between groups sum involves subtracting the overall mean from each category or group mean squaring the difference, and summing those numbers:

$$SS_B = \sum N_i(\overline{X}_i - \overline{X}_{tot})^2$$

The total sum of squares formula is:

$$SS_{tot} = \sum x_{tot}^2 - \frac{(\sum_{tot})^2}{N}$$

The F value is the ratio of the between group variation (the between group sum of squares divided by the *df*, or what is called the *mean squares*) to the within group variation (the within group sum of squares divided by the *df*):

$$F = \frac{ms_{Between}}{ms_{Within}}$$

Using the GPA example in Table 8.4, the F is not statistically significant because the variation (between group mean squares of .332 which comes from dividing the between sum of squares, .995, by 3, the *df*) of the category means (3.07 for first-year students, 2.91 for sophomores, etc.) from the overall mean (3.10) is not larger than the variation (within group) of the first-year students' GPAs from their category mean of 3.07, plus the variation of the sophomores' GPAs from their group's mean of 2.91, and so on.

this situation, there is no influence of the independent variable categories on the dependent variable. The larger the ratio is, the more likely it will be statistically significant. However, it is not a measure of strength like a Pearson r correlation, so the size of F does not tell you much. More variation among the three or more groups in comparison to the variation within the groups results in an F increasingly larger than one and likely to be statistically significant. In words, the independent variable categories make a difference in understanding the dependent variable when the between group variation is larger than the within group one.

Like the Levene F test for equality of variance used in the independent samples t-test, ANOVA involves analyzing (the "AN" of ANOVA) whether the two variances (the between and within ones, the "VA" of ANOVA) are equal or not. If the probability of obtaining that F by chance is less than .05, we conclude that there is a significant difference in variances; we reject the null of no difference and agree that the between group variance is larger. We then state that this is due to at least two of the categories having very different means from each other, because the original formula calculated how much these means differed from the overall mean. And that is why something called an analysis of *variance* is used to understand the difference among three or more *means*!

DIFFERENCES NOT STRENGTH

With both the t-test and the F-test, we learn about the differences between means among several subgroups or samples. These are alternative ways of providing information about the relationship between an independent and dependent variable. They do not tell us, like Pearson r, what the strength of the relationship is, or how much variance is explained in the dependent variable by the independent as PRE statistics do. Many researchers make use of several statistical techniques at the same time to gather as much information as they need about their hypothesized relationships. It is not unusual then to see a study employing crosstabs, correlation coefficients, and differences in means tests for the same research questions and hypotheses. Each provides alternative insights about the relationships. Your job as a researcher is to make the decisions about which statistics best assist you in answering your questions and learning what the statistics differently contribute to your understanding of the relationships.

We turn our attention in the next chapter to what happens when we want to analyze three or more variables at the same time. Social reality is such that behavior and attitudes are rarely explained by simple bivariate relationships. We often need to look at more complex relationships among multiple variables.

REVIEW: WHAT DO THESE KEY TERMS MEAN?

ANOVA	Independent samples	Paired samples t-test
Between Group and	t-test	Standard error of the
Within Group	Levene's F for	difference between
variances	equality of variance	means
Confidence interval	One-sample t-test	t-tests

INTERPRET: WHAT DO THESE REAL EXAMPLES TELL US?

1. Many times researchers want to describe their respondents before doing more complex data analysis. One way of seeing if there are any significant differences in subgroups is to use statistics that analyze differences in means. Here are some findings from Aiba and Wharton's (2001: 79) study of the pay gap between men and women in a Japanese company:

	MALES	FEMALES	T VALUE
Age	36.54	31.95	5.164 ***
Years of education	13.16	12.57	2.413 *
Days required on the job training	235	158	4.604 ***

*** $p < =.001$

a. Why is a t-test used for these data?
b. State the null hypothesis for this study and explain the significance levels and their relationship to the t values in terms of the null hypothesis.
c. Put into words what these findings suggest.

2. Xiao (2000) investigated child-rearing patterns and their relationship to social class in urban China. Specifically, she was interested in the valuation of autonomy (independence, imagination, determination) and conformity (obedience, hard work, thrift/saving) among five different social class levels from the highest level to the lowest ones (cadres: major decision-makers; professionals: skills like teachers, accountants; supervisors: administrative personnel; nonmanual: white-collar workers; and manual: blue-collar jobs). Respondents were asked to select the characteristics they believe children should be learning at home. Based on a scale of 0 to 3, where high scores represent high conformity and high autonomy, here are the findings (2001: 462):

	CADRE	PROFES-SIONAL	SUPER-VISOR	NON-MANUAL	MANUAL	F VALUE
Autonomy	1.65	1.62	1.24	1.73	1.57	11.91 ***
Conformity	1.09	1.24	1.59	1.17	1.30	11.68 ***

*** $p < .001$, df = 4, N = 984

   a. Why is ANOVA (F value) calculated for these data?

   b. State the null hypotheses for this study and explain the significance levels and their relationship to the F values in terms of the null hypothesis.

   c. Put into words what these findings suggest.

CONSULT: WHAT COULD BE DONE?

1. You've been asked by the university's financial aid office to compare the cost of textbooks used in five different majors: sociology, psychology, biology, history, and women's studies. Explain the steps you would take to do this and what statistic you would use to help you make a conclusion.

2. You've been asked by the Human Resources office at a company to assist in resolving a rumor going around the workplace. It seems that people believe that higher-educated employees are getting larger salaries than less educated ones. Describe what research you would do and the statistical procedures you would use to gather information to address the rumor.

DECIDE: WHAT DO YOU DO NEXT?

You are asked to do a study looking at the relationship between people's television viewing habits and their opinions about racial and ethnic issues and stereotyping, and their actions toward people from diverse backgrounds. Does TV viewing have an impact on their attitudes and behaviors toward diversity?

1. Look over your hypotheses and list the ones which could be assessed using a t-test. If none, develop a research question that uses t-tests. What would the independent variable look like and what information would you need for the dependent?

2. Look over your hypotheses and list the ones which could be assessed using ANOVA. If none, develop a research question that uses ANOVA. What would the independent variable look like and what information would you need for the dependent variable?

3. If you have actual data from a survey, develop a few hypotheses suitable to analyze with at least one t-test and one ANOVA. Interpret the results and put into words what you have discovered.

CHAPTER NINE

ANALYZING DATA
MULTIPLE VARIABLES

LEARNING GOALS

This chapter focuses on the analysis of three or more variables to answer more complex research questions. It discusses when to use various kinds of multivariate analyses and how to elaborate your findings with additional variables. By the end of the chapter you should be able to interpret multiple regression analyses and perform elaboration techniques with control variables.

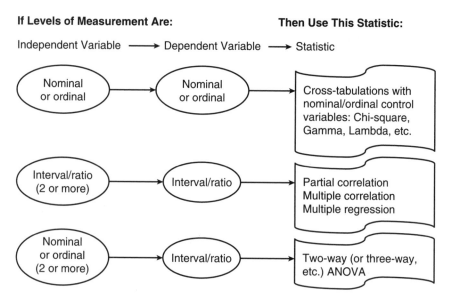

FIGURE 9.1   Statistical Decision Steps.

Although it may be tempting to try to understand people's behavior and opinions with just one simple explanation or cause, in reality there are probably multiple reasons for those beliefs and actions. If, for example, you are trying to understand why students' grades vary, the number of hours studying is probably just one reasonable answer. What else might explain differences in grades? Quality of the instructor, test-taking abilities, physical and mental health of the people at the time of doing the required work or test, difficulty of an assignment, basic intelligence levels, and the party the night before are all plausible alternative explanations.

One of the goals of research is to evaluate multiple explanations or predictors of some dependent variable or outcome. Sometimes it is also necessary to verify that the relationships we have uncovered withstand alternative explanations, or are consistent for a variety of subgroups in the sample. Unless the elimination of other variables that could possibly explain the main relationship occurs, we have not established cause and effect. Recall the three elements discussed in Chapter 1 that are essential to declaring causality. Most advanced methods books describe in greater depth the techniques that can be used to do multivariate statistics, but for our purposes, this chapter focuses on some basic techniques and concepts that are helpful when analyzing data for the first time.

ELABORATING RELATIONSHIPS: CONTROL VARIABLES

A typical question is whether the relationships you have discovered are strong enough to withstand other plausible explanations. What we need to do is something called *elaboration,* which extends our knowledge about the association to see if it continues or changes under different situations (see Rosenberg 1968). Researchers who use experimental designs use a control group as a means of verifying the results that occurred in the experimental group. Similarly, those of us doing survey research can control for other variables during the data analysis phase.

Consider an association you found that was statistically significant between respondents' educational level and yearly family income (Table 9.1). Let's first take the case where these variables are ordinal measurements— education: less than high school, high school graduate, and so on; income: under $25,000, $25,000 to $39,999, and so on. Minimally, a chi-square can be calculated for this cross-tabulation of data, along with some other statistics appropriate for ordinal measures, such as Gamma or Kendall's Tau-c. Perhaps you know, though, that women earn less than men and you wonder if educational level remains as good a predictor of total family income for

TABLE 9.1   Cross-tabulation of Income and Education, SPSS

TOTAL FAMILY INCOME BY RS HIGHEST DEGREE CROSS-TABLUATION

			RS HIGHEST DEGREE					
			Less than HS	High School	Junior College	Bachelor	Graduate	Total
Total Family Income	24,999 or less	Count	196	315	25	39	9	584
		% of RS Highest Degree	70.3%	40.4%	27.8%	16.7%	8.0%	39.0%
	25,000 to 39,999	Count	28	175	21	58	18	300
		% of RS Highest Degree	10.0%	22.4%	23.3%	24.8%	15.9%	20.1%
	40,000 to 59,999	Count	16	121	23	52	18	230
		% of RS Highest Degree	5.7%	15.5%	25.6%	22.2%	15.9%	15.4%
	60,000 or more	Count	39	169	21	85	68	382
		% of RS Highest Degree	14.0%	21.7%	23.3%	36.3%	60.2%	25.5%
Total		Count	279	780	90	234	113	1496
		% of RS Highest Degree	100.0%	100.0%	100.0%	100.0%	100.0%	100.0%

CHI-SQUARE TESTS

	Value	df	Asymp. Sig. (2-tailed)
Pearson Chi-Square	264.299[a]	12	.000
N of Valid Cases	1496		

[a]0 cells (.0%) have expected count less than 5. The minimum expected count is 13.84.

SYMMETRIC MEASURES

		Value	Approx. Sig.
Ordinal Measures	Kendall's Tau-c	.295	.000
	Gamma	.457	.000
N of Valid Cases		1496	

women. The question is whether the relationship is still statistically significant when *controlling* for sex of the respondent; that is, does it still apply equally to men and women? Sex becomes the test or control variable used to elaborate the original relationship between education and income.

As the chi-square and gamma indicate, there is a significant relationship and those with less education tend to be in households with less family income: 70.3 percent of those with less than a high school degree earn under $25,000 yearly, compared with 60.2 percent of those with a graduate degree who earn over $60,000 a year. Now let's see how well this relationship holds up when introducing a third variable: Respondent's sex, which has two categories or values, male and female. (See Table 9.2.)

Partialling

Two tables are developed, one showing the relationship between education and family income for males and one for females, along with two sets of chi-squares and gammas. There are now three variables involved in the multivariate analysis. When you introduce a control variable it is referred to as first-order *partialling*. You can continue to add multiple variables, called second-order, third-order, and so on, for more elaborate models, but interpretation can get complex at that point especially if each of those variables has numerous values or categories. The original bivariate association is the *zero-order* relationship.

Notice in the new partial tables that all the statistics remain significant, and the ordinal measures of strength (Gamma and Kendall's Tau-c) are about the same, although slightly stronger for men. You have replicated your original finding and can now conclude that there is a strong relationship between education and income, because it holds up even when controlling for sex. It is unlikely that being male or female directly affects total family income level; education appears more important. For example, 65.6 percent of men with less than a high school education tend to have under $25,000 a year in total family income; 74 percent of women with less than a high school education earn under $25,000 a year. This pattern is replicated across the other education and income categories. You now might want to test the original zero-order relationship again with a new control variable to see if it is sustained for other conditions.

Spurious and Antecedent Relationships

What would it mean when you introduced a third control variable and the relationship did not hold up? If the original relationship disappears or becomes less strong—it is neither statistically significant for the men nor the women, or the correlation coefficients decline substantially—you would claim the original relationship was *spurious*. You would verify this

TABLE 9.2 Cross-Tabulation of Income and Education, Controlling for Sex, SPSS

TOTAL FAMILY INCOME BY HIGHEST DEGREE
BY RESPONDENT'S SEX CROSS-TABULATION

Respondent's Sex				Less than HS	High School	Junior College	Bachelor	Graduate	Total
						HIGHEST DEGREE			
Male	Total Family Income	24,999 or less	Count	82	109	11	17	5	224
			% of Highest Degree	65.6%	35.9%	29.7%	15.7%	7.5%	34.9%
		25,000 to 39,999	Count	22	78	6	26	11	143
			% of Highest Degree	17.6%	25.7%	16.2%	24.1%	16.4%	22.3%
		40,000 to 59,999	Count	9	62	10	27	10	118
			% of Highest Degree	7.2%	20.4%	27.0%	25.0%	14.9%	18.4%
		60,000 or more	Count	12	55	10	38	41	156
			% of Highest Degree	9.6%	18.1%	27.0%	35.2%	61.2%	24.3%
	Total		Count	125	304	37	108	67	641
			% of Highest Degree	100.0%	100.0%	100.0%	100.0%	100.0%	100.0%
Female	Total Family Income	24,999 or less	Count	114	206	14	22	4	360
			% of Highest Degree	74.0%	43.3%	26.4%	17.5%	8.7%	42.1%
		25,000 to 39,999	Count	6	97	15	32	7	157
			% of Highest Degree	3.9%	20.4%	28.3%	25.4%	15.2%	18.4%
		40,000 to 59,999	Count	7	59	13	25	8	112
			% of Highest Degree	4.5%	12.4%	24.5%	19.8%	17.4%	13.1%
		60,000 or more	Count	27	114	11	47	27	226
			% of Highest Degree	17.5%	23.9%	20.8%	37.3%	58.7%	26.4%
	Total		Count	154	476	53	126	46	855
			% of Highest Degree	100.0%	100.0%	100.0%	100.0%	100.0%	100.0%

CHI-SQUARE TESTS

Respondent's Sex		Value	df	Asymp. Sig. (2-tailed)
Male	Pearson Chi-Square	136.855	12	.000
	N of Valid Cases	641		
Female	Pearson Chi-Square	145.194	12	.000
	N of Valid Cases	855		

SYMMETRIC MEASURES

Respondent's Sex			Value	Approx. Sig.
Male	Ordinal Measures	Kendall's Tau-c	.341	.000
		Gamma	.491	.000
	N of Valid Cases		641	
Female	Ordinal Measures	Kendall's Tau-c	.261	.000
		Gamma	.433	.000
	N of Valid Cases		855	

by creating a cross-tabulation for sex and education and another one for sex and income and see if indeed sex was *antecedent* to or came before the dependent variable of income, and if sex explained the dependent variable of education. If so, then the original relationship had the illusion of an association only because the independent and dependent variables were both related to a third antecedent variable for which you controlled.

Here is a classic example of a spurious relationship: The number of fire engines that show up at a fire (independent variable) is significantly related to the amount/costs of the fire damage (dependent variable). In other words, you might conclude that if only one or two fire trucks appeared, the damage would have been less. Here you can see the problem of making a cause and effect conclusion based on just a significant correlation. Clearly there is need for an alternative explanation, and perhaps size of the fire is one such control or test variable. Sure enough, the original relationship disappears when you demonstrate that fire size (independent variable) is highly correlated to the number of fire trucks that are called (dependent) and that fire size (independent) is highly related to the amount of damage (dependent). Fire size is the more direct reason for the amount of damage, not the number of fire engines!

Specification

Sometimes when you control for a third variable, you notice that the original relationship disappears only for some of the values of the test variable. Let's say that an elaboration of the education and income model showed that the original relationship applied only to the men in the sample, but not to the women. You would notice this by seeing that the statistical tests remained significant for the men, but were no longer statistically significant for the women or they were weakened. In such cases, you have *specification* because you determined very specific situations in which the relationship holds and those in which it does not.

Suppressing Relationships

Elaboration is also useful when you find no relationship or a very weak one between your independent and dependent variables. Don't give up and think that you found little. Elaborate on this nonfinding and introduce a control variable to see if for some reason this is *suppressing* or holding back the original zero-order relationship. Imagine we found a weak relationship between parents' educational level and respondents' income, despite reports about greater income for those growing up in higher educated families. So you introduce respondents' education as a test variable and see if the weak relationship between parents' education and income continues for each level of respondents' education.

Intervening Variables

Now imagine that you find that a strong relationship occurs within each level of respondents' education. In other words, for those with less than high school education, there is now a strong relationship between parents' education and income; among those who are high school graduates, there is also a strong relationship between parents' education and income, and so on. What you have shown is that respondents' education was suppressing the original relationship because it intervenes between parents' educational level and income. Respondent's education is an *intervening* variable that was mediating and keeping the original relationship weak, since parents' education is only an indirect influence on respondents' income. Parents' education is highly correlated with respondents' education, which in turn predicts income.

Partial Correlations

When variables are interval/ratio measures, controlling for a test variable can be done using partial Pearson r correlation (partial tau and partial gamma are also available for ordinal measures). A *partial correlation* takes into account the relationship between X and Y when the control variable Z is introduced. It calculates the Pearson r correlation between X and Y, X and Z, and Y and Z, and then recalculates the original zero-order relationship between X and Y after the effect of Z has been partially removed. For example, a Pearson r correlation of .084 was calculated for seniority on the job and current salary. That very low coefficient seemed to indicate that there was no statistically significant relationship between these two variables, somewhat counterintuitive to what you might think. After all, the longer people work someplace, the more raises they get and their salaries increase.

However, it's also possible that those who worked at the company the longest, started at lower salaries than those who began more recently, given the realities of inflation. Starting salary might be an antecedent variable that could elaborate on the original relationship found. So, a partial correlation was calculated, removing the relationship between starting salary and current salary, and sure enough the original relationship increases to .214 (Table 9.3). Starting salary (the control variable Z) was suppressing the original relationship between seniority and salary. Even though it is statistically significant, it remains somewhat low in strength, suggesting that there are other reasons besides seniority to explain current salary.

There are numerous ways to introduce additional variables for elaboration and to test various scenarios. For example, some categories of a political party control variable (such as "Independents") may be suppressing the original relationship, while other categories do not (such as "Democrats" and "Republicans"). Or an original relationship might be a strong positive one, but after controlling for a third variable, it becomes a strong negative one in some categories of the control variable but remains positive in the others. The important point to remember is that in order to establish any kind

TABLE 9.3   Example of Partial Correlation, SPSS

	CORRELATIONS		
			Seniority Months Since Hire
Current Salary	Pearson Correlation		.084
	Sig. (2-tailed)		.067
	N		474

Partial Correlation Coefficients
Controlling for . . . Beginning Salary

	Seniority
Current Salary	.2138
	P = .000

■ ■ ■ ■ ■

BOX 9.1

THE PROCESS OF ELABORATION

Zero-order relationship: X (independent variable) → Y (dependent variable)
First-order Partialling: Z (control/test variable with three values or categories)

1. Antecedent $Z → X → Y$ original relationship elaborated
2. Intervening $X → Z → Y$ relationship works through the test variable
3. Spurious $X → Y$ relationship is significant
   for Z (1), $X → Y$ relationship disappears/weakens
   for Z (2), $X → Y$ relationship disappears/weakens
   for Z (3), $X → Y$ relationship disappears/weakens
   because of antecedent $Z → X$
    $Z → Y$
4. Specification for Z (1), $X → Y$ relationship disappears/weakens
   for Z (2), $X → Y$ relationship remains (replicated)
   for Z (3), $X → Y$ relationship remains (replicated)
   or any other combination where the relationship disappears,
   remains the same (replicated), or is reversed, in some but not
   all of the categories of the test variable.
5. Suppressor $X → Y$ relationship is weak or none
   for Z (1), $X → Y$ relationship appears
   for Z (2), $X → Y$ relationship appears
   for Z (3), $X → Y$ relationship appears because the control
   variable weakened or suppressed the original relationship.

of cause and effect relationship you must be able to rule out alternative plausible explanations; the process of elaboration is a good way of doing this, and a good way of uncovering other kinds of relationships among your variables.

MULTIPLE RELATIONSHIPS

Using control variables is one kind of multivariate analysis, primarily focused on providing more elaborate understanding of initial relationships. Another important type is an analysis of additional independent variables that might contribute to a better and more complete understanding of the dependent variable or outcome. When these variables are interval/ratio measures or ordinal measures with equal-appearing intervals—instead of the nominal and ordinal ones better suited for cross-tabulations and the elaboration analyses just described—then some fairly sophisticated statistical procedures can be used.

Two-Way ANOVA

Let's say you are interested in the differences in mean income among several racial/ethnic groups. As you recall, when comparing means among three or more nominal or ordinal categories, use one-way analysis of variance (ANOVA). If the probability of obtaining the F value is less than .05, you declare that a relationship exists between race/ethnicity and income and specify which groups obtain higher average salaries. Yet, this seems too simple an explanation, so you introduce a third variable.

You could control for sex by rerunning the ANOVA for men and then another one for women, but another technique would be to introduce sex as a third variable (sometimes called a factor or covariate) and perform a *two-way analysis of variance*, or three-way or more, depending on how many new factors are included. In addition, you might want to see if there is another factor affecting the outcome that is a result of the possible combined impact of the two (or more) independent variables, not just their individual effects. This is what's called an *interactive effect*. For example, race might affect income, and sex might also have a main effect on income, but the combined impact of race and sex might be even stronger. The computer calculates the F values for the main effects of each of the independent variables, in this example sex and race, along with the F value of any interactive effects, sex by race. It is interpretable similarly to the F calculated in a one-way ANOVA. If F is statistically significant, the ANOVA would suggest that, for example, women of color receive lower salaries than white women, and so on. Details for doing multivariate and factorial ANOVA are available in advanced statistic books.

Multiple R

Another very common multivariate technique is *multiple correlation*. This is based on the Pearson r correlation coefficient and essentially looks at the combined effects of two or more independent variables on the dependent variable. These variables should be interval/ratio measures, dichotomies, or ordinal measures with equal appearing intervals, and assume a linear relationship between the independent and dependent variable. Rather than partialling out the impact of a third variable to see what remains of the original relationship, multiple correlation includes the effects of a third or fourth, or more, variable on the dependent variable. It is represented as the capital letter R and, similar to r, is a PRE when squared. However, unlike bivariate r, multiple R cannot be negative because it represents the combined impact of two or more independent variables, so direction is not given by the coefficient.

What multiple R^2 tell us is the proportion of the variation in the dependent variable that can be explained by the combined effect of the independent variables. Let's say you found that current salary depends on three explanations: Starting salary, seniority, and age of employee. Each of these independent variables is correlated to current salary, but you want to know their combined impact. The result is not simply the addition of the bivariate Pearson r correlations for each of these variables and the dependent one, because some variables, like age and seniority for example, are correlated with one another and this overlap needs to be taken into account mathematically.

The computer calculates a very strong positive multiple R correlation coefficient of .897 and an R^2 of .805. This tells you that approximately 80.5 percent of the variation in current salaries in your sample is accounted for by a combination of starting salary, seniority, and age. Which ones contribute more or less cannot be determined just by looking at the multiple correlation; however, as discussed later, there is a way of getting this information. R^2 also tells you that if you wanted to predict salaries, you would reduce your errors in predicting those figures by around 80 percent knowing three things: What the starting salaries were, how long the employees worked for the company, and ages of the workers.

Linear Multiple Regression

Uncovering which independent variables are contributing more or less to the explanations and predictions of the dependent variable is accomplished by a widely used technique called *linear regression*. It is based on the idea of a straight line that has the formula $Y = a + bX$, where

- Y is the value of the predicted dependent variable, sometimes called the criterion and in some formulas represented as Y' to indicate Y-predicted;
- X is the value of the independent variable or predictor;
- a is the constant or the value of Y when X is unknown, that is, zero; it is the point on the Y axis where the line crosses when X is zero; and
- b is the slope or angle of the line and, because not all the independent variables are contributing equally to explaining the dependent variable, b represents the unstandardized weight by which you adjust the value of X. For each unit of X, Y is predicted to go up or down by the amount of b.

The Regression Line.   Pearson r correlations and regressions assume linearity. If you were to construct a scatterplot, and the correlation was a perfect 1.0, then all the points representing a score on X and a score on Y would fall into a straight line. Most of the time, of course, a correlation is not perfect, so the points are more likely not to form a straight line. Therefore, through the scatterplot, a best-fitting line is drawn around which the points are the closest. This is similar to the idea of a mean being the point around which the scores in a distribution are the closest. This best-fitting line is called the *regression line*, which predicts the values of Y, the outcome variable, when you know the values of X, the independent variables. Linear regression analysis calculates the constant (a), the coefficient weights for each independent variable (b), and the overall multiple correlation (R). Preferably, low intercorrelations exist among the independent variables in order to find out the unique impact of each of the predictors. This is the formula for a multiple regression line:

$$Y' = a + bX_1 + bX_2 + bX_3 + bX_4 \cdots + bX_n$$

Methods for Entering Variables.   One method for generating a regression equation is to enter the independent variables in the order you believe—based on theory or prior research—they contribute to explaining the dependent variable. Another is to use what is termed *stepwise* multiple regression, which lets the computer enter the variables, either individually or in blocks or groups of variables, in the order of their correlation to the dependent variable. It selects the strongest predictor first, then the next, and so on, one at a time from the entire list of independent variables (or from within each block) until a variable is not statistically significant to enter the equation, usually set at the .05 level of significance. Another rule of thumb is to be sure that each new variable entered contributes at least one percent to the overall explanation of the variance of the dependent variable.

Beta Coefficients.   The result is an equation that can be used to predict values of the dependent variable. The information provided in the regression analysis includes the *b* coefficients for each of the independent variables and the overall multiple R correlation and its corresponding R^2. Assuming the variables are measured using different units as they typically are (such as pounds of weight, inches of height, or scores on a test), then the *b* weights are transformed into standardized units for comparison purposes. These are called Beta (β) coefficients or weights and essentially are interpreted like correlation coefficients: Those farthest away from zero are the strongest and the plus or minus sign indicates direction. If all the variables are measured in the same units, or if you are comparing a particular variable in one regression equation with the same one in another equation, then the unstandardized *b* coefficients are easily interpreted. With the Beta coefficients and the R^2 you have the most relevant information you need to arrive at some conclusions.

A multiple regression provides a description of possible influences on the dependent variable. It is a statistical technique designed especially for explanatory and predictive research hypotheses. Multiple regression is a robust statistical procedure that allows some flexibility in the kinds of variables used. Ideally your measures are interval/ratio ones that have a linear relationship between the independent and dependent variables. If not interval/ratio, then determine whether any ordinal measures have equal-appearing intervals (such as what typically occurs with Likert-type scales, or if income is in categories with equal ranges), or there are dichotomous variables with just two categories.

However, you cannot use nominal measures with three or more categories. Typically, you have to create dichotomous or *dummy variables* for nominal variables, such as religion. Because there is no order to the religions listed in your questionnaire, you might recode your data into Religious, Not Religious; or Protestant, Not Protestant; or Christian, Not Christian; or Jewish, Not Jewish; or any other possible dichotomy depending on the goals of your research. The same applies to such nominal demographic variables as race/ethnicity, sexual orientation, political party affiliation, and other variables with several nominal categories.

Let's hypothesize that there is a relationship between students' grades in college (CUM_GPA) and their high school grades (HS GPA), total scores on a standardized test (TOTSAT), and their participation in extracurricular activities (Extracurricular) where a score of 1 = high involvement and 3 = low involvement. This might be a model used to predict admission to a university where it is assumed that high grades, high test scores, and high involvement in activities represent the kind of well-rounded people an admission office would like to recruit to its university.

The first step is to decide how you want to enter the independent variables into the regression analysis. One method is to list them in the order you want them to be entered based on some theory or model. The order can make a difference: Given that high school grades and standardized test scores are likely correlated, if you enter high school grades first, then test scores will contribute less to the overall final prediction results. On the other hand, if you enter test scores first, then grades might get suppressed. Or you can let the computer program assist you by selecting stepwise method for entering the variables. With stepwise, the program calculates the unique contributions of the independent variables to the dependent variable and lists them according to their order of strength. Those that are not statistically significant, based on a t-test and alpha level of .05, are not entered. Think of it as requiring an ID to get into the party: If you are not of "strength," you have to stay outside!

Stepwise multiple regression is selected in Tables 9.4a–9.4d and the results are reported in several ways. Although more advanced statistic books go into details about all the components of a regression equation and output, for our purposes, the SPSS information most needed to interpret them is discussed here. The section numbered Table 9.4a is the overall summary of the regression model that has been calculated. Because it is stepwise, it presents the model in steps. Model 1 shows "HS GPA" entered first. Its correlation (R) with the dependent variable (footnote "a" reminds you what it is) is .400 signifying a moderate relationship. This one variable explains 16 percent of

TABLE 9.4   **Example of Multiple Regression, SPSS**

a	MODEL SUMMARY			
Model	R	R Square	Adjusted R Square	Std. Error of the Estimate
1	.400[a]	.160	.159	.56952
2	.425[b]	.180	.179	.56282
3	.440[c]	.194	.192	.55842

[a]Predictors: (Constant), HS GPA

[b]Predictors: (Constant), HS GPA, TOTSAT

[c]Predictors: (Constant), HS GPA, TOTSAT, Extracurricular

b		ANOVA[d]				
Model		Sum of Squares	df	Mean Square	F	Sig.
1	Regression	69.427	1	69.427	214.046	.000[a]
	Residual	364.579	1124	.324		
	Total	434.006	1125			
2	Regression	78.279	2	39.139	123.559	.000[b]
	Residual	355.727	1123	.317		
	Total	434.006	1125			
3	Regression	84.125	3	28.042	89.925	.000[c]
	Residual	349.881	1122	.312		
	Total	434.006	1125			

[a]Predictors: (Constant), HS GPA

[b]Predictors: (Constant), HS GPA, TOTSAT

[c]Predictors: (Constant), HS GPA, TOTSAT, Extracurricular

[d]Dependent Variable: CUM_GPA

(continued)

TABLE 9.4   CONTINUED

c						COEFFICIENTS[a]	
		UNSTANDARDIZZED COEFFICIENTS		STANDARDIZED COEFFICIENTS			
Model		B	Std. Error	Beta		t	Sig.
1	(Constant)	1.443	.108			13.420	.000
	HS GPA	.456	.031	.400		14.630	.000
2	(Constant)	.852	.154			5.526	.000
	HS GPA	.426	.031	.374		13.595	.000
	TOTSAT	6.042E–04	.000	.145		5.286	.000
3	(Constant)	1.410	.200			7.049	.000
	HS GPA	.362	.034	.317		10.499	.000
	TOTSAT	5.343E–04	.000	.128		4.665	.000
	Extracurricular	–.129	.030	–.131		–4.330	.000

[a]Dependent Variable: CUM_GPA

d			EXCLUDED VARIABLES[c]				
					Partial	COLLINEARITY STATISTICS	
Model		Beta in	t	Sig.	Correlation	Tolerance	
1	TOTSAT	.145[a]	5.286	.000	.156	.967	
	Extracurricular	–.151[a]	–4.991	.000	–.147	.796	
2	Extracurricular	–.131[b]	–4.330	.000	–.128	.780	

[a]Predictors in the Model: (Constant), HS GPA

[b]Predictors in the Model: (Constant), HS GPA, TOTSAT

[c]Dependent Variable: CUM_GPA

the variance in grades, according to R Square (R^2). It is also at this point the same as the simple Pearson r between high school grades and college grades.

Then the computer program looks for the second strongest predictor or independent variable. Model 2 finds "TOTSAT" and, as footnote "b" reminds you, at this step, it is high school grades and total SAT scores *combined* that correlate .425. R^2 tells you that 18 percent of the variance in college grades in this sample can be explained by respondents' high school grade point averages and total test scores, although including test scores only increased variance explained by 2 percent. This small increase in explanation likely occurred because grades and test scores are themselves related, thereby illustrating the partial effects of a new variable. If high school grades were not included in the list of independent variables, perhaps test scores would have correlated even higher with college grades.

The computer program keeps calculating and tries a third time and Model 3 shows the arrival of "Extracurricular" to the equation. Multiple R increases to .440 and over 19 percent of the explanation of college grades can be accounted for by these three variables together.

Table 9.4b tests the significance of the models that have been generated. Using ANOVA, an F value is calculated for the regression equation at each step. As can be seen, the final Model 3 is a statistically significant regression equation (p < .000). The footnotes also remind you of the dependent variable and the independent or predictor variables at each step.

By this point, the overall R^2 is known, but you still want to figure out how each of the independent variables is contributing to this R^2 in explaining or predicting the criterion or dependent variable. Each of them is not equally related or predictive of college grades, especially because there is some interrelationship among the independent variables themselves (called *multicollinearity*). The increase in R^2 at each step suggests that a good deal of the relationship is carried by the first variable, high school grade point average. Nonetheless, the other variables still contribute something, but they need to be given less value, or carry less weight. Because high school grades, test scores, and extracurricular participation are measured using different units (grades go from 0.0 to 4.0, combined test scores range from 400 to 1600, and extracurricular is measured on a 3-point scale from 1 to 3), the standardized Beta coefficients are used to compare the influence of each variable instead of *b*, the unstandardized ones.

Table 9.4c provides the Beta coefficients for all the independent variables entered at each step in the creation of the model, along with a t-test value and its significance level that tests whether the Beta coefficient is significantly different from zero. As the table shows, at step or model 3, high school GPA has a coefficient of .317, total SAT scores have .128, and extracurricular has a Beta weight of −.131. Similar to other correlation coefficients, the negative sign tells you that college grades and participation in extracurricular activities are inversely associated, in this case, those who score low on the extracurricular measure (that is, who circled 1 on the questionnaire and are highly involved in activities besides studying) are more likely to score higher on the college GPA measure. High school grades and test scores have positive relationships with college GPA.

In addition, Table 9.4d also shows you which variables have been excluded at each step and what their Beta weights would be *if* they are entered in the next step. Notice how at step one under Excluded Variables, the "Beta In" for TOTSAT is .145 and sure enough, at Model 2 of the

Coefficients table (Table 9.4c), it enters with a Beta weight of .145. Should there be some that never enter the models, as happens with stepwise technique, these would be listed at the last step under "Excluded Variables" with the Beta coefficients they would have had if they were entered into the model. Sometimes this information can tell you which variables may have been better predictors but were kept out of the model due to intercorrelation with the other variables.

Putting all the findings into words, this regression analysis tells you that around 19 percent of the variation in college grades among this sample of students can be explained by knowing their high school grades, SAT scores, and extracurricular involvement. Those in the sample who have higher grades in high school, have higher SAT scores, and are more involved in extracurricular activities tend to have higher college grade point averages. If SAT scores had a negative or inverse coefficient (which they don't), you would conclude that lower SAT scores are associated with higher college grades, and higher SATs are related to lower grades.

The actual equation for the regression line uses the b weights and looks like this: $Y' = 1.410 + (.362 \times X_1) + (.000534 \times X_2) - (.129 \times X_3)$, where Y' is the predicted college GPA (dependent variable), X_1 is high school GPA (independent variable 1), X_2 is total SAT scores (independent variable 2), and X_3 is the extracurricular involvement score (independent variable 3). Knowing nothing else, your predicted college GPA would be the value of the constant, 1.410, but your actual prediction is adjusted because you do have some information on the independent variables. High school GPA is giving you the stronger assistance in predicting college GPA, compared to both total SAT scores and extracurricular participation, but all three together help out in explaining something about why people get different grades in college. Assuming you are similar to the characteristics of the sample completing the questionnaires that led to the creation of this regression model, you could insert your high school grades, total SAT scores, and estimated participation in high school activities and calculate a predicted college grade point average for yourself.

Normally, you don't use a regression equation to calculate information about specific individuals, although many universities use such a model for admissions to predict success in college for individual applicants, and many businesses perform regression analyses to estimate future sales about a specific product. Regression analysis does not tell you about any one particular respondent, since the statistics are based on aggregated data. Mostly what you do with regression is construct a profile of characteristics related to the dependent variable from past data and use that to explain what already exists or to predict subsequent outcomes.

The regression does not tell you why any of the findings are so. You can't tell from this why participation in extracurricular activities improves your chances for higher grades in college. Unless you have other data from the questionnaire that can address this query, all you can do is offer some possible explanations based on theory or previous research. Or you can give some speculative interpretations and suggest that maybe those who are more involved in nonacademic pursuits are well-rounded people who exhibit commitment to, interest in, and curiosity about a wide range of issues. Perhaps curiosity and involvement translate into good study habits leading to better grades. Further research would investigate these new hypotheses and research questions, thus illustrating the continuous cycle of inductive and deductive social science research, as discussed in Chapter 1.

■ ■ ■ ■ ■

BOX 9.2

**MULTIPLE REGRESSION ANALYSIS
IN AN ACADEMIC ARTICLE**

Hibbing and Theiss-Morse (2001: 151) administered a survey assessing the public's preferences for governmental procedures, such as favoring direct democracy or wanting the government and its elected officials to make the decisions. In particular, they wanted to know which kinds of people were more likely to approve of the way the government has been doing its job and whether this was related to beliefs about the preferred process of making policy. Here are the results from a regression analysis; because all the variables were transformed into the same standardized units already, b coefficients are comparable, and Betas are not needed:

	b COEFFICIENT
Age	−.029
Income	−.030
Race	.037
Gender	−.005
Education	.017
Political Knowledge	.083 **
Party Identification	−.071 **
Personal Financial Condition	.045 *
Country's Financial Condition	.090 **
External Political Efficacy	.049
Perceived Policy Gap	−.160 **
Perceived Process Gap	−.095 **
$R^2 = .19$	

* $p < .05$; ** $p < .01$

The operationalizations for the significant independent variables are: "Political Knowledge" high scores demonstrate familiarity with current political information; "Party Identification" is coded 0 = Strong Democrat, to 6 = Strong Republican; "Personal Financial Condition" and "Country's Financial Condition" are

(continued)

BOX 9.2   CONTINUED

coded 1 = worse off, to 3 = better off than a year ago; "Perceived Policy Gap" is coded from 0, if the respondent believes government policy outputs perfectly match his/her preferences, to 6 if the respondent claims to be extremely liberal but sees federal policies as extremely conservative, or vice versa (in short a gap between the preferred and the actual); and "Perceived Process Gap" is similarly measured but focused on the political process of making policy with high scores indicating a gap between the preferred process and the actual process of making policy. The dependent measure, government approval, ranges from 1 = strongly disapprove the way the government is handling its job to 4 = strongly approve.

The authors (2001: 150) conclude that "the demographic variables are not particularly useful in specifying the kind of person likely to be dissatisfied with government. Among the political variables, the politically knowledgeable are more likely to approve of the federal government as are those who identify with the Democratic rather than the Republican party. . . . The policy gap variable has the expected negative sign and is highly significant. The farther governmental policies are from a person's own preferences, the less that person is satisfied with government. But do people only care about policies or do they also want these policies to be produced in a fashion they find acceptable? [The regression] offers a clear verdict. Process matters. . . . [A] process that matches a person's preferences for how the process should work increases approval of government. Apparently, people's approval of government is driven by more than just policy concerns. It is also driven by perceptions of the extent to which processes match what people desire processes to be."

Note how the authors interpreted these variables: A negative *b* coefficient for party identification, for example, means those who scored low on that measure (that is, 0 for Democrats), scored high on the government approval measure (that is, 4 for strongly approve), or vice versa (Republicans were more disapproving). Similarly, a positive coefficient for political knowledge means that those scoring higher on that measure (the more knowledgeable) score higher on the government approval item (strongly approve of government).

All together, though, these variables explain only 19 percent of the variation in approval/disapproval of the government. Clearly, other factors are important, but relative to each other, the significant variables in this model tell us part of the story and confirm the authors' ideas of the saliency of process in the production of government policies. Most respondents feel that elected officials have too much influence, and ordinary people have too little influence in making policy decisions. There is a gap between what people want and what they feel is actually happening, according to the results of this multiple regression analysis.

There are a variety of other widely used multivariate techniques, such as path analysis, factor analysis, MANOVA, and logit regression analysis, that are beyond the scope of this introductory book. But the underlying concept is similar: How do two or more independent variables work together in assisting you in making sense of the variation that exists in the dependent variable? How can we account for differences in the dependent variable knowing two or more independent variables? Similar to other statistical procedures, values are calculated and the probability of obtaining those values by chance are reported. If the odds are fairly small that chance played a role, then you are more confident in declaring results that deserve a press conference.

The research journey nears an end. You have completed data analysis and are now ready to put into words and tell others what you have discovered. How to interpret your findings and write a report is the focus of the last chapter.

REVIEW: WHAT DO THESE KEY TERMS MEAN?

Antecedent	Multiple correlation	Specification
Beta coefficients	Multiple regression	Spurious
Dummy variables	Partial correlation	Stepwise
Elaboration	Partialling	Suppression
Interactive effects	Regression line	Two-way ANOVA
Intervening	R square	Zero-order
Multicollinearity		

INTERPRET: WHAT DO THESE REAL EXAMPLES TELL US?

1. In their attempt to understand how some students perceive Asian Americans as the "model minority" who are more successful than others in achieving educational and occupational success, Wong, Lai, Nagasawa, and Lin (1998: 112) used multiple regression analysis. Here they wanted to explore the predictors of grade point average for a sample of Asian Americans:

	STANDARDIZED REGRESSION COEFFICIENTS (BETA)
Academically Prepared	.409 ***
Confidence to Finish Degree	.274 **
Employed Status	.057
$R^2 = .26$	

   ** $p < .01$, *** $p < .001$

"Employed Status" is measured as 1 = employed full-time, 2 = employed part-time, 3 = unemployed; and "Academically Prepared" and "Confidence" are measured from low to high scores.
   a. State the hypothesis being tested. Why is regression appropriate to use?
   b. What do the Beta coefficients and significance levels tell you?
   c. Explain R^2 and how it can be interpreted.
   d. Put into words what the study has discovered.

2. Consider the hypothesis that there is a relationship between sex of respondents and whether or not they graduate from college. Table 9.5 shows a cross-tabulation of sex and graduation for a sample of 555 students at a university.
   a. Put into words what the table says about the relationship between graduation rates and sex.
   b. What do the chi-square and significance level indicate?

   Yet, you feel there may be something else happening to explain graduation rates and wonder if introducing a control variable could elaborate your findings. Because other studies have shown that high school grades are a good predictor of college success, you control for them. Table 9.6 shows the results.
   c. Explain what each subtable says in words.
   d. What do the chi-square statistics tell you?
   e. What do you conclude about the control variable and the original relationship?

CONSULT: WHAT COULD BE DONE?

CNN calls you to be on one of its news shows to discuss the election results. The interviewer is planning to ask you about what seems to be a difference in the income of people who voted Democrat, Republican, or other parties. You are the expert and are going to be asked if this is so.

1. How can you be sure that income is related to political party choice? Describe the steps you would take to verify that relationship? What other variables might be relevant?

2. You will also be asked for whom people might vote the next time around. Just focusing on Democrat or Republican, what variables would you use and what would you do statistically to predict voting choice?

TABLE 9.5   Cross-Tabulation

GRADUATE BY SEX CROSS-TABULATION					
			SEX		
			F	*M*	*Total*
Graduate	No	Count	103	101	204
		% wthin SEX	32.2%	43.0%	36.8%
	Yes	Count	217	134	351
		% within SEX	67.8%	57.0%	63.2%
Total		Count	320	235	555
		% within SEX	100.0%	100.0%	100.0%

Chi-square = 6.79, df = 1, p = .009

TABLE 9.6   Cross-Tabulation of Graduate by Sex, Controlling for Grades

				SEX		
HS Grades				*F*	*M*	*Total*
B	Graduate	No	Count	43	59	102
or lower			% within SEX	40.2%	45.4%	43.0%
		Yes	Count	64	71	135
			% within SEX	59.8%	54.6%	57.0%
	Total		Count	107	130	237
			% within SEX	100.0%	100.0%	100.0%
B+	Graduate	No	Count	60	42	`102
or higher			% within SEX	28.2%	40.0%	32.1%
		Yes	Count	153	63	216
			% within SEX	71.8%	60.0%	67.9%
	Total		Count	213	105	318
			% within SEX	100.0%	100.0%	100.0%

For the HS grades B or lower subtable: chi-square = .647, df = 1, p = .421

For the HS grades B+ or higher subtable: chi-square = 4.518, df = 1, p = .034

DECIDE: WHAT DO YOU DO NEXT?

You are asked to do a study looking at the relationship between people's television viewing habits and their opinions about racial and ethnic issues and stereotyping, and their actions toward people from diverse backgrounds. Does TV viewing have an impact on their attitudes and behaviors toward diversity?

1. Suggest several test or control variables you could use to elaborate on the original relationship between hours watching television and attitudes toward racial equality. Be sure to include at least one antecedent and one intervening variable.

2. Look over your hypotheses and develop one to make it more suitable for a multiple regression. Which variables would you include? How would you recode any variables for a regression?

3. If you have actual data, run a regression, and interpret the results in words, Also, illustrate the process of elaboration and show you control for a third variable with a series of crosstabs.

CHAPTER TEN

PRESENTING RESULTS, MAKING CONCLUSIONS, AND WRITING REPORTS

LEARNING GOALS

In this final chapter, learning to write a report of the research project is emphasized, along with the key elements that go into a presentation of your study. Understanding the different audiences reading a report guides the preparation of the findings. By the end of the chapter, you should know the different styles for presenting your research and be able to put together a clear, concise report targeted to the relevant audience.

You've made it this far and now it's time to show off what you have accomplished. It all began with some idea, hunch, book or article you read, or maybe even an assignment at work or school. You managed to think up some fascinating research questions and hypotheses, operationalize your variables, and construct a reliable and valid questionnaire. Especially worthy was the sampling strategy you designed to generate representative respondents. You also demonstrated your skill in making decisions about levels of measurement and choosing the most relevant statistics to evaluate the research questions. After all this work, it's time to share it with others, and call a press conference to announce your major findings! But first, some important considerations must be kept in mind.

INTERPRETATIONS AND CONCLUSIONS

One of the key ideas to understand when doing survey research is that, although you uncover information with the best scientific methodologies you can employ, it is only one way of apprehending the world around you.

Just because you generated a random sample, used valid and reliable measurements, and incorporated the correct statistics does not guarantee in any way that what you discovered is therefore "the truth." However, you have at least used a more scientific way of achieving this information.

Limitations

It's important to remember that some data have not been uncovered, due to the scientific method you used. Some questions remain unanswered, and some information is out of reach. Perhaps qualitative field methods research would have resulted in additional findings, or even contradictory ones, and an experimental laboratory design could have arrived at a more detailed and concise explanation for your outcomes compared to what you discovered.

In other words, know the *limitations* of your methodology and be sensitive to them when interpreting your results and making conclusions. Most importantly, know that you have not "proven" anything, merely ruled out alternative explanations, or suggested relationships that seem more plausible than others. Knowledge accumulates incrementally and your contribution is but one step in that process, not the definitive answer to the topic you studied. Hence, avoid such phrases as "my findings prove . . . " or "my study conclusively answered all the questions about . . . " or "we found the answer to. . . ." It's much more accurate to say that "my findings suggest that . . . " or "it seems that in some cases . . . " or "for the sample of people I studied, we can conclude that. . . ."

Generalizing Findings

Of utmost importance is the question of *generalizability*. To which other groups or population can you conclude that what you found in your sample also applies? If you studied middle-level managers in a small organization in a medium-size town, can you safely state that the findings are also relevant to middle-level managers in other types of organizations in other kinds of localities? If the results were based on a sample of mostly white respondents, do they also apply to people of other races/ethnicities, or even whites of different educational or social class levels? A frequent problem in research is making conclusions about populations or subgroups that were not sampled appropriately. For most of the research we do, we can safely generalize only about those we actually surveyed or, at best, those similar to the people we studied.

Neutral Statistics?

People often say that statistics don't lie. Well, don't believe that lie (see Darrell Huff's 1954 and still reprinted classic *How to Lie with Statistics*). Sure, numbers are calculated without bias, but the numbers added and multiplied may have been chosen with intention. Perhaps, for some unethical reason, you decided to ignore the data from certain respondents and not others, or you legitimately eliminated extreme answers and only reported on the middle range of responses. Or maybe you inadvertently led the audience to a particular conclusion using such words as "only" or "very important" or "insignificant " and, in so doing, applied your biased interpretations on the "neutral" statistics.

Imagine you found that 10 percent of the high school sophomores used an illegal drug in the past month. The previous month 8 percent did so. That 2 percent change can also be presented as a 25 percent increase in drug use (25 percent of 8 percent is 2 percent). The headlines would say "Drug use is 25 percent higher than last month" when in fact it should also say that the starting point was 8 percent (see Glassner 1999 for many similar examples of how the media and many politicians misreport data). And what if you said that this month only 10 percent used drugs? The word "only" implies that either you expected more or that 10 percent is not a major issue. On the other hand, antidrug leaders could say that 10 percent is too high and would prefer saying "a disturbing" 10 percent of high school sophomores drank alcohol last month. So much for neutral statistics!

Using Hypotheses to Guide Interpretations

When making conclusions and summarizing findings, keep focused on what your research questions and hypotheses are. Sometimes researchers will write up their results and attempt to explain them using hunches or ideas that were not actually tested in the study. This could be done if the goal is to suggest further research and if the conclusions are written as speculative interpretations. It would not be unusual to say that "perhaps the reason those who studied more get higher grades is connected to the fact that they exhibit more motivation to succeed." But if you haven't included measures of "motivation to succeed" than you cannot say this as if it were discovered by you in your study. You should phrase interpretations in such a way that those reading your results know the interpretations are speculative, that you were unable to include variables to test them in your project, that you wished you had studied this topic further, and now you hope someone else will when the research is replicated.

Your summaries should always be in terms of the research questions and literature review you began the project with, and based on the data you actually collected. Certainly, you should not go back and rewrite your hypotheses based on what you have found after you collected the data. Although research does not go as linearly as described in most books like this one, it is not ethical to go back and change what you said you were going to do once you have already done it and arrived at your findings. However, it is good practice to develop new hypotheses and research questions when you uncover some fascinating findings that suggest additional research you can still incorporate in your project. Or perhaps you can adjust measurements and sampling, if you encounter problems along the way with the original design. In all such cases, you must report these modifications in detail in your report.

Cause and Effect Conclusions

Be careful of making conclusions of causality when all you have are measures of correlation without any sense of time sequence or having ruled out other plausible explanations. This is a very common error, even by professional researchers who occasionally imply causation when it was in fact never fully assessed. Often cross-sectional studies are used to suggest longitudinal changes or causation when the evidence is not actually there.

Unless you have data that demonstrate causation, you should conclude with findings focused on relationships and differences, and only speculate or hypothesize about cause and effect. In short, throughout the concluding interpretations, distinguish speculations from findings rooted in data. Remember to distinguish what you measured for descriptive or exploratory purposes, what you did for explanatory research, and what is being used for predictive purposes. Collecting data to describe relationships is not the same as collecting data for explanatory purposes.

For example, just because you report findings on gender and other information on salaries, does not mean there is a causal relationship between them. Let's say you found out that a particular company is 60 percent female and that the average wage is $60,000, compared to another company that is 40 percent female with an average wage of $70,000. You have merely described the organizations in terms of two variables, gender and salary. But to conclude that the percentage of employees that are female is the reason for the lower average has not been determined. You must do some additional data analysis that clarifies explanatory processes before you can make such a conclusion.

The Ethics of Reporting Results

In Chapter 2, the topic of ethics focused on the need to be forthright and up front about your project when recruiting subjects. Do no emotional or physical harm, and do allow for informed consent. However, the ethics of doing research don't end with the collection of data.

Data analysis, interpretation, and presentation of results each involve ethical issues as well. For example, if you recall from Chapter 6, when there is a skewed distribution, it's better to use a median than a mean when reporting a central tendency for the variable. Take income: Because few people earn millions of dollars, income is said to have a positive skew and if the few are included in the calculation of the mean, it could be distorted higher. Imagine a company reporting on the improvement of its employees' salaries by showing an increase in mean wages from one year to the next only to discover that it was just the executives who saw a dramatic increase in their earnings. If the median were used, the salary figures would likely have stayed about the same, because increasing the chief executive officer's salary from two million dollars to four million keeps the median the same, yet pulls the mean higher. Clearly, this is an unethical use of statistics.

What happens if you get findings that have major repercussions on public policy and people's lives? What are the ethical issues involved in reporting some of your findings and not others, especially those that may run counter to prevailing beliefs or to those of the sponsoring agency of your research? Writing up your report can have profound impact on people's opinions and behaviors, not to mention their faith in scientific research. How often have you heard that you can't believe what the polls say, yet they rarely have been wrong when done scientifically, as was shown in Chapter 5? How ethical is it for television stations or magazines to report the results of people who logged onto a web page survey or called in to vote in a phone poll without offering a disclaimer about the scientific accuracy of the research? What does this do, not only to people's sense of the quality of research, but also to their beliefs about the topic voted on?

Interpretations of findings should be informed, intelligent, creative, data-based, and ethical. They should not be speculative, selective, biased, and dishonest. Your conclusions should demonstrate a familiarity with the subject, theories, and prior research, and provide insights and ideas for future research projects.

AUDIENCES AND REPORTS

An important consideration in the preparation of a report is who will be reading it. This is a basic tip often given by people specializing in teaching good writing. Know your audience. If you visualize to whom you are addressing the remarks, writing ability improves. Any summary of what you have done will always contain some key pieces of information, especially about the methodology, but how it is stated and what elements need to be emphasized might vary depending on whether your audience is:

- the general public,
- a reader of an academic journal,
- a participant attending a presentation at a conference,
- a professor evaluating your thesis,
- an employer, or
- a funding agency.

Let's look at how the presentation of research findings might differ depending on the group to whom you are addressing your remarks.

The General Public

When communicating with the general public, avoid academic jargon from your field. There's nothing worse when describing the results of a project to lapse into concepts that carry very different meanings inside an academic discipline compared with what the public might understand them to mean. For example, someone might describe walking up to people on the street as "randomly" stopping them to ask for their participation in a survey. Or imagine reporting the results of a study on "anomie" and "cognitive dissonance" and failing to clarify those terms to a perplexed audience of non-social scientists. Too often we forget that the language we've become accustomed to is impenetrable to those not in our field of expertise.

In addition, most people are not familiar with statistical procedures, so presenting the results of a "multiple regression analysis" and the accompanying "Beta coefficients" will mean nothing to most people. Many of these statistics provide you with the information you need to decide whether your findings are statistically significant or not. For the purposes of a nontechnical audience, the results are the key point, summarized with clarity and insight, not laden with numbers that tell them very little. It is not the time to give a lecture on multivariate statistical analysis during a presentation of your conclusions.

When speaking with the popular press about a study, it is crucial that you clearly describe the limitations. There's nothing worse than reading in some local paper that you "proved" that men are less likely than women to ask for directions when lost, if in fact, you only demonstrated a slight tendency to do so in your limited sample of college-aged students in a small southeastern university. Frame results with such phrases as "some men demonstrated that . . . " or "it's not clear if these findings apply to older males or those living in other regions of the country . . . " and so on.

Readers of an Academic Journal

The best professional publications are those in a particular field that are refereed. This means that every submission is reviewed by readers who typically do not know who is writing the article. The author also does not know who is reviewing the paper. This is called a *double-blind* method because both authors and evaluators remain anonymous, thereby allowing for a potentially unbiased review without any preconceived assumptions about the level of expertise or skills of those involved. Reviews for the article are either a "rejection" or a "revise and resubmit," and occasionally an outright "accept." A "revise and resubmit" usually is a statement that the paper has some potential but that further clarification, reanalysis of data, rethinking of the interpretations, or other important changes need to be made before another critical review occurs. Then the revised paper is sent back to some or all of the original reviewers, and ocassionally to new ones, for another evaluation.

All professional journals (such as the *American Sociological Review, British Journal of Sociology, American Ethnographer, Journal of Clinical and Social Psychology* to name a few) provide a "style sheet" about the kind of information expected in the article, the standard format for writing the paper, and the bibliographic references. These guidelines, often published in issues of the journals or on their web pages, also tell you whether these are refereed journals. An academic article is normally organized in the following way (similar to the ordering of the chapters in this book):

- Abstract
- Literature Review
- Methods
- Results
- Conclusions and Summary
- References

Abstracts.   In general, most articles in the social sciences begin with an abstract, which is a one hundred to 150 word summary of the key points about the research. Consider it sort of a brief version of an *executive summary*, which is typically a short, one or two page summary of the key findings of a study, so termed because it is read by those in leadership positions who supposedly have very little time to read the entire research. An abstract gives readers enough information to get some key ideas about the paper but is not meant to include everything about the research. Remember that in this electronic age, many people learn about articles through computer databases that provide titles and abstracts.

Literature Review.   The body of the paper usually opens with a few sentences stating the focus of the article and its themes. Then a review of the relevant literature is presented, which serves to frame the paper in some theoretical and empirical context. This often ends with a set of research questions or hypotheses that are linked to the literature reviewed. Chapter 2 provides more details about writing concise literature reviews.

Methods.   Most important is the description of the research methods. This should be sufficiently detailed to guide readers in evaluating the quality of the data and research design. The methods section also should provide enough information to serve as a model for those who wish to replicate the study. Include specific information about the sampling procedures (how, when, where, who), composition and size of the final sample (demographics of respondents), the research design and methods used (questionnaire survey, interviews, experimental design, content analysis, participant observations, archival analysis, cross-sectional or longitudinal, etc.), description of the measurements (such as operationalizations, reliability and validity of any standardized instruments), and any other relevant information about the procedures used to gather data (mailed or distributed questionnaires, number and type of follow-ups to improve response rates, etc).

Results.   This section should be an unbiased and neutral presentation of the results in context of the research questions and hypotheses. Describe the statistical analyses, provide examples illustrating the results, and give quotations from the open-ended questions or interviews, if any. This is where your statistical skills are demonstrated as you correctly apply the best statistics for the kind of data you have. Be sure to present your results in clearly labeled tables, graphs, and other figures with a title describing in a few words what the figure or table represents, how many people responded, what statistics were used, and which ones are significant findings (usually with asterisks). See the examples presented throughout this book.

Conclusions and Summary.   The final section is where interpretations go and where you are encouraged to summarize and make sense of the findings. Here you need to clearly state what is based on speculations and what is rooted in the data. References to the theoretical and empirical findings described in the opening literature review section serve as a way of framing your conclusions. It is common to end your paper with some ideas for future research as well as with some caveats as to what went wrong, what the limitations of the study are, what should be interpreted with caution and why, and how far the results can be generalized beyond this sample.

References.   The last part of any paper is a complete list of references. A bibliography of what you have read should be in the format of the journal receiving your submission. Although most citation styles are slight variations of each other, one of the major differences is the use of footnotes or in-text citations. Most social science journals avoid footnotes for citing research (and if there are any, they tend to be endnotes and put at the conclusion of the paper before the references) and instead refer to a publication in the body of the article by listing the author's name, publication date, and page number if there is a direct quote from the source. The format for in-text citations and for the bibliographic information in the References section of the book you are now reading illustrates the American Sociological Association's publication style.

For example, if you were summarizing the work of Erving Goffman's *Presentation of Self in Everyday Life,* you would write "As Goffman (1959) said, the idea of a backstage and frontstage is central to social interaction." If there was a direct quote from the book, you would add the page number: Goffman (1959: 45). In the alphabetical list of references at the end of the paper, put

BOX 10.1

WRITING METHODS

Here's an excerpt from a published academic article explaining how the researchers accomplished their data collection. The information provided illustrates what is needed to assist readers in evaluating the quality of the data and the overall research project. Detailed methods sections also help those interested in replicating a study. The goal for writing a methods section of a report or article is to be as specific as possible with anything that was done that could affect the quality of the data, the interpretation of the results, and the generalizability of the findings.

Schuster, et al. (1998: 222–223) report the results from a questionnaire survey focused on sexual behaviors and sexual risk among high school students in a Los Angeles County school district:

> The district has two public high schools: a general school with about 2500 students and an alternative school with about 125 students considered at high risk for dropping out. Students in English as a Second Language classes and in intensive special education classes at the general school did not take the survey.
>
> About 12 percent of students were absent from class on the day the survey was conducted at the general high school; the absentee rate at the alternative school was not available but is typically about 35 percent. Of 2066 students present in appropriate classes on survey day, 2026 (98 percent) completed the survey, thirty-five did not (they or their parents declined participation), and five turned in unusable surveys. . . .
>
> The survey covered demographics; sexual beliefs, attitudes, and behaviors; and condom use. Male and female versions were identical except for pronouns and sexual behaviors. . . .
>
> To minimize confusion about types of sexual behaviors, we used both precise technical language and anatomic descriptions and avoided euphemistic language. . . . We adapted the anatomic descriptions from a Centers for Disease Control and Prevention survey and the *Surgeon General's Report on Acquired Immune Deficiency Syndrome*. All terms and concepts were part of the district's ninth-grade health curriculum. . . .
>
> Respondents completed the anonymous self-administered survey during a regular class period and sealed it in an opaque envelope. Survey administrators unaffiliated with the district proctored the classes. RAND's Human Subjects Protection Committee approved consent and administration procedures.
>
> The school district notified parents about the survey and gave them the opportunity to sign a form denying permission for their children to participate. Students could also decline participation, and names of respondents completing the survey were not recorded. Respondents were instructed to skip questions they preferred not to answer.

Notice how detailed the researchers are in describing everything from the ethical issues to the exact procedures for responding and sealing the questionnaire in an envelope. The article also presents information about the subjects, possible absentee rates, and items on the survey.

Goffman's name with the year of publication, book title, and other bibliographic information in the format of the journal's style, for example:

Goffman, Erving. 1959. *The Presentation of Self in Everyday Life*. New York: Doubleday.

A Presentation at a Conference

Similar to the readers of an academic journal, conference audiences are skilled in understanding the jargon of the profession and usually its methodologies. Hence, a paper presented at the meetings of a professional organization (such as the American Political Science Association, the American Psychological Association, and the British Sociological Association) typically follows the format of one submitted to an academic journal. The same kinds of information are required in order for it to be reviewed and judged acceptable for a conference.

However, presenting the paper is a different story. It is not usually the most pleasant experience to have a paper read aloud to you while sitting in uncomfortable chairs in an overly air-conditioned or heated hotel meeting room. Given only fifteen or twenty minutes to summarize what can be anywhere from twenty-five to fifty pages long does not allow for the details that should be in a written version for submission to a journal. Most conferences require that the paper has not been published already. This usually means it's a work in progress or very nearly a finished product. In either case, only key features can be presented at a meeting.

Begin with a brief statement describing the key focus and themes of the research. It is not necessary to review the literature in depth other than to say what your theoretical and empirical context is for the study. For example, instead of going through all twenty articles you researched on alcohol use among high school students, you simply state that your project grew out of sociological labeling theory and previous research that found an increase in substance use around the age of fifteen, or whatever the data have demonstrated. Then move on. Your goal is to share your findings not the background research you did before you collected your data.

Highlight just enough about the sample and methodology to provide general information to the audience to assist in interpreting the results. There rarely is enough time to go into details about the measures used and their operationalizations. Many of the specifics about the sample and the data collection procedures are best saved for a handout, overhead projection, or a computerized presentation. Similarly, reading numbers is sure to create a glazed look and droopy heads among audience members, so it's best to save the specific findings for handouts and other means of presentation.

Highlighting the key findings of the data analysis should be the central task. Invoke your creative skills to describe the numerical findings verbally and clearly. Rather than say that "there is a statistically significant t-test at the .05 level showing a difference in mean scores on a happiness scale where men scored 3.67 and women scored 3.84 (5 is very happy), and age has a Beta coefficient of .58 in a multiple regression predicting happiness," simply state that "there is a statistically significant difference in happiness scores between men and women, and age is the strongest predictor of happiness in a multiple regression analysis." Save the numbers for a handout or later publication.

After discussing the main findings, provide some interpretation of the results and end with a few limitations of the research and any suggestions for future research. Leave time for questions and discussion among the presenters and audience. It is crucial to prepare your presentation by rehearsing out loud and with a watch. Ideally, you should not read your paper; instead, talk about it. Imagine a conversation with a friend (or better yet, have such a conversation about your research with a colleague) and include all the pertinent information for your audience to get a clear sense of what you did and what you found.

Do not try to tell everything about your project. Stay focused on the main findings, highlight the methodology but do not get bogged down in its details, avoid extensive summaries of previous research and theories, and raise some provocative questions that the data have suggested. Your objective is to engage the audience in thinking about the topic in a new way, or to hear some fascinating findings. It is not necessary to report everything you found, because you have very limited time. Those details should be made available to anyone who would like to read the extended version, ideally when it is published in an academic journal. Think of your public presentation as an extended version of an "executive summary."

Professor Evaluating Your Thesis

Many undergraduates are expected to complete a "senior thesis" to graduate with honors or as part of the requirements for their major. For those in graduate school, a thesis or dissertation is central to most master's and doctoral degree programs. A thesis is a very detailed report of your research in which you demonstrate mastery of the literature, expertise in designing relevant methodologies, skills with statistical data analysis, and creative insights in interpreting your findings. Not unlike an academic article in a professional journal, most theses follow the same format, often written as chapters. What is specifically needed for your thesis and format should be supplied to you by those who supervise the research or who are in charge of overseeing the guidelines for conducting and reporting research.

After an initial introduction setting out the themes and purposes of the project, there is usually a very extensive literature review. Most reviews of prior research that appear in scholarly journals are abbreviated versions of what might be in a thesis. Here you are expected to "show off" your command of the field, demonstrate how extensively you prepared by citing relevant previous studies, and synthesize the broad literature into meaningful interpretive categories and themes. In many theses, this is where you develop some theoretical perspectives and perhaps create some new ideas and theories. It is also after this review that you present your research questions and hypotheses.

Within the limitations of what is likely to be an underfunded project, you next describe the methodology. Like the material required for a journal article, you spell out your sampling strategies, describe the respondents who filled out your questionnaire, explain the measurements and operationalizations, and discuss the procedures you used to collect the data. This section or chapter should provide enough information not only for others to evaluate the results properly but also to allow them to replicate the research design.

Presentation of your results and data analysis is the core of a thesis. This may take one or more chapters, depending on how the data are organized and what the research questions are. The use of tables, graphs, and other figures is an excellent way of showing what you have found. It is also important to remember that even if none of your hypotheses were supported, no findings are often a finding in themselves. Sometimes demonstrating that there is no relationship between some variables or that, for example, there are no gender differences in study habits and grades, can be a revelation.

Your conclusions reflect a scholarly interpretation of the data and should demonstrate your expertise in the field. Reference to the extensive literature you reviewed allows you to contextualize the research and the findings in the theories and empirical studies that came before. Here also is the place to mention any shortcomings about the project and ideas for future research on the topic. A bibliographic list of the extensive readings ends the thesis in the format required by the department or professional field. After it is evaluated and approved by your professor and perhaps other readers, you graduate with a sense of accomplishment and evidence of your abilities to carry out scholarly research.

Employer or Workplace Committee

And you thought doing theses to complete a degree was the last time you had to do this kind of research! Many people find themselves in work situations where they are asked to carry out some research for their company. Often this involves evaluation research where the effectiveness of some program or new policy implementation needs to be investigated. Or perhaps the nonprofit community service agency for which you volunteer seeks help in designing a study to evaluate its programs and the clients' satisfaction with them. You are asked by your employer or some board to present the results of your project.

In many cases, the suggestions described previously also apply here. Presenting this kind of research is often a combination of speaking to the general public and a professional conference. It is unlikely that you will be asked to go into the depths you normally would for an honors thesis, or with the jargon and theoretical details of an academic article. Yet, you must be able to demonstrate a sophisticated and scientifically sound research design because any related policy decisions can have profound impact on people's lives. In any case, you have to provide at least an "executive summary" that clearly and succinctly summarizes the key findings of your research and any relevant methodological points. Being able to condense a major project into one or two pages of information is a skill well worth working on when dealing with employers and other agency boards and organizations.

An extensive literature review is usually not presented in such reports, although doing one best serves your own personal interests because it becomes the source of information about what others have already discovered in this area. If you are hired by the university to study attrition and retention rates, it pays to read the numerous studies that were conducted previously. Why reinvent the wheel? See what measures other researchers used, what questions they addressed, and how they approached the topic, and then modify according to your own unique situation. However, it may not be necessary to write up as detailed a summary as you would be expected to do in a thesis or even an academic article. The key is to present the context for your study and the necessary comparison figures so that those hearing the results can properly interpret what you found.

Careful attention to the methodology is crucial because what you report can easily be discredited if there are major problems with the sampling, operationalizations of the measures, and the overall research design. It is necessary, then, to detail what you did when presenting your findings, whether in writing or in an oral presentation, and to explain your decisions.

Results of your data analysis are more than likely being distributed to people who do not have extensive knowledge of the range of statistical procedures employed. Again, some of the statistical analyses may be for your own background information, so that you can say with confidence what the findings are and whether they are statistically significant. Many agencies and workplaces are satisfied with descriptive data, cross-tabulations, and graphs. More complex data analyses, such as multiple regression, ANOVA, and even the simpler statistics like chi-square, Pearson r correlation, and t-tests, rarely get presented to employers and agency boards, unless there is some expectation to do so by those who are qualified to read and interpret the information. Statistics could be placed in an appendix with an occasional reference that statistical analyses of the data were completed and that these verify the significance of the results presented.

Many agencies or employers ask that you also present interpretations and suggestions for policy changes in light of the findings. However, some would rather leave that to the agency or another committee formed to make sense of the results and implement policy changes in the workplace. Again, this varies depending on the organization and you should be clear what the expectations are when assigned the project. So, for example, if you uncover with a multiple regression analysis that the quality of the campus facilities is a more important explanation than the quality of the courses for a rise in attrition rates at the university, then you may be asked to account for this and what you would recommend to change it. Or you might find that the data from an evaluation of a training program for new employees at the organization you studied indicate that they should be compensated for participation in a three-day orientation program. Depending on your role in the project, you might be asked to provide a recommendation, so you suggest that the employer should implement a training compensation program.

Grant or Funding Agency

If you were lucky enough to have your research funded through some grant or funding agency, then the requirements for disseminating the results of your study have likely been spelled out when you received the grant. Normally, a report is due and it can vary from a copy of the entire thesis or research project, to perhaps a long "executive summary" maybe five to ten pages long.

It is also very likely that, in order to have received the grant, you have already sent the agency a detailed proposal that included a literature review and extensive methodological procedures. Most funding agencies pay particular attention to the methodology and the ethical dimensions of the project when doing research with human subjects. A budget was probably requested and your final report may have to account for how the money was actually spent.

A grant report usually includes a summary of the data analysis, the statistics used, and your interpretations of the results. You are expected to demonstrate how the objectives and other goals you described in the initial grant proposal were or were not achieved. As always, reporting the limitations of the study and providing ideas for future research topics are good ways of concluding your summary to the agency. The format of a report follows the outline of topics and sections required in most academic articles and theses. The exact kinds of information requested are normally discussed in the granting agency's guidelines.

THE JOURNEY FINISHES

Congratulations are in order. You have completed your journey along the research trail. A few final words are in order: It's one thing to read about doing research; it's another to actually do it. Imagine reading about how to drive a car or play the piano and never actually driving or playing. Same with research. You cannot read it and think that you now know how to do it. Just like driving a car and playing the piano, you have to practice, practice, practice. You have to get out there and drive, play, and research.

Do not expect to do research exactly the way it sounds in this book. Research involves making trade-offs and compromises. It may seem ideal to get a random sample, but what happens when that generates a low response rate? You compromise and seek out a convenience sample. Sure you would like to have an interval/ratio measure of income, but when many respondents leave out their answers you realize that you might have to compromise to reduce nonresponses and ask the question using ordinal categories of income instead.

Typically research lurches forward, is set back for any number of reasons (delays in getting questionnaires back, typos and other errors only noticed later, computer glitches, and other petty annoyances), gets refined when some other unexpected finding emerges in your data, or reinterpreted when another article is discovered that sheds new theoretical light on your results. Your findings may lead to a modification of the theory you started out with in an ongoing deductive and inductive process. Although the report or article you complete presents a summary in a linear fashion and thereby reinforces the illusion, it might make for interesting reading if you included a list of shortcomings and caveats along with a few of the ways your project veered from the standard journey.

Positivism

Because this book focuses on survey research methods, and does not cover such techniques as content analysis, field methods, and other qualitative research methods, remember that writing a questionnaire to gather data carries with it some assumptions about the nature of reality and how we understand it. It is just one way of apprehending social phenomena and not the only way. It has its limitations and it has certain strengths. And it is based on a particular belief about understanding the world around us called positivism.

Positivism is the system of thought developed by Auguste Comte in the early 1800s in France which emphasizes empirical data and reasoning and the use of scientific principles to explain social phenomena. It is a philosophy of knowledge that stresses the experiential, that is, what is experienced through the senses and what is measurable using scientific techniques. Positivism believes reality is something that can be assessed, measured, and discovered logically. Opposed to this view of the world is the more metaphysical and humanistic belief that ideas are personal and cannot be measured scientifically. All human ideas, including the scientific method, are subjective creations. Truth is not something easily measured.

Whichever philosophy of knowledge makes sense to you, at least understand that choosing a questionnaire survey method implies signing on to a philosophy that assumes that the phenomena you wish to study are measurable and open to empirical assessment. Doing survey research can answer some questions, and then only with the limitations imposed by its methods. It is just one way of understanding the opinions and behavior of humans, but not the only one. The use of multiple techniques, what is sometimes called *triangulation,* to understand complex phenomena is ideal. Sometimes a self-report questionnaire should be combined with face-to-face interviews and participant observation of behavior to comprehend more fully the complex behaviors and attitudes you wish to study.

However, in face of the limitations imposed by funding and time, the selection of the most appropriate methodology must be determined by the nature of the phenomena and population under scrutiny, and the research questions you want answered. Clearly, a study involving young children who cannot read, or people with cognitive limitations, should not depend on survey research that uses questionnaires. Research focused on how people behave in particular situations, such as children at play or employees at work, may best be served with participant observation field methods. It is never ideal to begin by saying you want to write a questionnaire and then choose your topic.

Let the research problem lead you to the best methodology. And if a questionnaire serves the goals of your project, then let this book be your guide for the research journey.

REVIEW: WHAT DO THESE KEY TERMS MEAN?

Abstract	Executive summary	Positivism
Academic journal	Organization of a	Triangulation
Audiences	journal article	
Ethics		

INTERPRET: WHAT DO THESE REAL EXAMPLES TELL US?

For each of these excerpts from published academic articles, discuss what is included and what might be missing from the final write-up of the research:

1. Lindquist, Lagory, and Ritchey (1999: 696) designed a study to explore the differences between homeless people who stay in one place and those who migrate regularly in terms of demographics, psychosocial stressors, depression levels, and other factors:

. . . a census of street and sheltered homeless in the metropolitan area was conducted prior to the survey. The enumeration included residents of the thirty-seven shelters housing homeless persons in the metropolitan area as well as persons without residence sleeping in public places in a 368-square-block area of the city center. It was conducted in the early morning hours (2:30–4:30 A.M.) to reduce mistaking "homed" from homeless persons. . . .

Approximately one month after the census, face-to-face interviews averaging one hour in length were conducted with 161 homeless adults. . . . The survey instrument contained both structured and open-ended items on topics ranging from basic demographics, residential history, mental and physical health, everyday life experiences, work history, service utilization, and social networks and supports. The survey sample was a random probability sample based on quota proportions established from the census for the variables of race, sex, and geographic site. Quotas were filled with persons randomly selected from each shelter or public site.

2. As part of a research program funded by the World Health Organization and focused on the AIDS epidemic in Africa, Runganga and Aggleton (1998: 68–70) used focus groups and in-depth interviews to study the multiple factors affecting how young people in Zimbabwe learn about sexual behavior and form certain sexual expectations:

> The study reported on here was undertaken over an 18-month period at a rural growth-point [shops, night clubs, hotels, bank, and other structures where young people and sex workers gather] or small town of approximately 150,000 people, some 80 km from Harare. . . .
>
> A Rapid Assessment Procedure (RAP) was conducted in the early stages of the study to assess the feasibility of the study and to obtain a preliminary understanding of the sexual lives of adults and young people. Data were collected through focus group discussions and interviews with key informants who included community leaders. Issues identified were elaborated on in the main study that followed this RAP.
>
> Data collection techniques in the main study included individual in-depth interviews with young people, focus group discussions, participant observation and continuing key informant interviews with community leaders. . . . Respondents were recruited from one village near the growth-point and from another some 30 km away.
>
> In-depth interviews were conducted in young people's homes or at another convenient location such as at a quiet location in the town centre or beside the nearby river. Participation in the study was voluntary, and care was taken to ensure privacy and confidentiality in all interviews. . . . Relatively non-threatening issues such as upbringing and family interests were discussed prior to an exploration of sexual issues and concerns. Interviews most usually took the form of a dialogue, allowing participants the right to structure the direction of the discussion according to their own interests and train of thought. The majority of individual interviews were conducted by the first author, who was assisted by a small number of psychology and social work graduates. Detailed field notes were taken either during or after the interviews. . . .

Between ten and twelve respondents participated in each focus group discussion which lasted between sixty and ninety minutes. Focus group discussions were conducted with young women and young men separately with the age groups 13–15, 16–18, and 19–24 years. . . . The majority of focus group discussions were conducted jointly by the first author and one or more psychology or social work graduates. A tape recorder was used to maintain a record of the issues talked about.

CONSULT: WHAT COULD BE DONE?

The local newspaper has heard about a study looking at truancy at the town's high school that has data potentially damaging to the reputation of the teachers and administrators at the school. It also links truancy with substance abuse and violent threats to other students.

1. What kinds of questions would you advise the reporters to ask about the study?

2. What advice would you give the researchers who are about to release their findings?

3. What kinds of information about the study should be included in all reports of it by the study directors as well as the media?

DECIDE: WHAT DO YOU DO NEXT?

You are asked to do a study looking at the relationship between people's television viewing habits and their opinions about racial and ethnic issues and stereotyping, and their actions toward people from diverse backgrounds. Does TV viewing have an impact on their attitudes and behaviors toward diversity?

1. What different ways would you present your findings if you were reporting the results to (i) a committee of concerned citizens, (ii) the Board Members of the company that sponsored the research, (iii) racial organizations such as anti-defamation groups, (iv) an academic journal, (v) the local news media, and (vi) television network executives?

2. What ethical issues should you be attentive to when presenting the data in each of these situations?

Statistical Analysis Decision Tree

Determine which variable is *independent* and which is *dependent* in your hypothesis or research question.

Determine each variable's *level of measurement* (nominal, ordinal, interval/ratio). Remember dichotomies can be treated as any level and many ordinal measures with equal-appearing intervals can be used as interval/ratio measures.

Run *frequencies* and appropriate *descriptive statistics* (such as mode, median, mean) to assess whether each variable is really a variable (and not a constant) in your sample.

Decide on the appropriate statistics to use to *analyze* relationships between the independent and dependent variables.

To *compare means* of a dependent variable (interval/ratio) between *two* categories of an independent variable: use **t-test**. Among *three or more* categories of an independent variable: use **ANOVA.**

To test a relationship between *nominal* and/or *ordinal* variables: use **Chi-Square.** If at least one variable is nominal: use **Lambda.** If both are ordinal: use **Gamma.** If the variables are ordinal ranks: use **Spearman rho.**

To test a relationship between two *interval/ratio* variables: use **Pearson r** *correlation.* If there are two or more independent variables: use **Multiple Correlation** (R) and **Linear Regression.**

If the *probability* of obtaining that statistic by chance is less than .05 (p < .05), then *reject* the *null* hypothesis of no difference or no relationship, and declare there *is* a *significant* relationship between the two variables.

For Lambda, Gamma, Spearman, and Pearson r correlations, assess the *strength* of the relationship: around 0 to .25 is low, .25 to .60 is moderate, and .60 to 1.0 is strong.
The *direction* (+ or -) also tells you if it's a positive relationship (both increase or decrease in same direction) or an inverse one (as one variable increases, the other decreases).

REFERENCES

Adams, Richard E. and Richard T. Serpe. 2000. "Social Integration, Fear of Crime, and Life Satisfaction." *Sociological Perspectives* 43:4, 605–629.

Aiba, Keiko and Amy S. Wharton. 2001. "Job-Level Sex Composition and the Sex Pay Gap in a Large Japanese Firm." *Sociological Perspectives* 44:1, 67–87.

Babbie, Earl. 2001. *The Practice of Social Research.* Ninth edition. Belmont, CA: Wadsworth.

Baumann, Shyon. 2001. "Intellectualization and Art World Development: Film in the United States." *American Sociological Review* 66:3, 404–426.

Berg, Bruce L. 2001. *Qualitative Research Methods for the Social Sciences.* Boston: Allyn and Bacon.

Blake, Susan M., Rebecca Ledsky, Thomas Lehman, Carol Goodenow, Richard Sawyer, and Tim Hack. 2001. "Preventing Sexual Risk Behaviors Among Gay, Lesbian, and Bisexual Adolescents: The Benefits of Gay-Sensitive HIV Instruction in Schools." *American Journal of Public Health* 91:6, 940–946.

Budiansky, Stephen. 1995. "Consulting the Oracle: Everyone Loves Polls. But Can You Trust Them?" *U.S. News & World Report,* December 4, 52–55, 58.

Campbell, Donald and Julian Stanley. 1963. *Experimental and Quasi-Experimental Designs for Research.* Chicago: Rand McNally.

Catania, Joseph A., Dennis Osmond, Ronald D. Stall, Lance Pollack, Jay P. Paul, Sally Blower, Diane Binson, Jesse A. Canchola, Thomas C. Mills, Lawrence Fisher, Kyung-Hee Choi, Travis Porco, Charles Turner, Johnny Blair, Jeffrey Henne, Larry L. Bye, and Thomas J. Coates. 2001. "The Continuing HIV Epidemic Among Men Who Have Sex with Men." *American Journal of Public Health* 91:6, 907–914.

Denzin, Norman and Yvonne Lincoln (eds.). 1994. *The Handbook of Qualitative Research.* Thousand Oaks, CA: Sage.

Diaz, Raphael M., George Ayala, Edward Bein, Jeff Henne, and Barbara V. Marin. 2001. "The Impact of Homophobia, Poverty, and Racism on the Mental Health of Gay and Bisexual Latino Men: Findings from 3 US Cities." *American Journal of Public Health* 91:6, 927–932.

Dillman, Don A. 2000. *Mail and Internet Surveys: The Tailored Design Method.* Second edition. New York: Wiley.

Durkheim, Emile. 1951 [1897]. *Suicide: A Study in Sociology.* New York: Free Press.

ERIC Clearinghouse on Assessment and Evaluation and the Center for Equity and Excellence in Education (CEEE). 2001. "The Columbia Mental Maturity Scale" published by Harcourt Brace Jovanovich. Retrieved July 3, 2001 (http://www.ericae.net/eac/eac0069.htm) and "Language Proficiency Test" from Academic Therapy Publications (http://www.ericae.net/eac/eac0136.htm).

Glassner, Barry. 1999. *The Culture of Fear.* New York: Basic Books.

Guthrie, Doug. 1999. "A Sociological Perspective on the Use of Technology: The Adoption of Internet Technology in U.S. Organizations." *Sociological Perspectives* 42:4, 583–603.

Hansen, Wendy L. and Neil J. Mitchell. 2000. "Disaggregating and Explaining Corporate Political Activity: Domestic and Foreign Corporations in National Politics." *American Political Science Review* 94:4, 891–903.

Hibbing, John R. and Elizabeth Theiss-Morse. 2001. "Process Preferences and American Politics: What the People Want Government to Be." *American Political Science Review* 95:1, 145–153.

Huff, Darrell. 1954. *How To Lie with Statistics*. New York: Norton.

Jaret, Charles and Donald C. Reitzes. 1999. "The Importance of Racial-Ethnic Identity and Social Setting for Blacks, Whites, and Multiracials." *Sociological Perspectives* 42:4, 711–737.

Jobes, Patrick C. 1999. "Residential Stability and Crime in Small Rural Agricultural and Recreational Towns." *Sociological Perspectives* 42:3, 499–524.

Jones, Rachel K. and Ye Luo. 1999. "The Culture of Poverty and African-American Culture." *Sociological Perspectives* 42:3, 439–458.

Kibria, Nazli. 2000. "Race, Ethnic Options, and Ethnic Binds: Identity Negotiations of Second-Generation Chinese and Korean Americans." *Sociological Perspectives* 43:1, 77–95.

Kramer, Lisa A. and Steph Lambert. 2001. "Sex-Linked Bias in Chances of Being Promoted to Supervisor." *Sociological Perspectives* 44:1, 111–127.

Laumann, Edward O., John H. Gagnon, Robert T. Michael, and Stuart Michaels. 1994. *The Social Organization of Sexuality: Sexual Practices in the United States*. Chicago: University of Chicago Press.

LeBlanc, Allen J. and Richard G. Wight. 2000. "Reciprocity and Depression in AIDS Caregiving." *Sociological Perspectives* 43:4, 631–649.

Lindquist, Christine H., Mark Lagory, and Ferris J. Ritchey. 1999. "The Myth of the Migrant Homeless: An Exploration of the Psychosocial Consequences of Migration." *Sociological Perspectives* 42:4, 691–709.

Mackie, Marlene. 1980. "The Impact of Sex Stereotypes upon Adult Self-Imagery." *Social Psychology Quarterly* 43:1, 121–125.

Mears, Daniel P. 2001. "The Immigration-Crime Nexus: Toward an Analytic Framework for Assessing and Guiding Theory, Research, and Policy." *Sociological Perspectives* 44:1, 1–19.

Meyer, Ilan H. 1995. "Minority Stress and Mental Health in Gay Men." *Journal of Health and Social Behavior* 36, 38–56.

Miller, Delbert C. 1991. *Handbook of Research Design and Social Measurement*. Fifth edition. Newbury Park, CA: Sage.

Misra, Joya, Ivy Kennelly, and Marina Karides. 1999. "Employment Chances in the Academic Job Market in Sociology: Do Race and Gender Matter?" *Sociological Perspectives* 42:2, 215–247.

Mutz, Diana C. and Paul S. Martin. 2001. "Facilitating Communication across Lines of Political Difference: The Role of Mass Media." *American Political Science Review* 95:1, 97–114.

Nagasawa, Richard, Zhenchao Qian, and Paul Wong. 2000. "Social Control Theory as a Theory of Conformity: The Case of Asian/Pacific Drug and Alcohol Nonuse." *Sociological Perspectives* 43:4, 581–603.

Neuman, W. Lawrence. 2000. *Social Research Methods: Qualitative and Quantitative Approaches*. Fourth edition. Needham Heights, MA: Allyn & Bacon.

Plummer, Ken. 2001. *Documents of Life 2: An Invitation to a Critical Humanism*. London: Sage.

Reiss, Ira. 1993. "The Future of Sex Research and the Meaning of Science." *Journal of Sex Research* 30:1, 3–11.

Rosenberg, Morris. 1968. *The Logic of Survey Analysis*. New York: Basic Books.

Rossi, Peter and Howard Freeman. 1996. *Evaluation: A Systematic Approach*. Thousand Oaks, CA: Sage.

Runganga, Agnes O. and Peter Aggleton. 1998. "Migration, the Family and the Transformation of a Sexual Culture." *Sexualities* 1:1, 63–81.

Schuster, Mark A., Robert M. Bell, Gene A. Nakajima, and David E. Kanouse. 1998. "The Sexual Practices of Asian and Pacific Islander High School Students." *Journal of Adolescent Health* 23, 221–231.

Shaw, Clifford and Henry McKay. 1942. *Juvenile Delinquency and Urban Areas*. Chicago: University of Chicago Press.

Sherrod, Drury and Peter M. Nardi. 1998. "Homophobia in the Courtroom: An Assessment of Biases Against Gay Men and Lesbians in a Multi-Ethnic Sample of Potential Jurors." Pp. 24–38 in Gregory M. Herek (ed.), *Stigma & Sexual Orientation: Understanding Prejudice Against Lesbians, Gay Men, and Bisexuals*, Newbury Park, CA: Sage.

Sutherland, Edwin. 1934. *Principles of Criminology*. Chicago: Lippincott.

Swain, Scott O. 1992. "Men's Friendships with Women: Intimacy, Sexual Boundaries, and the Informant Role." Pp. 153–171 in Peter M. Nardi (ed.), *Men's Friendships*. Newbury Park, CA: Sage.

Weber, Robert Philip. 1990. *Basic Content Analysis*. Second edition. Newbury Park, CA: Sage.

Wong, Paul, Chienping Faith Lai, Richard Nagasawa, and Tieming Lin. 1998. "Asian Americans as a Model Minority: Self-Perceptions and Perceptions by Other Racial Groups." *Sociological Perspectives* 41:1, 95–118.

Xiao, Hong. 2000. "Structure of Child-Rearing Values in Urban China." *Sociological Perspectives* 43:3, 457–471.

Zuo, Jiping and Shengming Tang. 2000. "Breadwinner Status and Gender Ideologies of Men and Women Regarding Family Roles." *Sociological Perspectives* 43:1, 29–43.

INDEX

Academic article, 21, 208–210, 211
Aggregated data, 28
Alpha level. *See* Significance level
Analysis of variance, 174–177, 195;
  calculation of, 176; factors for, 174;
  two–way, 189
Anonymity, 29, 59, 84
ANOVA. *See* Analysis of variance
Archival research, 15–16
Attitudes, 62; measurement of, 64–72
Audience, 207–216; academic journal,
  208–210; conference, 212–213;
  employer, 214–216; funding agency,
  216; general public, 208; professor,
  213–214

Behaviors, 62; measurement of, 72,
  74–76
Beta coefficients (or weights). *See*
  Regression
Bias: in samples, 1, 5; everyday, 5; in
  questions, 3–4, 58, 71
Boolean logic, 24
Branching, 80, 90. *See also* Contingency
  questions; Filter questions

Cause and effect, 12, 13, 181, 206
Central Limit Theorem, 101, 133–136
Central tendency measures, 121–127. *See*
  also Mean; Median; Mode; Standard
  deviation
Chi–square, 144–148; calculation of,
  145–146
Closed-ended items, 59, 64–65
Coding, 54, 86–89; and codebooks, 87;
  missing answers, 89–90; precoding,
  87. *See also* Recoding
Coefficient of determination, 159
Concepts, 35, 37, 41–43, 62. *See also*
  Constructs; Variables
Confidence interval, 135, 170
Confidentiality, 29, 84

Constructs, 35, 50
Content analysis, 15–16, 54, 65, 87
Contingency questions, 65, 80. *See also*
  Branching; Filter questions
Contingency tables. *See* Crosstabs.
Continuous variables, 44, 46, 47
Control variables, 181–188; antecedent,
  183, 185, 188; intervening, 186, 188;
  specification, 186, 188; spurious,
  183, 185, 188; suppressor, 186, 188
Correlation, 12, 13, 52, 53, 54, 149–160;
  coefficients, 149; inverse (or
  negative), 149; multiple, 189–190;
  partial, 186; positive, 149. *See also*
  Pearson r
Cross-sectional samples, 109
Crosstabs (or Cross-tabulations),
  141–144; and marginals, 142

Databases, 23–24, 26
Degrees of freedom, 126, 147
Demographics, 62; measurement of,
  76–79
Dependent variable, 36–37. *See also*
  Variables
Descriptive research, 9–10, 116, 140
Dichotomous variable, 45, 46, 47, 89, 192
Discrete variables, 44, 45, 46, 47, 48
Double-barreled items, 71
Dummy variable. *See* Dichotomous
  variable

Elaboration, 181–188. *See also* Control
  variables
Empiricism, 7, 217
Equal-appearing intervals, 46, 48, 79. *See*
  also Likert scale
Eta, 160
Ethics, 29–31, 206–207
Evaluation research, 11
Everyday thinking, 1–6
Exclusive and exhaustive, 75, 78, 79